Political Economy of Cl
Caste and Gender

This book examines the structures of power and hierarchies within the agrarian political economy in India, with a focus on gender. It analyses various forms of inequalities within rural structures while situating the position of women and Dalit agriculture labourers within these discriminate networks of social exclusion, political marginalisation and poverty.

The book maps the impacts of neoliberal capitalist globalisation on agrarian relations to identify who labourers are and how rural diversification is shaped by class, caste and gender hierarchies specifically in the villages of eastern Uttar Pradesh. It looks at occupational patterns of women workers, labour relations and reconceptualisation of labour. The book documents the experiences of exploitation as well as forms of resistance and collective action of rural women labourers. In doing this, the book deals with processes witnessed across the global South – rural distress, depeasantisation, migration, feminisation of agriculture as well as identity-based inequalities in rural labour markets.

Rich in empirical data, the book will be useful for scholars and researchers of labour studies, women's studies, political economy, agrarian economy, agrarian sociology, rural sociology, sociology, development studies and political studies.

Ishita Mehrotra is an independent researcher with interests in political economy of agrarian relations, caste and gender, rural labour relations, labour movements and development theory. Previously, she has taught at the School of Development Studies and the School of Undergraduate Studies at Ambedkar University Delhi, India.

Political Economy of Class, Caste and Gender

A Study of Rural Dalit Labourers in India

Ishita Mehrotra

Routledge
Taylor & Francis Group
LONDON AND NEW YORK

First published 2022
by Routledge
4 Park Square, Milton Park, Abingdon, Oxon OX14 4RN

and by Routledge
605 Third Avenue, New York, NY 10158

Routledge is an imprint of the Taylor & Francis Group, an informa business

British Library Cataloguing-in-Publication Data
A catalogue record for this book is available from the British Library

Library of Congress Cataloging-in-Publication Data
A catalog record for this book has been requested

ISBN: 978-0-367-33623-3 (hbk)
ISBN: 978-1-032-22906-5 (pbk)
ISBN: 978-0-429-32189-4 (ebk)

DOI: 10.4324/9780429321894

Typeset in Sabon
by Apex CoVantage, LLC

Contents

Figures

Acknowledgements

This book was an almost forgotten dream of mine, happy and complacent as I was in everyday life and work. But being academicians themselves, Ena and Sejuti would not let me take it easy. It is only thanks to them that I put together a proposal for this book and here it is now. I am forever grateful to them for breathing down my neck until I took pen to paper because from that point on there was no turning back. Sejuti, thank you for being my greatest friend, mentor, colleague, critic – just thank you for being in my life and being you. In the journey of writing this book, Chandrani and Chotti Sejuti have been my constants. Chandrani, this book is in the shape it is all because of you and Chotti Sejuti, what would we do without you as our sounding board. The beautiful memories we made in our years together in Delhi will always keep us together even as each of us now lives and grows separately. Taneesha, I still think that the maps are the most beautiful part of this book and so a big thank you for all your help there.

Professor Pralay Kanungo at Jawaharlal Nehru University, Delhi and Dr Jens Lerche at SOAS, London turned me into the reader, writer, researcher that I am today and without them there never would have been me as a scholar to begin with. I will always be indebted to you both for your patience and encouragement. Over the years, I have taken great pride in your works and of having the privilege to have you both as my supervisors. I just hope that this book goes some ways in making you both proud of me.

This book took more than two years to be completed and parts of it were written under very difficult personal circumstances. But Shoma's unwavering support and patience kept me going. Thank you, Routledge and Shoma.

In my formative years, many a learning took place at Suman bua's knee. She continues to be our pillar of strength.

My parents and sisters are my world. My parents, Lalit and Neeru, made sure I had all possible opportunities and that I could travel, learn and work – all of which have stood me in good stead. We might not have always agreed, but their faith in me, their love and strength remained unshaken. My sisters, Tanushri and Rakshita, have stood shoulder to shoulder with me always. They are my heart and soul and without them I would not have made it this far. Ashish, you are a remarkable person and Rakshita and I are forever

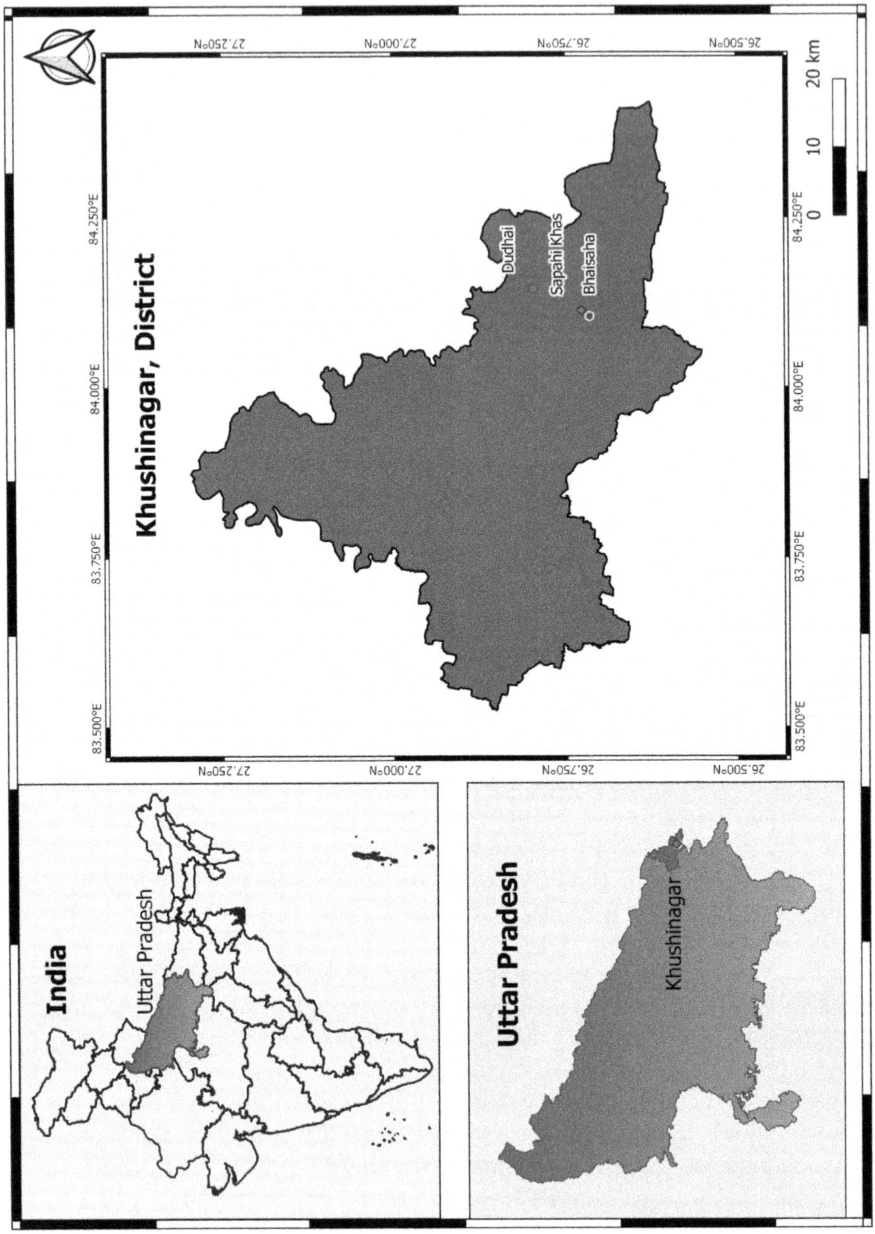

Figure 1.1 Fieldwork Area, Kushinagar, Uttar Pradesh

grateful for being the almost son and brother that my parents are so proud of. Tanish and Abeer, you both have brought much happiness and meaning to all our lives. Thank you for keeping us on our toes and running around!

I lost my father before this book could be published. He always encouraged me to write a book, more so in his last few months. I did not tell him about this book earlier as I wanted it to be a surprise, for him to be the first person to hold a copy. Unfortunately, this wish will remain unfulfilled, but I know for sure that wherever he is, he is happy and proud about this book and very much hankering for a party. In the last year and a half, stuck as we were in our homes due to the pandemic, during our early morning conversations, Papa often expressed his wish to chronicle his work life. To do so is now my burden of love. Till then, Papa, rest in peace. And with this book, I wish you a very happy 75th birthday.

1 Introduction

This book has been a long time coming. For me, this book symbolises the end of one journey and the beginning of another. I began this journey in 2008 as a doctoral student in the Department of Development Studies at School of Oriental and African Studies (SOAS), University of London. This book is the culmination of this journey of learning, doing research, writing and the struggles of making and holding an academic career. Though this journey has been fraught with self-doubt and many highs and lows, I am glad that I undertook it. The new journey that I hope to embark on emerges from the very writing of this book which has inspired and encouraged me to return to my original fieldwork areas and themes. This chapter and this book are an introduction to this endeavour.

This book is about rural Dalit female labour relations in the context of eastern Uttar Pradesh (UP), India. My fieldwork was conducted in three villages of Kushinagar district. Why did I write this book? I see this book as an opportunity to study women and their work within the wider social relations of power and inequality as well as a study of the constant negotiations with these structures of domination that all women are engaged in everyday. But not all of us can write and not all of us get heard. There are works on rural labourers which focus on UP, where women are mentioned only in passing while documenting their position and contributions with respect to male labourers. There is certainly a dirth of literature on women labourers in eastern UP. This book documents their story.

Research on rural Dalit female labour relations is interesting and important. Labour studies in the Indian context have broadly focussed on the role of the state and the informal economy. Within agriculture, the emphasis has been on the implications of reduced state support and trade liberalisation vis-à-vis disparately defined agrarian classes. In most empirical studies, the female labour is implicit. It is not directly studied but referred to in relation to what is happening to the male labour. This is ironical given the disproportionate concentration of female labourers in agriculture. These studies deny the importance of women as independent economic actors, more so in a context of labour fragmentation and mobility, and as the primary everyday providers of household sustenance. Implicit in this indirect

DOI: 10.4324/9780429321894-1

and under-representation of female labourers is the tendency to assume that men and women confront capitalist forces in a similar manner, that they are incorporated within capitalist social relations similarly and that their experience of capitalist exploitation is undifferentiated. More importantly, the lack of nuanced investigation is problematic for it reifies existing unequal power relations. It is only when female labour is directly studied can these questions and other generalisations be substantively interrogated, such that policy provisions can take into account ground realities.

The aforementioned also indicates the significance of this research, derived from its focus on one of the most socially and economically discriminated and marginalised population and from their absence in the literature despite the fact that identities of gender, caste, tribe and religion are the primary markers of segregation in rural India.

The few studies dealing with rural female labour relations are concerned with quite specific regions of India, that is either South India or selected green revolution areas. But most of rural labour lives in less developed areas of north, central and eastern India. One such area is eastern UP. The north Indian state of UP is characterised by regionally unequal levels of development. However, with the exception of certain case studies, most work on UP centres on the more developed western part of the state. Even today, eastern UP is a much under researched area, despite being one of the most backward areas in the country and state. One possible reason for scholarly focus being restricted to the western region of the state is that it was one of the first regions where green revolution was introduced. Agrarian political economy in India during and immediately after the green revolution period was dominated by three key questions – capital creation, surplus extraction and socio-economic differentiation – questions considered the domain of economists primarily. But naturally then, western UP became a preferred site for research. Gradually, with the diffusion of the green revolution, comparisons between the more developed western region and the less developed eastern region of the state were undertaken. The emergence of farmers' movements in the late 1980s, especially the Bhartiya Kisan Union under Mahendra Singh Tikait, in western UP, kept the attention of scholars on this part of UP. Another possible reason for this could be that western UP districts are easily accessible from the National Capital Region, while the eastern region is in the interior and logistically speaking (transport, place to live, challenging social environment), difficult to penetrate.

The state of UP was also thought to make for an important study given the regional political context. Since the mid-1990s, the state has been governed by three different political regimes (independently or in alliance) – the Bahujan Samaj Party (BSP hereafter) which came to power on a Dalit vote base, the Samajwadi Party (SP hereafter) whose vote base has been the Other Backward Classes (OBC hereafter) and Muslims and the BJP that had steadily built on the traditional Hindu vote base through communal polarisation and in recent years sought to attract those Dalits and Muslims who had been sidelined by the BSP and SP. Despite political regimes that claimed to represent Dalits, this constituency which disproportionately makes up for agricultural labourers remained on the margins. In fact, successive governments prioritised industrial and infrastructural development over agriculture. The purpose of this book is not to study the developmental or governance failures in UP, but rather to study these Dalit labourers and women especially. Currently, no substantive contribution to this topic based on empirical work in east UP exists.

The study should be understood on the background of the agrarian transformations under the advance of neoliberal capitalist globalisation, as this has major implications for rural classes. An understanding of these developments is essential because agriculture is the preferred entry point to study rural labour. One reason for this is that in the available literature female labour is posited as village based and agrarian. Another is that changes in agrarian production structures and social relations are encompassed within its political economy. This is key in understanding such historical transformations. It is widely acknowledged that these agrarian transformations have had a varied impact on rural classes and these processes of differentiation are further refracted through gender, caste and other such categories.

Capitalism is constantly evolving and leading to changes across the board. Capitalist developments in agriculture have led to significant changes in processes and relations of production in agrarian village economies. My concern here is to find how neoliberal capitalism has impacted the rural class structure in general and in my field area specifically. What are the main rural classes in my field villages? What are their features? How can they be theoretically captured? What are the relations between classes? Given this, I chose a political economy approach for my work. A political economy framework uses class analysis to investigate relations of power, of domination and exploitation and how the political nature of public policy brings into effect an institutional infrastructure and economic policy which has differential consequences for the position of various classes. Such an approach enables a comprehensive understanding of how capitalist social relations are premised on labour exploitation to secure accumulation. Therefore, a political economy analysis of agrarian change and rural labour was chosen.

An obvious question here could be why I did not choose feminism as a theoretical reference point for this work. To answer this question, I borrow from Nancy Fraser's (2012) work. According to her, mainstream liberal feminism ends up being an ally of capitalism in focussing on 'productive labour'. This restricts analytical focus to women from relatively privileged women in terms of colour, class and caste. Those on the margins are neglected – blacks, Dalits, poor immigrants, etc. Such feminism is limited also in the sense that it does not trace the structural causes of women's subjugation. Women have multiple identities – race, caste, sexuality, religion, etc. which influence how women participate in the economy and how they experience exploitation. Women are a heterogenous group and they have conflicting interests, but it is important to realise their common enemy that is neoliberal capitalism. Without this, analysing and challenging structural sources of exlploitation is not possible. Here, political economy frameworks are definitely more useful becasue they tell us about the overall structural context in which individuals are incorporated and how they operate that is the nature of capitalism and relate this to ground reality (for example, see Mezzadri, 2017). Feminist scholarship focusses on the family or the private. In this book, I attempt to study women who are labourers, so my entry point is the category of class. My field methods were designed to seek information on women's work in the public, productive domain. But of course, what women do and why cannot be understood in isolation of their other social roles and responsibilities. This is precisely what Professor Bernstein's work helps me to capture – how class positions and relations are shaped by non-class identities. Locating this work in political economy is by no means a negation of the sophisticated analysis of intersectionality extended by feminist and Dalit literature in the Indian context. But these tend to emphasise more on sociocultural differences rather than on hierarchies within caste, gender and between and within classes. Nonetheless, works such as those of Bina Agarwal (1994), Radhika Govinda (2014, 2017), Manuela Ciotti (2002, 2009) and the Jefferys' (1996) offer very useful insights.

I chose to locate my work in agrarian political economy; using Bernstein as my theoretical framework becasue it explained the nature of contemporary neoliberal capitalist globalisation, how this impacted traditional class structures leading to the breakdown of erstwhile 'pure' categories like agricultural or rural classes and formation of classes of labour and extended analytical tools that could be put to use in fieldwork. According to Bernstein (2010), central to political economy works are questions of who owns what, who does what, who gets what and what do they do with the surplus? This book throws light on some of these aspects.

In the following paragraphs, I present the outline and main arguments of each chapter in this book.

Chapter 2 lays out the nuts and bolts of this book. In other words, it explains the theoretical framework in which this work is embedded and the analytical tools that were deployed in the process of my doctoral research which is the subject matter of this book. The chapter presents an extensive literature review of relevant themes – the classical agrarian question and its reinterpretation, labour relations and labour struggles. Following Professor Henry Bernstein's scholarship (2010), I use the agrarian question approach to show how agriculture and rural labourers have been impacted by neoliberal capitalist globalisation generally and more specifically, in the context of India and eastern UP, where this work is located. Since this is about labourers, the focus is on the agrarian question of labour, reinterpreted by Professor Bernstein as a question of 'reproduction squeeze'. This is clearly borne out by small farmers and labourers struggling to keep themselves productively employed, often simultaneously straddling different odd jobs across sectors and spaces. This new reality necessitates a rethink on classical categories used in agrarian political economy scholarship. For example, can class be understood as just an economic category, is the term peasantry still useful given the commoditisation and corporatisation or are there labourers who can be identified with prefixes such as agricultural and rural? In this context, I find Professor Bernstein's framework on petty commodity production very relevant to the Indian context and moreover it extends analytical categories such as classes of labour which can be deployed for fieldwork-based class analysis. The strengths of Bernstein's framework clearly come across in my review of other seminal class analyses in the context of rural India. A common observation in political economy works, discussing the nature of rural class structure in village India, is the interconnectedness of class, caste and gender. It therefore becomes imperative to discuss these concepts and how they relate to each other. I do this in another part of the second chapter. An important point raised here is that there might be divergence between the concept and its lived reality. Moreover, identities of caste and gender underscore one's experience of exploitation. But do these identities preclude any collective action by women labourers against their employers? This is dealt with in the section on rural political expression wherein I discuss classic works on collective action by peasants and farmers. The purpose is to get a sense of what form does such action take, under what circumstances and the consequences thereof. After this, the second chapter makes the shift from a general theoretical discussion to the state of agriculture and agrarian relations in the state of UP and what this has meant for rural labourers and women labourers, more specifically.

Chapter 3 maps caste-wise occupational patterns. Within caste groups, this is further nuanced along the lines of gender. This mapping exercise serves several purposes. First, it informs the reader about the rural class structure in the region. Second, we learn about the features of these classes by way of looking at their occupations, ownership of land and other assets, gender and intergenerational relations, etc. Third, this occupational mapping is also indicative of social and power hierarchies, inequality and poverty that characterise the region and actually much of village India and defines the everyday lives of Dalit labourers. Finally, this mapping exercise reiterates that Bernstein's petty commodity differentiation is more attuned to ground reality. Overall, this chapter is of immense importance because it creates a type of knowledge database for eastern UP that does not exist till date. Also, it also establishes that labour markets and labour relations are not just a reflection of the economy. These are very much constructed on and shaped by one's religion, gender, socio-political networks, life cycle changes and family structure and so on. The worst off are the Dalits and women. In fact, I argue that the mobility, job prospects of men and their sense of pride and honour are all built on the backs of women who are held captive in the least paid and most demeaning tasks, and it is women who entirely bear the burden of unfree labour. I flesh out this in Chapter 4 wherein I go into a detailed description of wage relations, recruitment process, labour control mechanisms, evidence on unfree labour and intra-labour relations of Dalit women from the classes of labour category. What also comes out clearly is that employment relations are best understood against the wider village-based social, economic and political relations of domination and subjugation.

Chapter 5 is on labour struggles, that is, the various ways in which labourers attempt to improve their positions vis-a-vis their employers or capitalists. Some of the questions that will be answered in this chapter are – what are the forms that labour struggles take, under what conditions do they occur, what are the outcomes of these struggles, etc. Also, I consider how women Dalit labourers relate to local political issues and the everyday state. This chapter gives readers an insight into the nature of the local state and the myriad ways in which the state–class nexus operates to ensure the continued dominance by a few and the continued marginalisation of Dalits in general. Based on my fieldwork, I argue that 'weapons of the weak' (Scott, 1985, 1986) and 'negotiations' (Jeffery and Jeffery, 1996) are the most common forms of labour struggles. Such actions seek small wage increases, respect and recognition by employers and are reflective of labourers' politicisation and assertion. This is in contrast with the ongoing farmers' protests which draw on relatively larger mobilisation efforts of farmer organisations, cutting across identities and classes, organised around meso- and macro-level issues and that directly challenge the state.

The final and the concluding chapter recaps and weaves together the main arguments of the preceding chapters. Overall, this book contributes to agrarian political economy in several ways. One, the novelty of this book is that it creates a knowledge base on rural labour regime in eastern UP and the labour relations of village-based Dalit women labourers that is difficult to find. Similar stories have been written but from other regions of the country. Second, it brings out the benefits of using Henry Bernstein's theorisation of differentiation in petty commodity production and helps us to understand the heterogeneity of small farmers in India, especially the role of non-class identities in class formation and class relations. His concept of 'classes of labour' is indicative of larger processes of informalisation. This idea has been applied by Jens Lerche (2010) in the Indian context. His development of a hierarchy of jobs in terms of stability, income, rights, etc. finds strong resonance in this book as also his and Chen's (2008) argument that this is also a hierarchy of power, caste and gender. Third, an important argument made in the book is the feminisation of unfree labour. Fourth, at a broad level, this book contributes also to our understanding of power and inequality. Power is a multi-level process and operates in complex ways. For example, this book shows how work relations have to be located in women's everyday relations of domination and subjugation, how women bear disproportionate burden of unfree labour but nonetheless they are not powerless, ignorant or passive. Women labourers seek better work terms and conditions by resorting to weapons of the weak and occasionally resort to open confrontation. One would assume that with feminisation of agriculture and in the absence of their male relatives, women would have greater agency in taking decisions. Unfortunately, this has not been the case and internalisation of patriarchy is a major barrier. While inequality has not been a conceptual concern of this book, it does highlight some important concerns on this front. A high level of inequality (income, asset, social exclusion, political marginalisation) characterises village India. This is also indicative of poverty and deprivation, which have a strong female connection.

2 Who Is a Labourer? Reconceptualising and Understanding the Agrarian Question of Labour Today

In this chapter, I will build a historical narrative on the classical agrarian question and how this has been reconceptualised in the context of agrarian political economy. Drawing on the works of Byres and Bernstein, I will argue that, traditionally, the classic agrarian question was that of capital. Using Bernstein's theoretical framework, I will then go on to show that today's agrarian question is that of the very survival of labourers as understood against a backdrop of agrarian neoliberalism. Juxtaposing Bernstein's schema of petty commodity differentiation with other important schema on rural class differentiation in the Indian context, I will conclude that Bernstein's conceptualisation of differentiation amongst small farmers and especially, his category of classes of labour is analytically more enabling and suitable to the ground reality. He, however, does not study or analyse the struggles of labourers – an important aspect in my research. Here I will use other scholars' work as an entry point to my research. This chapter will also look at the literature on labour struggles and labour relations and I will conclude the chapter with a methodological note.

Labouring poor today cannot be typified as just rural or agricultural labourers. Labourers are in constant movement across diverse locations attempting to secure individual and household reproduction. To achieve this, they variously combine insecure and exploitative forms of labour commodification, self-employment activities and other non-remunerative but value-adding work with small-scale farming. Against this reality, how best to understand rural labourers? Are they rural? Are they agrarian? Is this picture true of labourers from all caste groups and for both men and women? Can rural labourers still be understood with theoretical conceptualisations such as the peasantry? Answering these and therefore the need to re-imagine categories of capital and labour, one needs to first understand how the idea of agrarian itself has undergone massive transformations in the post independence period.

This chapter is organised in the following manner. The first section provides a brief description of the changed contours of agricultural development under neoliberal capitalist globalisation and their consequences for the rural labouring classes in developing countries and especially in India.

DOI: 10.4324/9780429321894-2

This is important because, though subject to much debate, rural labour continues to be either perceived as predominantly agrarian or at least originating from the village agricultural economy. In much of the literature, such labour is treated as a fuzzy category to which certain general characteristics are attributed on the basis of observed empirical tendencies. Following this, the concern of the second section is to understand rural class differentiation today. To this end, the classic agrarian political economy perspective on class differentiation and Bernstein's development of it is discussed. The third section locates Bernstein in the Indian context. The fourth section is a select overview of literature on how rural political expression or the relation between peasants and politics has been understood. The fifth section introduces the fieldwork area. It does so by discussing the available literature on labour relations and labour struggles and identifying knowledge gaps. I will conclude this chapter with a note on the method and methodology deployed in the research undertaken for this book.

Exploring the Context: Neoliberal Agricultural Development and Rural Labour

Agriculture was attributed a central role in the industrial transition of developing countries. Agriculture would supply cheap labour, cheap food and raw materials to industry. Agrarian surplus would finance the industrialisation project of developing countries. As such, the primary questions of study were: How has agriculture contributed to the development of capitalism and indeed, to what extent has capitalism emerged and developed?; What role did rural classes play in this transition and how were they impacted and reconfigured and in the larger political context of national struggles against colonial regimes and their influence on emerging post-colonial states? Post-independent India initiated an ambitious industrialisation drive in the context of a Nehruvian mixed-economy socialist state. In colonial India, works on peasantry focussed on their struggles against colonial exploitation and their role in the freedom struggle. A major debate in India in the early post independence years was to what extent has capitalist mode of production been established in the countryside and the socio-economic differentiation that has emerged in the process of this transition. At the time, agrarian political economy in India was dominated by three key questions – capital creation, surplus extraction and socio-economic differentiation. The works of Utsa Patnaik are a classic here (1986, 1987, 1988). Thematically, even today, there is continuity in that analyses of state, capitalist developments in agriculture, rural class structure, and class struggles are the continued preoccupation of scholars working in the field of agrarian political economy. Unfortunately, while ground reality on these has changed drastically over the decades, there has not been much theoretical re-engagement. But first, what is the nature of the capitalist system in which these analyses of state, rural class structure and relations and their politics is taking place?

Since the 1990s, neoliberal capitalist globalisation has culminated in a continued situation of rural distress and agrarian crisis. Since the central concern of this work is with labourers, the focus is on how neoliberal agricultural restructuring has implicated the small and marginal farmers.

I discuss this here to show why we need to rethink traditional conceptual categories and it is here that Bernstein comes into play.

The theoretical foundation of the neoliberal policy logic is found in the neoclassical economic theory. In this perspective, the state is corrupt, inefficient and creates distortions. The market is non-hierarchical, neutral and composed of free and rational individuals seeking to maximise utility and benefit through market-based exchanges. Therefore, the state should concern itself with creating conditions to promote unfettered functioning of markets; for example, political stability, secure property rights and minimal transactions costs and informational asymmetries. The spread of the market would lead to economic growth and development (Saad-Filho, 2005; Oya, 2007).

This paradigm shift effected a change in the fundamental role of the agricultural sector in concerned developing economies. Earlier, agriculture's role was that of sourcing labour and financing industrialisation (for example, Saith, 1990). This state-led development model tackled agricultural modernisation and social inequalities in a bid to create a more productive agriculture (Bernstein, 2010). But at the same time, these policies accentuated regional imbalances and class-based contradictions (Cleaver, 1972). Under neoliberalism, agriculture is seen as an important driver of economic growth, poverty reduction and food security in the developing South, excluding the more industrialised East Asian countries (World Bank, 2008). Introduced as aid conditionality, these policies were a part of IMF–World Bank-designed structural adjustment and economic reform programmes. The timing, pace and extent of the structural adjustment programme varied from country to country and was marked by the internal characteristics of each country and region. These policies have not been clear successes and their impact has been much debated. Even in the limited cases of success, the causes of growth have been difficult to ascertain or specifically attribute to the market reforms (for example, see Rodrik, 2004; Khan, 2007).

Agrarian neoliberalism included, among other things, reduction of government expenditure on rural infrastructure (credit, power, irrigation, subsidies on seeds and fertilisers, extension and support services), limiting the scope of Public Distribution System (PDS hereafter), revision of land ceilings, trade liberalisation with regard to agricultural commodities and increasing dominance of multinational corporations (MNCs hereafter) in input markets (for a detailed discussion on the main features of agrarian neoliberalism, in general, see Bernstein [2010] and for India specifically, see Chandrasekhar and Ghosh [2002], Ghosh [2005], Reddy and Mishra [2009], Ramachandran and Rawal [2010] and Chandrasekhar [2017]).

While India's regional diversity precludes a uniform picture, the unpacking of agrarian neoliberal agenda, together with other historical changes relating to technological developments, changes in cultivation practices, fragmentation of landholdings with successive generations, etc. have culminated in a situation of rural distress and agrarian crisis with its class, caste and gender specificities.

Indian agriculture is numerically dominated by small and marginal farmers, majority of them being Dalits[1] or Adivasis[2] and women labourers who are left behind in the villages due to socio-cultural restrictions and continue to work in agriculture due to lack of alternative village-based employment opportunities (NCEUS, 2007, 2008; Mehrotra, 2017). Various works document how they have borne the brunt of the crisis over decades. For example, Utsa Patnaik (2003) has written that neoliberalism has compounded the problems of poverty, unemployment and food insecurity in India. Laws such as those relating to SEZ, land pooling or liberalisation of laws governing agricultural land are devised and deployed to dispossess the poor of their means of production and livelihood so as to enable capitalist accumulation and real estate business. On this, detailed case studies have been done by Sud (2009), Levien (2012) and Sampat (2016). Ghosh (2015) and Ramachandran et al. (2010) have described how, over the years, declining public spending and privatisation of rural infrastructure, facilities and services have resulted in a high incidence of indebtedness, reverse tenancy, decreased investment in farm, reduced food intake and outmigration in general.

There are exceptions to the aforementioned story. For example, Das Gupta (2019) has written about capitalist farmers who are socially and politically powerful and have benefitted from agrarian neoliberalism in a major way. They straddle rural and urban locales and cultivate new non-traditional crops which are exported or meant for upscale domestic consumption. This is in addition to the trade and industry that they may already be engaged in. Moreover, what is to be noted is that much depends also on the nature of the ruling political regime. For example, Indian agriculture did find some relief under the United Progressive Alliance period (2004–2014) and the most stark instances of these are the rights-based legislations. Mahatma Gandhi National Rural Employment Guarantee Act (MGNREGA hereafter), for instance, insured a minimum wage to the poorest and created crucial rural infrastructure; the Forest Rights Act (2006) ensured the livelihoods of Adivasis.[3] Juxtapose this with the current regime of the National Democratic Alliance (NDA) government which, immediately after coming to power in 2014, sought to dilute MGNREGA and Right to Fair Compensation and Transparency in Land Acquisition, Rehabilitation and Resettlement Act (2013) and cut funds for subsidies and social sector (Ghosh, 2015). Even after more than six years of being in power, the NDA government has failed to deliver on its electoral promise of high Minimum Support Price (MSP) or affordable and good quality rural health services.

As such, the agrarian distress and crisis that we speak of is one that is lived every day. In the increasing marginality of the 'rural/agrarian' – which tends to occupy public imagination and debate only when cases of farmer suicides pop up – there is a further marginalisation and muting of small farmers and agricultural labourers – who today constitute the bulk of agricultural-cum- rural workers.

Over the decades, how has this situation of agrarian crisis impacted livelihoods and jobs in village India? It is factually borne out that agriculture is not the mainstay of rural livelihoods. Usami and Rawal (2018) use NSS data (2004–05 and 2011–12) to show that the share of total employment in agriculture fell sharply from 73.7 per cent in 1993–94 to 59.4 per cent in 2011–12. However, the fact that almost 75 per cent of rural women are still engaged in agriculture (Mondal et al., 2018) means that dependence on agricultural employment is a gendered phenomenon. In rural India, the non-farm sector – for example, construction, brick kilns or factories, mills or shops – is an important source of employment outside of agriculture. These jobs pay more than agricultural labour but can also be very exploitative. For instance, in brick kilns debt bondage and unpaid family labour are very common (see Guerin, 2013 for a detailed description). Also, social identity regulates one's 'eligibility' to do a specific job. For example, I noted during the course of my fieldwork that a Dalit women could not enter the kitchen of her Rajput employer and had to wash utensils in the courtyard. So while it is true that there is diversification away from agriculture, this is true more for men than women who are held back due to a patriarchal ideology. More on this in the subsequent chapters.

In view of these dynamic processes, how is rural labour best understood? In the mode of production debates that dominated in the early post independence decades, Indian scholars operating within a political economy analyses have spoken of landlords, big capitalist farmers and differentiation within peasantry (rich, middle and poor peasantry). The term peasant denoted small holders, largely subsistence oriented, rooted in traditional agricultural village economies. Peasants, agricultural labourers and the landless – these were seen as conceptually different categories on the basis of criteria such as landownership, exploitation and wage labour. But considering that market forces are all pervasive and that subsistence itself is commodified, how relevant is it today to use pre-capitalist terms like landlords and peasantry? As discussed earlier, class categories cannot be reduced to just the economic, they are not fixed and closed categories. Therefore, the need to re-engage with theoretical categories.

I now discuss Bernstein's formulation, making a case for why his theorisation on differentiation amongst petty commodity producers is theoretically and analytically closer to ground reality and more enabling. Subsequently, I discuss works of some prominent political–economy scholars such as Utsa Patnaik, Ashok Rudra, Andre Beteille, Jan Breman and Barbara Harriss-White. I juxtapose their analyses on rural class structure with that of Bernstein to reiterate the relevance of using the latter's theorisation.

Bernstein: The Agrarian Question of Capital and Labour

A leading scholar of agrarian political economy, Henry Bernstein has focussed on the impacts of neoliberal capitalist globalisation on agriculture and class relations. Bernstein (2001, 2006b, 2010) uses the approach of agrarian question in his analysis. He begins with how agriculture has come to be dominated by global agri-business corporations in areas of agricultural production, farming techniques, organisational techniques, processing, marketing and even in shaping in demand patterns. Capital concentration and labour fragmentation are common tendencies. Bernstein approaches the agrarian question from two perspectives, that of capital and labour. He reformulates the classical agrarian question as one of labour in the context of globalisation. This is a question of 'reproduction squeeze' – how to ensure its survival; labour is in constant movement across diverse locations attempting to secure individual and household reproduction. But before detailing Bernstein, a brief note on the classical political economy perspective on the agrarian question and the nature of class differentiation.

Byres (1977, 1996) and Bernstein (1996) deconstructed the classical agrarian question into three meanings. Drawing on Engel's work, the first meaning has to do with political alliances between a growing industrial working class and peasantry to bring about structural transformations in the context of capitalist development. The second meaning was derived from the works of Kautsky and Lenin. It refers to the form and extent of capitalist development in agriculture and obstacles to such development. Here, Lenin considered whether capitalist development could occur in conditions of economic backwardness, and he argued that this was indeed happening in Russia. The third meaning of the agrarian question was derived from Preobrazhensky's work and referred to the generation of an agrarian surplus to finance industrialisation and the creation of a domestic market.

Debates on the classical agrarian question have centred on the transition to capitalism, the continued relevance or not of the classical agrarian question and alternative interpretations of it in the context of neoliberal globalisation (Byres, 1996; Bernstein, 1996, 2006a, 2010; Lerche, 2008; Akram-Lodhi et al., 2009a, 2009b, 2010a, 2010b). The concern here is not with agrarian transition or its relevance per se, but more with what this means for rural social classes in general and agricultural labour in particular, how this has been theoretically reformulated in the current context and whether and what analytical tools it extends.

According to Bernstein (2010), the capitalist agrarian structure that emerged out of feudalism in England (fifteenth to eighteenth centuries) was based on 'capitalist landed property, agrarian capital and landless labour' (Bernstein, 2010, p. 28). Capitalist landed property referred to landowners with private property rights who could sell, rent or lease out land (now a commodity). Tenant farmers were representative of agrarian capital who rented land to produce for the market and make profit. The commodification of land resulting in the dispossession of peasants (subsistence-oriented farmers) created a class of landless labour working for the aforementioned classes or providing 'free' wage labour for industrialisation. The England case is seen as one of successful agrarian transition.

Byres's (1996) reading of Lenin's analysis of the Prussian case (sixteenth to nineteenth centuries) indicates a successful resolution of the agrarian question, but here capitalist farming was a gradual development and land relations retained semi-feudal features for a considerably longer time. Feudal landlords who dominated the processes of capitalist transformation became capitalist farmers. Differentiation of the peasantry was limited as only a minority of big peasants, in association with landlords, were transformed into capitalist farmers. Majority of the peasants became landless. Lenin described this type of capitalist agrarian transition as 'capitalism from above'. In contrast, Lenin described the American case (nineteenth century) as 'capitalism from below'. In the absence of feudalism, capitalist relations in agriculture emerged from within the peasantry, mainly from rich peasants who were transformed into a capitalist class. At the other extreme, the poor peasants were transformed into agricultural or urban wage labourers. This case reflected greater social differentiation among the peasantry reconfigured as petty commodity producers under spreading commodity relations.

The resolution of the agrarian question is conditioned by the evolving structural context shaping and influencing agrarian processes. As such, there is no one manner of its resolution. Over the years, the macro-level structural context has significantly changed with attendant consequences for agriculture and rural classes. In the context of decolonisation and within the framework of state-led development, different conceptualisations of rural differentiation were furthered. In general, these were articulated with reference to the historical trajectories of agrarian transition, growing commodity production, integration of developing economies into a global economy, access to means of production and regional specificities of land and labour patterns, patterns of accumulation and investment, cropping patterns and production methods, government policies, etc. (for example, Raikes, 1978; Deere and de Janvry, 1981; Kay, 1981; Akram-Lodhi, 1993).

In Bernstein's (2003, 2004, 2006b, 2008, 2010) view, the classical agrarian question was that of capital, concerned with the establishment of the capitalist mode of production, marked by transformation of feudal landlords into a capitalist class and peasant labour into wage labour. Characterised by generalised commodity production, it entailed transition from a predominantly agricultural to industrial economy by way of investing agrarian surplus into industrial development. Bernstein's argument is that the classical agricultural question of capital has lost its relevance. At their independence, Asian and African colonies were characterised by agricultural petty commodity production and capitalist social relations more generally. Petty commodity producers combine elements of capital and labour and are subject to tendencies of differentiation. Class locations are influenced by other factors like gender or labour and income patterns in families.

Bernstein (2010) has qualified that the establishment of generalised commodity production does not mean complete commodification. In capitalism, those variously referred to as peasants, small-scale farmers or family farmers are transformed into petty commodity producers (they are not subsistence-based family farmers). They combine class locations of capital and labour and depend on subsistence and commercial agriculture and other forms of labour commodification. They are subject to market imperatives. Bernstein refers to this as commodification of subsistence. In addition, it has been suggested that with the shift from developmentalism to conditions of globalisation, industrial growth is in many cases de-linked from the agricultural sector. Developing states are ascribed a minimal role with limited power to redirect agrarian surplus for industrialisation and with trade and financial liberalisation, alternative sources for financing industrialisation are available (Lerche, 2008).

As such, Bernstein has argued that the classical agrarian question of capital does not exist anymore, that is, it has either been resolved or is not relevant in the current context. Byres (1986, 1996; Lerche, 2008) does not agree with this generalisation. For example, according to him, successful capitalist agrarian transition in India is limited mainly to Punjab, Haryana and west Uttar Pradesh. Byres stresses on the possible persistence of pre-capitalist rural classes and modes of appropriation in other regions of India. In hindsight, Bernstein's assertions have proved to be closer to ground reality in India.

In a Marxian political economy framework, class is a social relations and capitalism is a necessary stage towards the establishment of communism. It is a progressive stage based on the central contradiction between capitalists and wage labourers. Both capital and labour had a common interest in dismantling the feudal structure. As such, according to Bernstein (2004), to the extent that a successful capitalist agrarian transformation results in changes in rural social formations, enhances technological productivity and provides a surplus and wage labour for industrialisation (the transition from agricultural to non-agricultural labour), the classical agrarian question of capital is also a question of labour. Bernstein has established that the classical agrarian question is no longer a question of capital. But is there still an agrarian question of labour? What have changes in capitalism meant for an agrarian question of labour? An important element of the agrarian question of capital was the disintegration of pre-capitalist landed property as a viable political and economic force and this was accomplished (albeit in diverse ways and with somewhat different outcomes) through land reforms. Land reforms remained a significant feature of agricultural policy in the period of state-led development, that is, up to the 1970s.

According to Bernstein (2002, 2006b, 2008, 2010) then, from the perspective of labour, the classical agrarian question referred to redistributive land reforms with the state as the main agent of development. Land reforms could take various forms, for example, confiscation and redistribution of ceiling surplus land, conferring title of land on tenant cultivators or nationalisation of large commercial farms and plantations. They were often accompanied with rural development policies such as provisioning social and economic infrastructure like schools and credit facilities or employment and skill generation programmes, etc. These were undertaken either in response to the threat of or actual conflict and unrest. The intention was to deliver social justice, alleviate poverty, lead to development of productive forces in agriculture and thereby generate a surplus which could be directed into industrial development and accumulation. These policies were supported by or made possible by a political alliance between different social classes and an economic rationale where they were perceived as modernising. These agricultural and rural development policies followed different historical trajectories in various regions, but what was mostly common to them was the expansion and increase of commodity production and tendencies of regional and social differentiation (for example, see Cleaver, 1972).

Proponents of market-led agrarian reforms criticised the state-led agenda of land reforms for their huge implementation costs, corruption, bureaucratic legalese, top-down approach, distortion of the land market, and so on (Borras, 2003). Promoters of neoliberal globalisation further market-led land reforms. Borras (2003) summarises the key features of these as follows. Land reforms are envisaged as voluntary, that is land to be bought from willing buyers rather than state acquisition. The approach is demand driven, that is those who explicitly want land will benefit and land sales to be negotiated according to the type of land in demand. This was a departure from the earlier expropriation and redistribution model. Other advantages of this model include decentralised implementation allowing transparency and accountability, creation of a more free, efficient and informed land market, and commercial farming is encouraged through the provision of various grant schemes. Subjection to market imperatives and provision of land to small farmers would increase productive efficiency and weed out inefficient farmers.

However, according to Bernstein (2002), underlining this reform agenda are issues of land commodification and private property rights and the mainstream development rhetoric of ending rural poverty that serves a legitimisation function. Both Borras (2003) and Bernstein (2002) have criticised this model for completely overlooking the nature of and the interplay between social, economic and political power relations in the countryside that influence land prices, information and financial flows, bargaining position, etc.

Relating the classical agrarian question of labour to the nature of capitalism today, Bernstein (2001, 2002, 2004, 2006b, 2010) suggests the unlikelihood of land reforms based on broad political alliances occurring because ruling classes are no longer dependent on agrarian surplus for industrial development and rural classes of capital and labour no longer subsist on agriculture only. In addition, as petty commodity production reflects possibility of class differentiation, class alliances are likely to be tenuous and temporary. The struggle between classes is limited by within class divisions of caste and gender which mediate experiences of oppression and exploitation. Finally, in view of the changing role of land in agriculture and farming practices and by association, the role of agriculture in the livelihoods of petty commodity producers, the demand for land reforms has given way to questions of capital–labour relations (i.e. understanding labour against capital and not agriculture). The structural context of neoliberal globalisation is marked by capital concentration in advanced economies (mostly) and labour employment and income insecurity and fragmentation. Petty commodity producers simultaneously pursue different employment and income sources, straddling various locations in the social division of labour and are subject to differentiation and exploitation (Lerche, 2010). So, labour is increasingly involved in non-agricultural wage labour to sustain itself, but the move is partial as non-agricultural wage labour is undertaken in combination with farming. This partial move is indicative also of distress and crisis of labour reproduction. Finally, in a country like India, this needs to be gendered.

In this scenario, Bernstein has indicated it is difficult to envisage a common ground in demanding land reforms. While land continues to be an important buffer against food insecurity and socio-cultural pride is associated with its ownership, the extent to which land reforms can possibly benefit rural labour remains a vexed issue. Also, it is in this context that Bernstein has argued that the demand for land reforms (the classical agrarian question of labour) has lost ground to the relationship between capital and labour and that rural labour is better understood in relation to capital rather than agriculture. As such the classical agrarian question of labour is reconfigured and the structural source of this agrarian question of labour is the increasing insecurity of employment in contemporary capitalism that cannot provide the minimum reproduction costs (Arrighi and Moore cited in Bernstein, 2006b, p. 457).

As pointed out earlier, in petty commodity production, the possibility of class differentiation arises from the fact that petty commodity producers combine elements of capital (land, agricultural machinery and implements, seeds, etc.) and labour (individuals). This gives rise to the possibility of their disintegration into classes of capital or labour as they pursue reproduction through a variety of combinations of wage labour and self-employment with farming. The process of differentiation is in turn influenced by non-class identities like gender and ethnicity.

At the top of the hierarchy are the petty capitalists, rich farmers or emergent capitalists, able to reproduce themselves as capital over a prolonged period of time. They pursue diverse economic activities and are an accumulating class (Bernstein, 2010).

Bernstein's (2010) second stratum is composed of petty producers or medium farmers. These combine family and wage labour and are able to reproduce on a simple basis. They are not an accumulating class. These farmers may hire wage labour or they themselves work as wage labour on others' farms as and when needed and lease in or lease out land as part of various sharecropping arrangements. They exploit wage labour but can also be exploited themselves as the boundaries between middle and poor farmers or rural labour are blurred. At the bottom are the classes of labour. These are unable to reproduce themselves as capital and increasingly find it difficult to secure their survival on a daily basis. To achieve this, they variously combine insecure and exploitative forms of labour commodification, self-employment activities and other non-remunerative but value-adding work with small-scale farming. In the process, they reflect a high degree of mobility across different production locations and positions in the social division of labour.

To reiterate, this process of labour fragmentation/class differentiation is underscored by social, economic and political factors like gender; caste; access to and control over resources; changing farming practices and production costs; marginalisation and proletarianisation of middle farmers; role of livelihood diversification and so on. As such, classes are understood as dynamic categories.

Following Bernstein's development of the classical agrarian question and his perspective on social differentiation, it is now clear that categories such as rural labour or agricultural labour no longer capture the empirical reality or extend a partial ground picture. The erstwhile agricultural labour is best understood as classes of labour and the agrarian question of labour is that of a reproduction problematic resulting in a crisis of labour (Silver and Arrighi, 2001).

There are several reasons for choosing Bernstein as the theoretical reference point for my research. First, Bernstein clearly theorises and links the evolving nature of capitalism to labour. Other political economy frameworks do capture the ground reality correctly but continue to work with pre-capitalist class categorisations such as peasantry. Second, he provides concrete categories which can be used as analytical tools rather than simply seeing petty commodity producers as a homogenous or fuzzy category to which are attributed general features like footloose nature, deagrarianisation, proletarianisation and so on. Third, given that my primary concern is with rural labourers, Bernstein's preoccupation with petty commodity producers and the nature of their differentiation made it very suitable to delineating who actually constituted rural labour and their characteristics. Moreover, Indian agriculture and my fieldwork area in eastern UP is largely smallholder. Fourth, his concept of classes of labour captures the ground reality, that is the increasingly fluid class locations that may combine elements of capital and labour and the possibility and complexity of internal differentiation within class categories. His derivation can be used to understand most of the empirical class categories documented in the field sites. This is not to deny the existence of comparatively large capitalist farmers as indicated earlier, but theoretical distinctions do not map onto empirical reality very neatly. I will take up the capital side of the story later in this book. Finally, that analytical categories other than class may underline the process of class differentiation is easily related to the Indian context.

Locating Bernstein in Indian Context

A scrutiny of Bernstein's theorisation in Indian context is interesting considering that despite periodic high growth rates in the first two decades of this millennium, jobs remain a huge challenge. This has to be understood with reference to the lopsided nature of Indian growth. The services sector accounts for more than half of India's GDP, but it does not make a significant contribution in employment generation (Chandrasekhar and Ghosh, 2018). While the share of agriculture in GDP has fallen over the years to about 14 per cent today, almost half the workforce (about 49%) still directly or indirectly depends on agriculture for livelihood (Rustagi, 2015). Share of agriculture in GDP for the year 2019–20 stood at 16.5 per cent, but one should note here that rather than crop production and income, allied activities such as livestock and fishing are growing faster (GoI, 2020). Moreover, according to an NCEUS report (2008), in the early 2000s, when India reported about 8 per cent growth rate per annum, 77 per cent of the population was poor and vulnerable (Sengupta et al., 2008). In fact, according to an ILO report (Saha and Verick, 2016), overall rural employment grew at an average of less than 1 per cent per annum in the periods 1999–2000 and 2011–12. Simply put, India is recording high growth but at the same time, large sections of its citizenry are struggling to survive on the margins. That capital is accumulating more and more and that the share of labour is falling is a reality across countries (Oxfam International, 2016, 2017).

Figures provide one side of the story. In a country like India, which is characterised by deep inequalities, labour markets cannot be understood solely in an economic sense with reference to percentage of employment created, poverty effects, extent of unemployment or underemployment, wage rates, etc. Labour markets, especially rural labour markets, are arenas of social relations where unequal power relations are a norm. Labour relations are based on a political economy of difference – of caste, gender, religion, region, asset base, capabilities, etc. These factors influence who can access what type of jobs, under what terms and conditions and with what labour market outcomes. Discrimination actually starts before one even enters the labour market.

India's working poor (just under 60 % taking USD2 as poverty line) are characterised by structural inequalities, degrees of informality, low wages, little or no social protection, very low levels of education, skills and health standards (Institute for Human Development, 2014). There is a strong correlation between poverty and social identity. India's poor are also more likely to be Dalits, Adivasis, Muslims and then OBCs (Kannan, 2018). Clearly then, India's growth has been unequal and based on exclusions. Based on detailed fieldwork from different regions of India, Shah et al. (2018) have documented that capitalist modernity and accumulation are in fact premised on inherited social identities.

Can one then agree with Bernstein's assertion that that the agrarian question of capital has been bypassed or resolved in India and what exists is an agrarian question of labour that is, the very matter of labourers' survival? Lerche (2008) highlights two grounds for Bernstein's assertion that the agrarian question of capital has been bypassed or resolved. First, generalised petty commodity production within capitalist social relations already existed at the time of decolonisation. Second, not only neoliberal globalisation has opened up new sources of funding industrialisation (doing away with dependency on agrarian surplus), but also the state's power to redirect agrarian surplus is much constrained under this regime. Moreover, contrary to the classic agrarian transition's assumption, linkages between the agricultural and industrial sectors are considerably weakened. This is seen in the lopsided Indian story of high growth rates in recent years. On these fronts, Lerche agrees with Bernstein. On the agrarian question of labour also, Lerche agrees that broad-based redistributive land reforms are difficult to achieve. The only difference is that while Bernstein does not consider the possibility of redistributive land reforms, Lerche thinks it is possible but highly unlikely. Lerche also believes that even if land reforms were to occur, unless substantive, the extent to which they can benefit rural labour is debatable. He agrees with Bernstein that given the predominance of capitalist relations of production and reproduction, rural labour is best understood vis-à-vis capital and not agriculture.

However, the establishment of the capitalist mode of production and declined dependency on agricultural accumulation do not undermine the importance of studying the diverse processes of capitalist agrarian transformation in India, for instance, a class-based analysis of the creation and appropriation of surplus (Lerche, 2008). Lerche (2011) believes that capitalist agrarian transformation in India is uneven, slow and in accordance with Bernstein's framework, that is the nature of India's capitalist growth indicates that the agrarian question of capital has been bypassed without a classical resolution. Moreover, there are others like Byres (2003) who do not agree with Bernstein. In the case of Arunachal Pradesh, Harriss-White et al (2009) argues that capitalist developments outside agriculture and the state's integration with the global economy in this sense conform to Bernstein's assertion that the agrarian question of capital has been bypassed. At the same time, the pace of capitalist agrarian transformation is very slow, and it still reflects pre-capitalist social relations. However, she also admits that reproduction outside the market is increasingly becoming difficult. In West Bengal, she shows a different picture, that of agrarian accumulation being diverted into related activities such as agri-trading and processing and other commercial activities (Harriss-White, 2008; Lerche, 2011).

The strengths of Bernstein's framework become all the more clear when compared with the dominant empirically informed class analyses in the context of agrarian political economy in India.

The class structure of rural India has been widely debated and there is no agreement on any one class structure as being representative of the Indian countryside. Alice Thorner (1982) has explained this as inevitable given India's regional diversity and the varying objectives of scholars. There are many perspectives on the structure of agrarian class relations in India. It is not possible to detail them all here. Some of these viewpoints refer to aspects of rural class structure in their broader scheme of things and agrarian change and processes of class differentiation were not the direct concerns of these analyses. For example, in analysing economic stagnation in India in the 1980s, Bardhan (1984) wrote of a class of rich farmers as an organised and politically powerful interest group influencing state policies. Another example is that of John Harriss (1999), who highlighted the high degree of caste and class overlap in rural India, while analysing how the character of 'political regimes' influenced state performance. Ashok Rudra (1978a, 1978b, 1978c) wrote about the dualistic character of Indian agriculture and rejected the view of class differentiation.

Andre Beteille (1996, 2007) has written about the rural society in general. Beteille defined class in terms of ownership of means of production and based on his fieldwork carried out in Sripuram village in Tanjore in Tamil Nadu in the 1960s; he described the agrarian class structure as composed of landowners, tenants and agricultural labourers. He defined class in terms of ownership of the means of production. Patnaik (1987) has challenged Beteille's class categories for being of little analytical value because it does not take into consideration exploitation in deriving classes. Classes so derived are theoretically confusing because a landowner could be a landlord or tenant and a tenant could be a middle or small peasant. If landownership is the principal criterion for defining classes, then on what basis should a landowner be classified as a landlord or an agricultural labourer? Is it landholding size in combination with factors like participation in labour process, cultivation practices, occupational patterns, etc.? If both capitalist and labouring classes diversify into other types of employment, then what should be the defining criteria? These are not elaborated. Andre Beteille's work on agrarian class structure is historically significant and indicative of trends like emergence of new classes, intra-class differentiation, fluidity regarding class position, occupational multiplicity, etc. It is rich in descriptive detail but not foregrounded enough explanation for the processes he identified. He does not explain processes of surplus creation and appropriation; how systemic exclusion and exploitation allow a minority to appropriate from the subordinated majority. In what type of structural context and power relations do the various classes operate? These are important questions for any political economy analysis and Bernstein's analysis does this well.

In the following, I therefore restrict myself to discussing the works of Patanik, Breman and Harriss-White, who have either been directly concerned with the nature of agrarian change and its implications for rural classes or made important and directly relevant interventions on the topic of my work.

Utsa Patnaik: Peasant Differentiation to Peasant Pauperisation

Operating with an agrarian political economy approach, Patnaik (1976, 1986, 1987, 1988) makes two important assertions with reference to capitalist developments in Indian agriculture. One is the semi-feudal nature of these developments considering that landlords continued to dominate through semi-feudal characteristics such as caste oppression. Second, green revolution has heightened rural class differentiation; and class was defined on the basis of exploitation. Arguing against traditional Marxian notions of class based on just landholding size or initial resource endowments, she asserts that class position is influenced also by factors like family size, cropping pattern and intensity of cultivation, level of technology employed, etc. One indication of this is the extent to which a household hires outside labour and the extent to which the household members work for others. This and the exploitation criteria are used in Patnaik's method of labour use index for identifying classes.

Based on this, Patnaik (1976, 1987) identified five rural classes. At the top are the big landlords with large resource endowments who undertake no manual labour and depend on hired labour. The peasantry is differentiated. Rich peasants, like big landlords, are an accumulating and exploitative class, but they do some manual labour on their farms and equally depend on hired labour. The middle peasantry is primarily dependent on family labour and is subsistence oriented. Though self-employment is the most important element here, middle peasants may be further sub-classified as upper and middle peasants. The former are net exploiters of labour as they hire some labour and are able to generate and retain small surpluses. The latter do not hire labour at all and therefore are not exploiters. Since, it is more difficult to ensure subsistence, they may resort to wage labour to supplement self-employment and as such, they themselves are exploited to some extent.

The fourth class identified by Patnaik (1976, 1987) is that of poor peasants whose subsistence is dependent on working for others, irrespective of whether they own some land or not, as wage labourers or lessees. Further, poor peasants can be subdivided into two categories. A petty tenant makes rent payments and is less dependent on wage labour. An agricultural labour cultivates a tract of land, whether owned or rented, but is more dependent on wage labour. Poor peasants are barely able to meet their reproduction costs. At the bottom are the landless or full-time labourers having no resource endowments and therefore no self-employment possibility. They are completely dependent on working for others. In comparison to poor peasants, full-time labourers face even greater uncertainty in securing survival. It is the strata of poor peasants and full-time labourers that constitute 'rural labour' for Patnaik.

Since the derivation of labour-exploitation criterion in the 1970s, the context in which rural classes of capital and labour operate has changed profoundly. At that point of time, Patnaik's method was advantageous. For example, she argued against a reductionist class definition and asserted the differentiation in the peasantry. She was not blind to the limitations of her framework – it was applicable to only cultivating households and not very robust for situations of weak differentiation or where factors like caste are over-determining (Patnaik, 1976, 1988). There is no one position on the mode of production debate (see Lerche et al., 2013 for an overview). On the one hand, some scholars stress on the persistence of semi-feudal features like landlordism and bonded labour (Lerche et al., 2013). On the other hand, there are scholars who emphasise on capitalist agrarian relations as seen in processes of commodification, proletarianisation and the diversification of rural livelihoods, albeit with regional variations (Lerche et al., 2013). It is precisely this conflict that also explains why some scholars believe in the continued salience of the idea of peasantry. Patnaik's was a static model that captured class locations at that point of time. Patnaik considers agrarian relations outside the production process as secondary to those arising within the production process and therefore does not consider how classes interact with the market or are involved in exploitative relations outside the immediate production process. She agrees that these would need to be studied for any dynamic conception tracing changes over time.

Bernstein's formulation overcomes these problems. In circumstances where even susbsistence is commodified, it is not clear what is to be gained by sticking to pre-capitalist concepts like peasantry. In fact, 'semi-feudal' features like bonded or unfree labour are very much capitalist in nature (Guerin, 2013), and other features like landlord dominance and dependence on farming and land for livelihood and accumulation are declining. Bernstein's formulation takes accumulation as a central concern in addition to a consideration of means of production, labour use patterns, surplus/deficit situation and combinations of labour commodifications, self-employment activities and non-remunerated activities. These are important contributions to survival, though they are not without their attendant forms of exploitation or even very limited mutual benefits as in the case of debt maximisation or buffer against food insecurity within patron–client relations of neo-bondage. Unlike Patnaik, he takes into account commodity relations of labouring poor outside cultivation. In an era where agriculture has a declining role in rural livelihoods, an empirically derived model of class classification has to consider other commodity relations and overlapping socio-economic relations outside of agriculture that are central to the rural poor. Also, Bernstein's is a dynamic conceptualisation that can capture shifting class positions and trace changes over time, unlike Patnaik's formulation. He explicitly states that non-class factors like gender and ethnicity underscore processes of class differentiation. Bernstein's model appears as a closer approximation of the current ground reality.

In recent years, Patnaik (2006) seems to have made a shift in her position from stressing on peasant differentiation to peasantry similarly affected by the onslaught of agrarian neoliberalism, resulting in its pauperisation. In doing so, the idea of differentiation is displaced by a peasant–globalisation contradiction – contradiction between 'all the toiling masses and imperialism'. She highlights the emergence of peasant struggles against this drive but does not elaborate much on this aspect, beyond emphasising on the adoption of policies that will allow the labouring poor to live a life of dignity and expansion of internal markets for growth (Patnaik, 2010). In this analysis, the idea of differentiation as Patnaik elaborated in her earlier work seems to have lost importance. Using a framework such as that of Bernstein where class formation is a key concern is more useful for research agendas such as this book.

Jan Breman: Capitalism and Labour Exploitation

Breman has worked on rural labour relations in India for more than forty years. Steeped in ethnographical tradition, his historical account of changing rural class relations in Gujarat is seminal. The issue with Breman is that he has not written much on theory and conceptual categories. Nonetheless, based on a reading of Breman (1985b, 1994, 2003, 2007) it can be concluded that his work is grounded in a class analysis. Broadly, three themes can be identified. First, agricultural modernisation and associated rural development are associated with class differentiation and diversification of rural economy. Related to this is the second aspect which traces the impact on labouring classes of changing accumulation patterns. The third theme is that of increased labour mobility and fragmentation along regional and communal lines. The overriding concern of Breman is to show how capitalist processes and class inequality (overlapping with caste) result in exploitation and pauperisation of agrarian labour and proletariatisation of migrant workers.

In one of his early works, Breman (1985b) referred to small owners, middle and large farmers and landless proletariat. The class of large (above 15 acres) farmers are identified as the main drivers and beneficiaries of agrarian change and associated rural developments. This class is also the dominant regional caste. Large farmers either occupy or are in a position to influence political authority and accumulation from agriculture is invested in alternative acquisitions such as better jobs and education.

Middle farmers (5–15 acres) are also usually from similar caste backgrounds. Their holdings are not as fragmented as in the case of landless proletariat. Like the large farmers, middle farmers also reflect economic diversification. Their upper caste status and social networks are crucial in enabling their access to better non-agricultural employment opportunities. Nevertheless, agriculture continues to be the main source of livelihood for a majority of middle farmers. Though numerically dominant, small landowners (less than 5 acres) represented a very small share in the overall land structure. Small landowners are usually from middle to lower castes. Majority of these were marginal owners with holdings of less than two acres. Dependent on family labour, small landowners undertook wage labour also. Debt is a common and in certain cases could result in land dispossession. These farmers lack capital and are excluded from access to markets and resources, institutional support, etc. At the same time, small landowners prevent absolute impoverishment by simultaneously engaging in employment made available as a result of diversification of rural economy.

The landless proletariat is the largest class composed mainly of tribals. They are dependant upon low-waged agricultural labour for their reproduction and seek to supplement this with other casual labour across different locations. In his later work (2007), Breman has highlighted how the neoliberal regime reinforces this. In a situation of surplus labour competing for scarce employment opportunities, non-class affiliations like caste, region, religion acquire great significance in accessing even the most exploitative and insecure jobs. This fragmentation and circulation of labouring class prevents any collective action and weakens its bargaining power.

Breman is an extremely important scholarly reference for any work on labour relations in India. His description of how capital accumulates, dominates, exploits and prevents labour resistance is a useful reference point in studying and comparing labour–rural labour relations elsewhere in India. It serves as a good guide to a researcher on what to look out for in fieldwork. But as stated earlier, its lack of theorisation leaves one with no conceptual tools to work with. Breman's work is also limited on the gender front. Though he highlights their marginalisation in the labour market and their 'double burden', this is not accorded much attention. For example, how gender shapes and is shaped by class relations is not investigated.

Barbara Harriss-White: Discrimination Through Social Identities

Barbara Harriss-White (2004; Harriss-White and McCartney, 2000) explains the economic decline in India in the period of the developmental state with reference to the notion of intermediate classes as coined by Kalecki and applied by P.S. Jha in the Indian case. However, of more relevance here is her work on social structures of regulation and accumulation (Harriss-White, 2003, 2004, 2005).

Barbara Harriss-White's (2003, 2004, 2005) concern is with the way in which certain social and political institutions – gender, religion, caste and space – influence class formation, regulate labour participation in markets, shape accumulation strategies and contain tensions created by capitalist development. Class conflict is contained by the labouring poor's daily struggles for survival, their mobile and fragmented nature and their non-class affiliations in a context of employment scarcity and insecurity (Harriss-White and Gooptu, 2001). How do these identities suppress and exploit the majority in favour of capitalist domination and accumulation? In her various works, Harriss-White (2003, 2004, 2005; Harriss-White and Gooptu, 2001) has described how gender, caste, religion, etc. regulate the majority of Indian labour operating in its informal economy and how capital and its agents deploy these to their benefit.

For example, to escape the exploitative and humiliating social relations in which village and agrarian class relations are embedded and to supplement their meagre wages, labourers migrate to urban areas for casual labour. But this takes place along gender and age lines. Women largely remain in villages because of responsibilities of domestic chores and own cultivation. Not only are they excluded from better waged off-farm work, but even in villages they are concentrated in least paid agricultural tasks. In the case of male labourers, local or migrants, debt relations and patronage provide capital access to them and attached unpaid family labour. Poverty, food insecurity, exclusion from public and common resources and the political and social clout of the landed are some of the bases of labour bondage.

How does gender interact with class and caste? From the aforementioned example, it can be drawn that feminisation of agriculture is distress induced and has not done away with the sexual division of labour. Where women can be found in non-agricultural employment, it is usually menial, casual, unpaid or very lowly paid in cash and/or kind and they are subject to harassment. These are more likely to be found in the case of scheduled castes, men and women. At the upper end of class hierarchy, women do not participate in productive employment. Marital alliances are arranged to access capital investment (dowry) and for men to take over family businesses. Across the class spectrum, women are subordinate to men and lacking asset ownership.

Another way in which caste interacts with class is evident in the manner in which dominant classes create caste-based associations which function as interest groups vis-à-vis the state. At the other end, intense competition for reserved jobs creates divisions among scheduled castes. In situations where employers and labourers are from similar caste background, the rhetoric of caste unity is used to repress labour. Labourers have resorted to caste-based organisation to maintain control over certain types of jobs or organised in social movements or around political parties. This is one way in which these labourers assert their dignity, but at the same time, this resort to caste appeal undermines the struggle against class-based exploitation. Religious principles and practices like unequal property inheritance laws and female seclusion also facilitate capital accumulation. As in the case of caste, religion-based associations can circumscribe the flow of information and distribution of resources, create closed business networks, etc.

Harris-White, through such examples drawn on her research, has argued that caste and class reinforce each other. Class contradictions are diluted and strategically contained. Sporadic labour action, either individual or collective, is ruthlessly repressed by state-backed authorities. Such action, when it occurs, is directed against the direct oppressor on some issue. They are not broad based, sustained or against a common enemy. Economic stability, so central to capital's agenda, is ensured through these identities which are social and political constructions and this regulation of the economy has intensified under neoliberal globalisation as 'free' markets gained more and more ground at the expense of state which either cannot regulate or deliberately 'deregulates' under the neoliberal mandate (Harriss-White, 2003). At the same time, such facilitation of capital accumulation reinforces patriarchal relations, adversely affecting the welfare of women.

Harriss-White's is an important contribution. Her description of capital control over labour through class and non-class identities, as well as how labour exploitation and resistance are structured around these is well related to the objective of this book. Her works provide an invaluable insight into the conditions of labour. However, it is conceptually weak. Operating in a political economy framework, she provides a well-researched and comprehensive analysis, but it is not theoretically grounded. For example, while it is clear that class cannot be interpreted in narrow economic terms, no explanation is extended as to how it should be conceived when conducting research. But then her concern is not to provide a class schema. In comparison, Bernstein's framework provides not only a theoretical framework and analytical categories to work with but also a detailed picture of the changing nature of capitalism, key features of agrarian change and how rural/agricultural labour is implicated in these transformations. In other words, not only does he consider the importance of non-class identities, but his area of focus is more suited to this book and also conceptually strong.

This discussion underlines the relevance of Bernstein's position. Some of them agreed with Bernstein on certain grounds. For example, Patnaik, Beteille, Breman and Harriss-White all agree that rural change and class differentiation are to be understood in relation to the nature of capitalism. Their description of labour conditions attests to the relevance of Bernstein's agrarian question of labour in India. All these scholars emphasised on the interconnections between class and caste and gender to varying extents. Bernstein spoke also of how gender and caste shape class differentiation. Given that the primary objective of this book is to study rural low caste female labour relations from a class perspective, the importance of how caste, gender and class mediate cannot be undermined. Given this, the following section briefly refers to the key features of the caste system and its intersection with gender. This discussion is important as we see in the subsequent chapters how everyday lives of Dalit women are mediated by these identities.

Caste and Gender: Power in India

In much of the literature, caste and gender appear as interconnected factors determining the position of individuals in the (unequal) society. Here, I mention some features of the caste system and gender relations which operate to keep certain sections of a society subjugated, beginning with caste. The former is discussed first.

The Government of India (GOI) has a three-fold caste classification: at the bottom are the scheduled castes (SCs) and scheduled tribes (STs) who have been so categorised on the basis of their specific features. SCs are the former untoucables, the historical victims of social and economic injustices perpetrated by a hierarchical caste system. STs refer to communities so classified by the GOI on account of their economic backwardness, unique cultural traits and geographical and social separation from the mainstream Indian society. Classes, other than SCs, STs and General category, with low levels of social, economic and educational development are classified as Other Backward Classes (OBCs). All others are lumped in the General category, at the top.

While the idea of caste[4] is widely debated, two things are commonly agreed: one, it is premised on a notion of inequality (Srinivas, 1966, 1989; Fuchs, 1981; Mandelbaum, 1972), and two, caste identity is bound to be contested for several reasons – India's regional diversity, political use of caste by colonial power in pre-independence India, significance of caste in the electoral arena and in various social movements and finally because of the political and economic implications that follow from one's caste identity (Srinivas, 1957, 1966; Mendelsohn and Vicziany, 1996; Beteille, 1997; Dirks, 2002). Moreover, though in recent years the focus on untouchability may have been displaced by emphasis on the poverty of SCs, in reality, this shift is just symbolic (Dilege, 1997; Mendelsohn and Vicziany, 1996).

Srinivas (1966, 1989) defined caste (or *jati*)[5] as a hereditary identity, applied to an endogamous group of people, engaged in specific occupations associated with their position in a hierarchical society. Position in the caste hierarchy depended on notions of purity–pollution, on regional features, linguistic affiliations or it could be due to differing principles. Affluence, asset ownership, political and economic power were also important determinants. Castes are internally divided.

At the top of the caste hierarchy are 'dominant castes' (Srinivas, 1987). They may or may not be a numerical majority in a village but are large landowners and are politically and economically influential. They are most likely from higher castes. Fuchs (1981) identified those at the bottom of the caste hierarchy as SCs (former untouchables). The historical practice of untouchability is associated with their poverty, low educational standards and discrimination in daily life (Fuchs, 1981; Mendelsohn and Vicziany, 1996). It is this which distinguishes them from the other poor.

Based on this caste hierarchy was a division of labour (Mandelbaum, 1972; Srinivas, 1987). Depending on their caste position, various castes were assigned occupations. This traditional division of labour regulated economic and social relations in the village. This was called the *jajmani* system. Along these lines, patron (usually upper castes) and client (usually lower castes and service providers) relations also developed. Though considerably weakened by capitalist developments, the *jajmani* system was seen as a convenient way of securing labour or employment, as a source of credit and securing other services as and when required. Mendelsohn and Vicziany (1996) noted that SCs mostly worked as agricultural labourers in addition to providing their traditional service. With capitalist penetration of agriculture and its declining capacity to absorb labour, these agricultural labourers had to resort to other non-agricultural casual wage labour in urban areas.

There are divergences between an understanding of caste at a conceptual level and caste as seen in practice on ground (Srinivas, 1966; Mandelbaum, 1972). According to Deliege (1997), this ambiguity arises because government classification of scheduled caste does not neatly fit with sociological realities existing on ground. To put it simply, there are degrees of untouchability. Some castes are less clean than others or are permanently 'polluted'. However, these castes are not rigidly separated (Mandelbaum, 1972). According to Deliege (1997), nature and conditions of castes may vary from village to village which makes a uniform characterisation difficult. But more than this, the decisive point in being classified as a scheduled caste or a touchable low caste is whether a particular caste was historically engaged in slave or bonded work and whether it is served by other lower castes.

In comparison to caste, the issue of gender has not been as politically charged. In an autobiographical essay, Ilaiah (2005) describes how caste and gender ideologies and lifestyle were inculcated in children from a young age. The very process of socialisation serves to create a caste-based and gendered consciousness, they become a way of life, a natural order of things while in reality they are used to control and marginalise women. For instance, sexual division of labour is perceived and accepted as a traditional order rather than as stabilising and legitimising a form of structural inequality (Beneria and Sen, 1997). If this is the case, then female agrarian labour relations, determined as they are by patronage and familial ties by caste position and gender ideologies, can be said to subsidise (male?) capitalist accumulation. How does the ideology of gender intersect with capitalist relations?

Srinivas (1989) stressed on a straightforward correlation between caste and class vis-à-vis gender, that is, upper caste women lived a secluded life bearing domestic and reproductive responsibilities, whereas lower caste women, in addition to these responsibilities, performed wage labour which could bring them in direct contact with men. Imitation of upper caste practices in the case of upwardly mobile lower castes was also associated with female exclusion and stringent observation of rituals and traditions (Srinivas, 1977). More recently, this caste–class overlap with adverse consequences for women has also been documented in the case of Kanbis and Halpatis in Gujarat (Ebrahim, 2000). Even within the households, the gender hierarchy operated along the lines of age with the eldest female member commanding the most authority (Ramamurthy, 1994).

Agricultural modernisation is associated with intensified female participation in own cultivation and in wage labour to save labour costs and to provide for the household in the face of male outmigration and irregular remittances. This has had some positive outcome in terms of increasing female visibility and mobility, but these are distress induced. As women are perceived as dependents, their work and income are seen as supplementary to that of the male breadwinner. Their labour in own cultivation and livestock rearing is invisible and rendered unimportant. Such gendering of roles underlines exploitation of women labours (Mazumdar et al., 1992). Importantly, Ilaiah (2005) noted that though gendered division of labour is found across the caste spectrum, it is less rigid and oppressive among the SCs than in the upper castes. For instance, scheduled caste women were perceived as productive agents, they openly retaliated against domestic agents, were involved in independent social relations, etc.

Dube (1996) highlighted the role of gender in reinforcing caste hierarchies. Men migrate to take up new and relatively better paid work for reasons such as low wages, inadequate employment in traditional occupation or agriculture or because of the stigma attached with their traditional occupations. Women, on the other hand, have had to continue with traditional occupations to provide for the household and to maintain socio-economic relations in the village. Notions of purity, family dignity and honour are strictly tied to a woman's behaviour and observation of cultural practices and marital alliances are arranged to maintain these. Violation of traditions invites harsh punishments in the case of women but not men.

Another line of debate on the intersectional nature of gender and caste comes from within feminist and Dalit scholarship which talk of different forms of patriarchy. The works of Guru (1995), Rege (1998), Geetha (2009), Chakravarty (2012–2013) are seminal here. An obvious question is why a work on Dalit women such as this book does not use these as its theoretical reference points. My work is located within the framework of agrarian political economy; the focus is on class and class relations as the entry point. Bernstein's framework allows me to do this and at the same time shows how class relationships are shaped by non-class identities of caste and gender. This work is not about socio-cultural differences or to how patriarchy operates within a community, how multiple forms of patriarchy are different from each other and so on.

A logical question that follows from this note on caste and gender is whether this common experience of exploitation and subordination of the SCs and women overcomes their internal differences and lead to any action against their oppressors. Does caste, class or gender form the basis of such action? In other words, if capitalism has incorporated and structured various social differences to serve its purposes, has there been any viable challenge to this from labouring classes? What form does this rural political expression take? The following section investigates these.

Rural Political Expression

Bernstein's framework does not deal with this per se, though he refers to struggles for land, better wages and other issues of 'agrarian politics' more generally (Bernstein, 2001, 2004; Bernstein and Byres, 2001). In Marx, class contradictions ultimately culminate in a revolution leading to progressive change. However, so far, it emerges from this chapter that petty commodity producers are greatly differentiated. Class interests among them and between petty commodity producers and other rural classes are also bound to be divisive and contradictory, unlike in the case of Marx's working class. Capitalist exploitation is also differentially experienced by men and women and by upper castes, other castes and scheduled castes. If their interface with structural constraints is varied, how are seemingly common interests such as resisting domination and oppression articulated? This section looks at some of the ways in which these have been achieved more broadly and in India specifically.

Eric Wolf (1969) highlighted the role of the peasantry in effecting structural change. The background to his 'peasant wars' was the spread of capitalism and how it resulted in the economic and social alienation of various sections of the population. This paved the possibility of broad-based class alliances as seen in the case of the emerging Chinese working class, the peasantry and the students against the capitalist upheavals. Wolf does not undermine the differentiated nature and interests of the peasantry classes. Rather, the coming together of diverse interests at specific historical points for purposes of political action has to be explained with reference to local or regional power matrices, social configurations and external influence.

Hobsbawm (1973), on the other hand, strongly discounted the possibility of peasant revolts occurring on a grand scale as in the case of Wolf. Also, he wrote in the context of traditional or transitional societies. According to him, peasant rebellions are mostly local or regional in character. Though, like Wolf, Hobsbawm too considered external influence an important factor in transforming small-scale peasant action into a broader movement. However, this singular and broad-based peasant political action was nothing but a temporary agglomeration of small peasant movements. At the same time, Hobsbawm does not deny the possibility of such action wielding considerable influence, depending upon their physical proximity to the capital state.

An internalised sense of backwardness and demands of the agricultural production cycle are major limitations on the political potential of the peasantry. Hobsbawm argued that nonetheless this should not be equated with powerlessness because it might be a deliberate front behind which peasants seek to maximise benefits. What was more crucial in interpreting peasant inaction or action was how peasants related to local or national power structures.

As with Wolf and Hobsbawm, Alavi (1973) too was concerned with understanding the context of the peasantry's political response. Drawing on empirical work in Punjab (Pakistan), Alavi argued that peasant action had to be understood in relation to the wider socio-economic structures that peasants are embedded in. She identified three such structures. The first referred to the patron–client relationship between landlords and sharecroppers and labourers. Both, sharecroppers and labourers are dependent on the landlord for wage labour. Middle peasants either hire seasonal labour or work for others but to a much lesser extent. The second structure was that of kinship. Kinship ties were the strongest among middle peasants and weakest among sharecroppers and labourers as a landlord's authority extended into their private lives. Kinship ties were weak among landlords as each sought to outdo the other in political and economic power. The third was political structure. Landlords served as middlemen for villagers vis-à-vis government structures, and the government in turn sought inroads into local power structures through landlords. How do these relationships bear on the possibility of political action by peasants? In case of sharecroppers and labourers, economic dependence on rival landlords prevented kinship solidarity among them which could be an important factor in political mobilisation. Middle peasants share strong solidarity links and could organise against landlords with the help of political parties or peasant unions. In the case of landlords, kinship did not enable class solidarity. Rather, kinship networks served as political base.

In the latter half of the twentieth century, James Scott's (1985, 1986) 'weapons of the weak' found much resonance in micro-level empirical works and still continues to. As such, it is critically looked at here. Weapons of the weak referred to routine ways in which the exploited such as the peasantry sought to minimise their oppression; for instance, foot-dragging, slander, feigned ignorance, pretensions, slander, etc. These are deliberate actions that do not require collective coordination. Importantly, they extend anonymity to their users as direct confrontation is absent. They are easily accessible and possible in a context where the peasantry is an increasingly diverse, geographically dispersed and unorganised category. Though symbolic in nature, they can influence policy options of the state. For a recent application of this formulation, see Kerkvliet and Tria (2009).

The reasons that prevent or diffuse overt class conflicts, as seen in the previous section, offer one explanation as to why everyday forms of peasant resistance come across as the most viable expression of class conflict.

However, Scott's formulation has been criticised for various reasons. Hart (1991) criticised Scott for not taking into account the gendered nature of labour arrangements. Drawing on her fieldwork in Malaysia, she argued that patron–client relations constrained actions of male labour who cultivated these ties for various reasons. Moreover, political marginalisation of women allowed female labour to openly challenge oppressive structures. White (1986) criticised Scott's approach for undermining the socio-economic differentiation between and within peasant households and for not adequately elaborating on what/who was being resisted and the effectiveness of the resistance (White, 1986). Turton (1986) also criticised Scott for not focussing on the oppressor but portraying only one side of the class relation. Walker (2008) criticised Scott for a weak and conservative portrayal of the peasantry.

The 1980s were also witness to collective political action as encapsulated in the farmers' movements in India. They were representative of broad-level rural political agitation or agrarian conflict. In a volume edited by Brass (1994), it is evident that farmers' movements emerged and mobilised around issues of neoliberal economic policies, crisis of green revolution and underdevelopment of India. Their actions were shaped by their regional specificities. The class composition of these movements was also much debated. The more common view though was they represented the interests of surplus-producing farmers at a crucial time of capitalist development in agriculture, where some accumulated to the exclusion of others. Not only did farmers' movements not represent the interests of rural labourers, but they also fanned caste consciousness because the landlord–peasant divide overlapped upper caste–scheduled caste divide.

The issues of class, caste and gender have figured prominently in labour struggles which themselves are highly diverse in terms of their mobilisation, objectives, the level at which they take place, the nature of struggle, etc. What is common to most of them is their local or regional nature, labourers featured as principal actors and these agitations derived from capitalist developments, particularly in agriculture, which directly affected them. Two of the early examples come from Maharashtra: that of the Shahada movement in Maharashtra (Mies, 1976) and the successful organised militant action on the part of women agricultural workers for employment and against price rise (urban women mostly) in the early 1970s (Omvedt, 1978). More recently, Tanner's (1995) study of labour union participation in rural Andhra Pradesh highlighted that political response of labourers is conditioned by various factors such as the local history of confrontation, the degree of caste solidarity and economic differentiation within castes, personal motivations, risk perception, etc. Tanner moreover stressed on the greater possibility of success of female agitation which draws on social and work-based relations and is conditioned by ideological factors. However, Jeffery and Jeffery (1996) proposed a different understanding of resistance by women. They argue that in the case of women, resistance cannot be understood simply as visible collective action. It has to be perceived as women's agency and the covert ways in which they use political dynamics, social structures and power relations to negotiate spaces for themselves. A narrow definition of resistance risks stereotyping women as passive victims of oppressive structures.

Then there are other types of 'agrarian politics' such as those represented by transnational agrarian movements (for example, see Borras et al., 2008) or in the Indian context, the role of political parties with an overwhelming scheduled caste and/or agricultural support base (for example, see Lerche, 1999).

Despite this variety of ways in which the agrarian classes can politically express themselves, in recent years the terrain of Alavi, Scott and local- or regional-based sporadic, dispersed and temporary issue-based labour struggles are more common, as one would assume in the context of Bernstein's agrarian question of labour. These are not class struggles as traditionally understood in a Marxian sense. They do, however, reflect the contemporary ground realities of fragmented classes of labour, embedded in particularistic identities and structures of power and negotiating between class in itself and class for itself action.

In recent years, India has seen the rural dispossessed organising themselves into protest marches, for example, the Nashik–Mumbai march in 2018 or the demonstrations of farmers from Tamil Nadu in Delhi in 2017. These protests are a melting pot of the rural – farmers, labourers, artisans, adivasis, Dalits – often joined by urban activist intellectuals. Through these marches, they seek to draw the attention of the state to very pressing issues such as minimum support prices, remunerative prices for their products, relief from indebtedness, credit crisis, water crisis, landownership rights and so on. On the one side, there is the spectre of farmers' suicides and on the other side, we now see that farmers are organising themselves peacefully, capturing public space and imagination in prominent cities and forcing the state to listen to them at the very least. Sainath has argued that these marches, which the government dismissed as urban Maoism, have actually been the strongest form of democracy.[6]

Agrarian Structure and Relations in Rural UP

Here I will foreground the discussion on agrarian crisis and agrarian relations in the context of UP. I begin with a historical overview of agrarian structure and relations in UP, and it is against this framework rural labour in the state is understood.

A basic knowledge of agrarian developments in UP is essential to set the context for rural labour or labour originating from agriculture. This review is limited by several factors.

The state of UP is divided into four regions – western, eastern, central and Bundelkhand. But it is the east–west comparison that dominates the literature. On this, most of the existing studies are located in western UP. With the exception of a few micro-level field studies, recent changes in agrarian structure and relations in the east of the state have not been comprehensively captured. Central UP and Bundelkhand do not find independent studies focussing on them and in early works were discussed as extensions of other regions of the state. Here, the agricultural history of the eastern part is considered in relation to that of west. One reason for this is the availability of secondary literature and second, this comparison captures the main agricultural development patterns in the state. This review is also constrained by the fact that evidence on agrarian distress in the state is rather patchy. Finally, most literature on UP does not extend a historical analysis of agrarian structure and relations with reference to gender. There is some evidence on gendered impacts of capitalist diffusion in agriculture vis-à-vis female labour (for example, Sharma, 1985) and this will be subsequently discussed.

Historically, land has been the primary asset around which agrarian relations revolved. Brass (1980) and Hasan (1998) extend a historical analysis of agrarian change and rural class relations in UP. At independence, UP had a small number of large zamindars who had been politically and economically favoured by the British and therefore were already in a dominant position in rural India.[7] The main nationalist organ at that time, the Indian National Congress (INC) sought to build its support on the platform of the medium and small zamindars and the high-caste tenants of the zamindars. For this purpose, the Congress rallied for tenancy reforms in the colonial era with partial success. As the undisputed rulers in post-independence India and in UP, the congress enacted reforms to abolish the zamindari power hold and break up large holdings by imposing ceiling limits.[8] However, these reforms fell far short of their mandates. While the zamindar's role in revenue collection was eliminated as were various tenancy rights and some large holdings were broken up, in reality the former zamindars managed to evade law and retain their land base. Therefore, land redistribution was little and inequalities in ownership persisted. Over the years, the economic and political position of these landowners has been further entrenched through land consolidation, the green revolution and panchayati raj institutions.[9] Some middle castes who were tenants of zamindars also benefitted.

Brass (1980) and Hasan (1998) agree that at the beginning of the 1970s, in both the eastern and western regions of the state, the numerically small upper castes like Brahmins, Bhumihars, Rajputs, Thakurs and a few middle castes like the Ahirs and Kurmis owned most of the land. At the bottom end, lower castes were overwhelmingly agricultural labourers. Beyond this common caste–class overlap, there were significant regional disparities. Unlike western UP, eastern UP had a disproportionately high number of small holdings, a few medium holdings and a large number of agricultural labourers. The situation was the same in the early 1980s (Hasan, 1998; Sharma and Poleman, 1994). One implication of this was the presence of extreme inequality in eastern UP, where a small number of non-cultivating upper and middle castes controlled most land. In contrast, western UP had comparatively numerically significant cultivating caste-classes that controlled much more land, constraining class polarisation. It is clear that in the case of UP, economic and social inequality largely show a straightforward correlation and in fact, it had been argued very early on that land reforms were unlikely to extend social and economic equality (Neale, 1962). In subsequent years, this became a major basis for politicisation of various sections of rural classes.

The period between 1970s and 1990s saw a few other changes in agrarian land relations in UP: redistribution of gram sabha land among SCs prevented absolute landlessness to some extent, inheritance laws accentuated fragmentation of holdings across the socio-economic spectrum, some SCs and OBCs purchased land in the market or leased in land from upper caste Hindus and Muslims (Srivastava, 1999). These factors have been associated with increasing rural class differentiation, class polarisation to varying extents and proletarianisation of the poor peasantry (Saith and Tankha, 1972; Subas, 1984). Between the early 1980s and 2000, the proportion of SCs among large landowners increased, but at the same time, they reflected a disproportionate share at the bottom of land hierarchy (Srivastava, 2007). In other words, slight improvement in the position of SCs was accompanied by greater differentiation among them. Overall though, upper castes maintained their hold at the top of the land hierarchy, while agricultural labourers were primarily SCs (Srivastava, 2007; Lerche, 1998).

As suggested by Hasan (1998) and Srivastava (1999), the different trajectories of agrarian change in eastern and western UP can, to a large extent, be explained in relation to the land structure in combination with other government-sponsored policies extending rural infrastructure, credit, subsidies, etc. Green revolution was first introduced in western UP in the mid-1960s given its favourable agro-climatic conditions, land structure, infrastructural and resource base (particularly with respect to irrigation and electrification) and the industrious nature of its farmers. Resultantly, the western region reflected high agricultural growth till years later. Just as in the case of regional inequality, gains accrued to economically better-positioned farmers in western UP and an emerging surplus-producing middle caste peasantry which in time became politically and economically dominant in the region (for an overview, also see Lerche, 1998).

Economic and social change was slow and uneven in eastern UP during the 1960s (for example, see Singh, 1970, 1976; Jetley, 1977). However, it is generally agreed that the situation in eastern UP began to change from the mid-1970s under government tutelage leading to the development of an irrigation network and adoption of green revolution technologies and by the early 1980s, inter-regional disparities had narrowed (Sharma and Poleman, 1994; Srivastava, 1999). An important factor in this was the evolving class structure under the impact of changing cultivation practices, accumulations patterns and labour arrangements, particularly in the case of middle and rich peasants (Srivastava, 1999). Some of these aspects will be mentioned later. Lerche and Jeffery (2003) point out a north–south divide in addition to the one between the east and the west regions. According to their analysis (1961–91), the northern districts in west UP and central districts in east UP reflected higher agricultural growth than other districts. For example, in east UP, agricultural growth has been more pronounced in the north where capitalist agriculture pursuing small peasants are concentrated in contrast to the south-east where labourers are predominant (for example, Mirzapur, Allahabad, Banda).

At the same time, these developments in agriculture reflected another trend; decreasing labour requirements of agriculture due to several reasons: mechanisation displaced some labour, increased cultivation of sugarcane or shift to orchards that do not provide year-round employment, miniaturisation of holdings, increased participation of owners in cultivation and greater availability of better paid and less exploitative non-agricultural employment. In the 1970s and 1980s, off-farm employment availability was a consequence of government's rural schemes and emergence of industrial, manufacturing and service activities in response to capitalist developments in agriculture (Sharma, 1994; Ruthven and Kumar, 2002). However, it has been suggested that these peaked by the mid-1980s as public expenditure decreased or government-sponsored work could be accessed only through patron–client relations, and competition for local employment increased because of incoming migrant labour (Ruthven and Kumar, 2002). Logically, it would then follow that marginal and small holders and agricultural labourers (predominant in the eastern region) would be adversely affected.

Recent figures show that all is not well in agriculture in UP. As per agricultural census 2015–16, in UP, 80.18 per cent of the operational landholding fall under marginal land size, followed by 12.68 per cent in small land size and only 0.1 per cent belongs to the large land size (GoI, 2019). The same cites approximately 65 per cent of the workforce in agriculture. According to Verma et al. (2017), the average monthly income of an agricultural household in UP is third lowest (₹4701) in the country and the state also accounts for the largest share (16.9%) of all indebted agricultural households in India – 90.4 per cent of these being marginal and small agricultural households. Growth in agriculture and allied activities in UP has averaged at 2.5 per cent per annum between 2000–01 and 2014–15, which is below the all-India average of 2.9 per cent during this period, at 2004–05 constant prices. The share of foodgrains has declined while allied activities like livestock, milk and fisheries have done well. This is in line with the national picture.

Extending definite conclusions applicable to the entire state, in a vast and diverse state like UP, is not possible, but the aforementioned tendencies and observations do provide a general understanding. A report by the erstwhile Planning Commission of India, GoI (2007) and a report by the GoUP (2006) recognised the need for higher public investment in agriculture but emphasised on developing the private sector. They suggest elimination of subsidies to increase efficiency and promulgation of leasing laws to encourage long-term contract farming under corporate tutelage. The state government's intention to allow large private actors to purchase directly from farmers is a further reflection of the continuing corporatisation of agriculture (Ghosh, 2007; Mahaprashasta and Ramakrishnan, 2011). More generally, underlying these policies is the failure of various governments to invest adequately in agricultural subsidies, extend rural credit, provide supporting facilities and protection from the damaging consequences of corporatisation of agriculture occurring at various levels.

Unlike for some other states, comprehensive fieldwork-based political economy analyses of the status of UP agriculture in recent years are not available (for example, which agrarian classes have gained and which have been marginalised and why?). However, low agricultural growth rates, with continued concentration of the workforce in agriculture, do indicate that all is not well with the agricultural sector, as is evident from farmers' suicides under debt burden (Verma, 2011). Small, marginal and even well-off farmers in western UP have been forced to sell their produce at very low prices (Tripathi, 2004). Here the problem is not of damaged crop or low output but one of 'overproduction', lack of market, weak procurement efforts by the government and unremunerative prices (Tripathi, 2004). According to Nayyar (2011), the state invested in building a huge road network. But such types of investment are more likely to benefit corporate interests by acquiring farmers' land and displacing them rather than improving the social and economic conditions of UP's masses (Ramakrishnan, 2012). The government's neoliberal stance continues in its emphasis on private investment in agricultural sector and acquisition of farmers' land at below market rates for private development (Srivastava, 2011; Ramakrishnan, 2012).

Bernstein's understanding of agrarian neoliberalism and its implication for rural labour find resonance in the earlier description. There is no doubt whatsoever that the recent economic growth seems to have largely bypassed agriculture and rural labour. State policies have increasingly given capitalist interests a definite toehold on crucial assets like land and more generally in the agricultural sector by relaxing land laws, facilitating investment by large companies in agricultural retail trade. The numerically predominant small and marginal farmers are increasingly forced to look for alternative sources to augment their minimal incomes from agriculture. Not only are these opportunities an erratic source of income, but they are increasingly hard to come by as numerous labourers compete for casual work at the bottom of India's informal economy under very oppressive conditions. In terms of social, income and power status as well, they are situated at the bottom of Indian society (Lerche, 2011). More importantly, the relevance of Bernstein's classes of labour as an analytical tool is reiterated in this context of a fragmented labouring class moving in and out of agriculture and other occupations and for understanding the social relations it is involved in.

Capitalist Agrarian Transformations and Female Labour: A General Note

Given the hitherto intertwined relationship between agriculture and rural labour, the next logical question then is how has this transformation implicated rural labour and specifically female members of low caste labouring households? If the agrarian structure does not show insignificant continuities (landownership, caste–class overlap), then have rural labour relations also remained unchanged? I now move on to discussing the implications of such developments in agriculture for rural female labour in particular. My primary focus is on female members of low caste rural labouring households. However, most Indian case studies on rural labour focus on male labour while female labour remains a muted subject. The few field-based case studies, where female labour is the primary subject, draw on evidence from South India or selected green revolution areas. Studies on rural labour in UP concentrate mainly on the western region. Very few cover the eastern part of the state, the focus of this book. These works only occasionally refer to female labour. Considering the dated and limited evidence in the case of UP, I will juxtapose evidence on various aspects of low caste rural labour from various regions with evidence available on these from east UP. As much as possible, gender and caste aspects will be highlighted.

Most of the works on rural labour are village-based studies and the obvious starting (rather, turning) point for these studies is the capitalist penetration of agriculture, particularly in the form of green revolution, as an entry point to discuss rural labour relations. At the same time, they rightly emphasise on the importance of local histories, particularly regarding land reforms and the regional political context and state interventions, in understanding evolving agrarian relations. Here, I will focus on labour relations. Though the importance of migration in rural livelihoods is acknowledged, it is not discussed here because rural female labourers are primarily agricultural and village based (NCEUS, 2008[10]; Breman, 2007). Reference to the state of agriculture is therefore a good starting point before moving on to the more specific aspects of labour relations.

Agriculture as main source of rural employment has been on the decline since the 1990s. Analysis of National Sample Survey (NSS hereafter) data by Usami and Rawal (2018) shows that share of total employment in agriculture fell sharply from 73.7 per cent in 1993–94 to 59.4 per cent in 2011–12 and it continues to decline (for example, see World Bank, 2020). Since rural women labourers are disproportionately concentrated in agriculture, they are also the worst hit by the contraction of employment opportunities in agriculture. Since the 1990s, there has been increasing diversification away from agriculture. This has been more the case for men than for women. According to NSS data, in 1993–94, 75 per cent of men and 86 per cent of women were engaged in primary sector activities (including agriculture and other sectors such as mining) which reduced to 59 per cent for men and

75 per cent for women workers in 2011–12 (Mondal et al., 2018). For a variety of reasons, women engage in only certain types of rural non-farm employment – most commonly in manufacturing and construction (this showed a huge increase partly due to public interventions such as MGNREGA). Manufacturing accounted for 9.8 per cent of total rural non-farm workers in 2011–12 and construction accounted for 6.6 per cent in 2011–12 (Ibid.). Social identity and roles, such as caste and gender, continue to be important determinants of occupational profiles. According to the NSS 68th Round, in rural India, households reporting casual labour as the major income source was the highest for Dalit (52.6%) and Adivasi (38.3%) households. The percentage of rural women in casual labour is 35.1 per cent; Dalit women constituted 50.6 per cent of this and ST women 39.3 per cent.

Land relations are a good starting point to study labour relations. Landownership is linked to political and economic power. It is a major indicator of asset inequality in rural India. NSS 70th Round reports that landless households declined from 10.04 per cent in 2002–03 to 7.41 per cent in 2012–13. But does this decrease mean anything significant considering that NSS 70th Round defines landlessness as less than or equal to 0.002 hectares and also includes under 'landless' category plots where area is not reported? (NSSO, 2013a). The share of land owned in rural India by different social groups was 13.06 per cent for STs, 9.23 per cent for SCs, 45.68 per cent for OBCs and 32.03 per cent for others (NSSO, 2013b). According to Thorat and Madheswaran (2018), in livestock and farm equipment, the share of SCs is 11.7 per cent, 43.8 per cent for OBCs, 25.5 per cent for higher castes and 18.9 per cent for the rest. The high degree of landlessness among Dalits also means preponderance of Dalits in casual labour – as comes across clearly from the figures mentioned here. According to the India Exclusion Report 2016, even where Dalits own land, they are mostly marginal and small farmers, and their land is of very poor quality. It reports that about 56 per cent of women-headed households were landless – indicating multiple layers of exclusion. Field-based village studies show that there is a strong overlap between caste position and not just land but also asset and wealth ownership (Ramachandran et al., 2010; Swaminathan and Rawal, 2015; Kumar, 2017; Swaminathan and Das, 2017).

The incidence of landlessness is high among women in general. According to an Oxfam report, about 85 per cent of rural women in India are engaged in agriculture but only 13 per cent of them owned land (Oxfam International, 2018). In the case of Dalits, landlessness is high and given patriarchal norms and cultural bias, it is possible that landownership among Dalit women would be even worse. One would assume that in the absence of agricultural land, men from Dalit labouring households would migrate to towns and cities in search of employment. This is the general picture but needs to be nuanced further. For example, landless Musahar men from eastern Uttar Pradesh did not migrate. As men are more likely to find employment in and around villages, they needed to stay behind in the village to provide for their families. This was also because they live in a nuclear family set-up and there were no other family members to take care of their families while they were away. So, the landless and the poorest are not always likely to migrate. de Haan (1997, 1999) has argued that in certain cases, the landless are less likely to migrate because they cannot afford the expense of it and they lack the necessary social contacts. Guerin et al. (2012), in the context of brick kiln migration in Tamil Nadu, found that in a wet area, labourers are less likely to migrate. Labourers derive a strong sense of identity from the village or lack connections or do not want to miss out on the benefits associated with patron– client relations.

Figures can only tell us so much. I now look at land relations through some early qualitative fieldwork.

Kapadia's (1995) village study in post green revolution rural Tamil Nadu showed increasing economic polarisation and proletarianisation of the scheduled caste Pallars. In the 1970s, landlords had primarily sold land to better-off middle caste tenants, some of whom over the years managed to consolidate their holdings. This emerging rich peasantry coexisted with the traditional rich landowners. On the other hand, the Pallars, who were small tenants and marginal peasants, became agricultural wage labourers and some of them lost all land in due course. Unlike the middle peasantry, they have been unable to access non-agricultural employment. Their extreme poverty meant the lack of a minimum start-up capital and their untouchable status meant that others were unwilling to lend them. At the same time, there have been increasing economic divisions within caste groups on account of education or jobs which have strained caste and kinship relations and limited the development of class consciousness (Kapadia, 1995). One consequence of this has been the strengthening of caste identities (Kapadia, 1995). For instance, Kapadia shows that while the Pallar female labourers are aware of their common economic interests, they remain divided along neighbourhood and caste ties which play an important role in accessing employment.

At the same time a blanket generalisation is difficult. The extent of polarisation and proletarianisation may vary according to local ecological conditions. The work of Athreya et al. (1990) in Tamil Nadu showed greater polarisation in the wet area where the middle peasantry constituted a small class and, less polarisation in the dry area where the middle class is significant. The wet area had a higher number of landless labourers whereas the dry area had more poor peasants. The study of Djurfeldt et al. (2008), also from Tamil Nadu and covering a span of twenty-five years, showed a limited degree of polarisation and differentiation. Yet, another study from Tamil Nadu shows that overall landlessness doubled from the early 1980s to late 2000s, but the proportion of landless SCs slightly declined reflecting decreased land inequalities as the SCs came into land (Harriss et al., 2010). In the context of rural Tamil Nadu, Ramachandran (1990) also attested to economic differentiation in his area of field study.

Based on her work in rural AP, Garikipati (2009) has pointed out that men were the primary beneficiaries of land redistribution which allowed them to withdraw from exploitative agricultural wage labour and tied labour relations into own cultivation. Women had no such option. da Corta and Venkateshwarlu's (1999) work also supports this. Gupta (2002) also concluded that even in a state like West Bengal, which is reputed to have performed better than other states on land reforms agenda, women remained marginalised. According to Gupta, part of the problem is the socio-cultural identification of women as a part of a family and not as an autonomous individual. Even where joint titles have been granted, it is men who control such assets. On top of this, left organisations do not accord priority to 'women's issues' for it would undermine the class struggle.

Around the green revolution period, a common observation made in relevant literature is that the adoption of new farming practices, technological applications and changing cropping patterns led to new patterns of labour demand – concentrated at peak season time and in certain tasks that were still done by hand. This is where casualisation of labour and feminisation of agricultural labour are also noted.

Kapadia (1995) has pointed out that while the primary male task of ploughing was mechanised, female tasks like transplanting and weeding were not. The sexual division of labour based on the culturally superior status of men was not challenged. Consequently, there has been a **feminisation of agricultural labour**. Breman has also referred to a **gendered division of labour** wherein women work as casual agricultural labourers, primarily inside or near the village because of their domestic and reproductive responsibilities and that they are preferred certain tasks like picking fruits because of their diligence (Breman, 2007). This is an indication of the centrality of the gendered division of labour in new cropping patterns as well (also see De Neve, 2002 for gendered work perception in a rural but non-agricultural setting).

Drawing on her work in another area of Tamil Nadu, Heyer (2001) associated feminisation of agriculture with movement of male labour into non-agricultural employment, cultivation of less labour-intensive crops and emerging new accumulation strategies of rich farmers in the face of declining agricultural productivity. More importantly, as pointed out by Kapadia (1995), women do perform male tasks in own cultivation and occasionally as wage labourers as well. As such, women bear an unequal burden of household responsibility and indeed contribute more regularly to household expense. da Corta and Venkateshwarlu (1999) and Garikipati (2009) also found this to be the case in rural AP.

Drawing on their fieldwork in rural AP, da Corta and Venkateshwarlu (1999) agree that feminisation has occurred but the explanation of it is derived from rapid decline of male participation in agricultural tasks like threshing which was jointly done by men and women. One reason for exit of male labour is that these jobs are low paid. Another is that having benefitted from government policies providing land, credit and other assets, men increasingly moved into own work. At the same time, men continued to rely on female wages for household reproduction. da Corta and Venkateshwarlu (1999) have described such gendered division of labour as also reflecting a class division between 'a non-propertied/waged workforce composed of women . . . and self-employed men' (Da Corta and Venkateshwarlu, 1999, p. 104). Garikipati's (2009) evidence from rural AP also attests to higher involvement of women in agricultural wage labour. This is because men are largely into better paid work involving the use of assets owned by them, and alternative employment opportunities and migration are mostly the preserve of men.

The feminisation of agricultural labour is more of a fact today as men are moving out of agriculture into rural non-farm employment or are migrating to work in other productive sectors in towns and cities. In the case of rural women in general, there has been very limited occupational diversification. Mondal et al.'s (2018) study of NSS data shows that almost 75 per cent of rural women continue to be in agriculture. Outside of agriculture, rural women work as para-teachers and health workers, in construction, garments, domestic work, etc. Much of this diversification is because of government initiatives such as Sarva Shiksha Abhiyan (SSA), Rashtriya Madhyamik Shiksha Abhiyan (RMSA), National Rural Health Mission (NRHM) and MGNREGA. Again, this highlights the role of government in employment generation in rural areas, specifically for women. However, in comparison to regular jobs, much of this employment is contractual and remunerated at a lower rate. In fact, Accredited Social Health Activists (ASHA)s and Auxiliary Nurse Midwives (ANM) are categorised as volunteers and paid honoraria. In much like the upper caste-class employers of these women workers, the *mai-baap* government actually benefitted from a readily available cheap labour force, in the process reifying occupational segregation. My own research indicates that even these are much coveted jobs and captured by the not so poor. These are coveted because they pay much more than agricultural wage labour and are perceived as relatively prestigious clean jobs, reflecting some educational attainment, and workers hold the hope that eventually the *Sarkar* would regularise them. Along similar lines, Chakravarty (2013) writes about 'Viramma' from Racine and Racine's work (1997) where she says how Viramma talks about a Dalit's entry into government services and other government institutions which have remained unreachable in the past but has now become accessible. This is also therefore coveted because these jobs apart from being a bit more lucrative than agri labour has more respect and therefore becomes a point of assertion for both men and women.

Moving on to the issue of **wages**. Wages are distinguished on the basis of the type of employment primarily and can be paid in cash, kind or a combination of the two (Ramachandran, 1990; Kapadia, 1995). Irrespective of this and despite the fact that wage rates are more than what labourers received in the 1970s and 1980s, a gender wage gap is commonly observed in most literature (Athreya et al., 1990; Kapadia, 1995; Heyer, 2001). High male wages are attributed to the higher status and more arduous nature of male tasks (Kapadia, 1995). Even where there is a possibility of women earning more, as is likely in better paid contract work, a portion of the wages are appropriated by their male relatives who recruited them for the job (Kapadia, 1995). Also, this unequal wage system is mediated by the existing patron–client relations between male employers and male labour. Kapadia has noted that when men took paddy, threshed by women, to the employer's house, men would receive some paddy as 'gift'. Wage rates could also be influenced by rates in neighbouring villages, individual economic status and labour availability vis-à-vis its demand at different times in agricultural season and the socio-economic position of the employer (Kapadia, 1995). Local availability of alternative employment opportunities, government policies like the MGNREGA and the politicisation of labourers are also known to influence the wage structure (Harriss et al., 2010).

An important area of change has been the **modes of employment**. This has to do with the decline of traditional social relations and casualisation of the labour force. The two most prevalent types are daily wages work and piece-rate or contract work (Athreya et al., 1990; Kapadia, 1995; Heyer, 2001). The former implies a fixed rate for specified hours. Labourers are supervised by the employer or recruiter. Contract work implies a prior agreed amount for a fixed job, irrespective of the time taken to complete the work. Supervision is not required. According to Heyer (2001), male and female labourers preferred contract work because it paid better. Athreya et al. (1990) and Kapadia (1995) noted the decline of the system of labour exchange among small farmers and labourers. However, in transitional societies like that of Arunachal Pradesh, exchange labour could still be significant (Harriss-White et al., 2009). Hired labour may be common even on family labour-based farms because of caste considerations or farmer's access to better paid non-agricultural employment (Athreya et al., 1990). Gidwani (2001) writes that labour practices can be shaped by caste and cultural ideology also. He describes how scheduled caste Koli labourers prefer group-based contract work because it does away with the need for close supervision and spares them the constant nagging and humiliation by the employer. At the same time, it allows the Patel (a cultivating caste) employers to project themselves as progressive and superior.

Recruitment depends on the mode of employment. In daily wage work, any person who is aware of work opportunity can recruit others, while in contract work the contractor recruits young and skilled people (Kapadia, 1995; Athreya et al., 1990). Recruitment is overwhelmingly shaped by locality and caste ties (Kapadia, 1995; Athreya et al., 1990). Recruiters exercise significant power and influence as sources of employment and credit (Kapadia, 1995, Athreya et al., 1990).

Debt plays an important role in labour relations. For example, Athreya et al. (1990) show that in wet areas, in cultivation where demand for skilled labour is high, employers extend loans to their workers so that these skilled workers would continue to regularly work for them. Heyer (2001) highlights the role of debt in curtailing labourers' attempts at independence from their oppressors but which paradoxically ended in them becoming more dependent on the employers. For example, government provided partial funding for house construction. Labourers borrowed from their employers to invest in this and in the process ended up being more dependent on them. Debt has for long been a ground for capitalist social and economic dominance and a basis for labour mobilisation and relations. Though based on inequality, such arrangements are not feudalistic but found in capitalist social relations and perceived as insurance (for example, Bardhan and Rudra, 1980). It should be noted that debt-based labour relations are not the same as traditional bonded labour (Bardhan and Rudra, 1978).

It is widely agreed that traditional bonded labour is no longer found in villages. Breman (1985b) has documented this in the context of Gujarat's capitalist agricultural development, displacement of Brahmin landlords by commercially oriented Patidars as the dominant caste and various government interventions. According to him, traditional bonded labour or *halipratha* has disintegrated. He described it as a feudal mode of exploitation, a debt-based bondage between large farmers and *Halpati* agricultural labour (and by extension his family) (Breman, 1985b). This system was rooted in the servility and ritualistic inferiority of the *hali* (bonded labourer) and could also involve physical violence. Central to *halipratha* was a complex web of economic and other obligations on both sides. **Neo-bondage**, on the other hand, is more of an economic and impersonal relationship, contractual and comparatively of shorter duration and does not involve family members by extension. It is rooted in exploitative capitalist social relations.

In contrast to Breman, Ramachandran (1990), in his study of agrarian relations and unfree labour in a Tamil Nadu village found that these are increasingly a characteristic of non-wage labour relations between landlords and agricultural labourers, though he denied a strict segregation between the two; for example, guarding crop, working as a driver for the landlord, running errands like buying things from the market and various household chores. These are either unpaid or remunerated at very low rates and are often delayed. Despite this an agricultural labour provides these '**labour services**' to landlords because they are a source of food, work and credit when required. The relationship involves obligations on both sides such as the employer providing the labour with employment and a place to live while the labourer is obligated to work off his loans or provide priority services to this household. Labour services can be provided by men or women of any age and even children.

As pointed out by da Corta and Venkateshwarlu (1999) green revolution did increase agricultural productivity initially, but it also increased labour (given availability of new employment opportunities) and production costs. Rich capitalist farmers responded by adopting mechanisation and diversifying into related activities such as trading, processing, transport, investing in education of their sons, etc. **Tied harvest and labour arrangements** were another way by which they sought to economise on costs, more so with falling agricultural returns.[11] Under tied harvest arrangements, rich farmers engaged in trading, advanced loans to small farmers to cover production costs and other expenses in the off-season. In return, small farmers had to pay back the agreed amount with the produce. Rich farmers might lease out a small plot of land also to small farmers in return for a 50 per cent share in the harvest. Tied labour arrangements involved debt/lease arrangements also. In return, labourers are expected to provide priority services to creditors, plough their fields, tend to livestock and perform other household chores as required. The arrangement assures the creditors or rich farmers of a regular and cheap labour supply, particularly in the peak season. The lease arrangement also tapped into the labour of women of the attached household. Garikipati (2009) found similar tied labour arrangements in her survey of two villages in AP.

According to da Corta and Venkateshwarlu (1999), tied labour arrangements are different from the old system of labour bondage: they are of shorter duration, not rooted in violence or ritualistic discourse of purity/pollution and the terms are contested. Nonetheless, they are based on expectations of patronage and an obligation to provide 'labour service'. To the extent such ties restrict the mobility and ability of labourers to sell their labour power in the market for higher wages, it is an unfree relation.

Rural labour is engaged in patron–client relations and varying degrees of unfree labour relations for various reasons. Some have already been indicated earlier. More generally, these have to be understood in the contemporary structural context of poverty, socio-economic dominance of a minority, caste and gender discrimination and the role of dominant classes as 'gatekeepers', that is, in mediating/controlling access to and distribution of public resources (Pattenden, 2011). Pattenden (2011) has argued that 'gatekeeping' also served to discipline labour as well as maintain dominant class interests by co-opting low-level gatekeepers who performed monitoring and other functions for the main dominant class/gatekeepers.

Dissolution of old-style labour bondage, decline in the political status of upper castes, rural economic diversification, higher wages than in the past, some minimum economic improvement in the position of labourers, a growing consciousness of their exploitation and organisation have been associated with a more vocal and confrontational labouring class (Breman, 1990; Kapadia, 1995; Heyer, 2001). But as pointed out by da Corta and Venkateshwarlu (1999), there is a gender angle to this struggle. Since men refuse to perform low-waged or demeaning wage labour, the burden has increasingly fallen on women to secure household subsistence by undertaking even those wage labour activities refused by men. In this manner,

women's exploitation and humiliation subsidises male labour struggles. Another indication of this is that while men have managed to move away from tied labour arrangements, the number of women in such arrangements has increased – as unpaid attached family labour independently incurring debt against their labour. This and the lack of women's ownership of productive assets are responsible for their **weak bargaining position in the households and in the labour market** (Da Corta and Venkateshwarlu, 1999; Garikipati, 2009).

From this description it is clear that rural labour relations have definitely changed. Women are disproportionately concentrated in agriculture. Economic differentiation and rural proletarianisation exist to varying extents. Though caste and class overlap to a significant extent, there are internal differentiations, and this is a ground for labour fragmentation. Within agriculture, a gendered division of labour and a gender wage gap are common. Locality-based networks, caste identities and gendered ideologies underline recruitment processes. Female labourers are involved in unfree labour arrangements. This, coupled with their income and asset poverty, has perpetuated the exploitation of female agricultural labourers. Does this description apply to female labourers in eastern UP? I explore this here.

Capitalist Agrarian Transformations and Female Labour: Eastern UP

What follows is a general overview of available literature, highlighting caste and gender aspects as much as possible. In the process, I will raise questions also on which my main areas of enquiry come to be based; for example, class structure, patterns of labour commodification; patron–client relations; interlocked land, labour and credit relations; bondage; etc.

As mentioned previously, most studies on UP draw on field evidence from the western part of the state. Wiser and Wiser (2001), Wadley (1994), Lanjouw and Stern (1998) and Dreze (1997) are long-term fieldwork-based studies that describe rural society and economy in western UP. Such longitudinal works are not available in the case of east UP, though there is a set of literature that sheds light on rural society generally, for instance, Singh (1970) and Cohn (1987). On rural labour per se, Srivastava (1989, 1999), Lieten and Srivastava (1999) and Lerche's (1994, 1995, 1998, 1999, 2003) village-based studies from eastern UP are the main sources of information and I draw heavily on them in the subsequent discussion.

The picture one gets from a reading of early village-based studies from eastern UP is that of an upper caste-dominated economy and society, with SCs at the bottom (Singh, 1970; Cohn, 1987).

This can be seen in Singh's (1970) depiction of a village in north-eastern UP. According to Singh (1970), Rajputs and Thakurs who were the big farmers were involved only in a supervisory capacity in agriculture. The middle castes like Ahirs and Kurmis were directly involved in cultivation while the

SCs, who were mostly agricultural labourers, were primarily dependent on wage labour. Those at the top of this hierarchy wielded the most political and economic power. The 1950s and 1960s also witnessed conflicts between various classes on wage and land issues. On such occasions dominant castes closed ranks in view of their collective class interest, though otherwise factionalism within castes was not unknown. Though there was some evidence of castes taking up non-traditional occupations, such mobility was not seen in class status (Singh, 1970). Purity–pollution discourse still dominated social life and among other things, this was reflected in the spatial organisation of the village and the seclusion of upper caste women. At the same time, some change was visible; for instance, changes in local revenue and political institutions under land and other reforms and more importantly, a changing social environment in which SCs could move more freely.

Since then, agrarian relations, as well as the political scenario have shown significant change, but some continuity as well, for instance, **upper castes are still the dominant landowners while agricultural labourers are overwhelmingly SCs** (see Lerche, 1998, pp. 74–75; Srivastava, 1999; Lieten and Srivastava, 1999). Between the 1970s and 1990s, rural social differentiation increased owing to land reforms, green revolution and other public policies. The period saw mechanisation, fragmentation of landholdings, shifting cropping patterns with different political economies of labour, rural economic diversification, etc. The Indian government's policy turn, in the early 1990s, saw the introduction of agrarian neoliberalism marked by a much 'trimmed' state and agricultural corporatisation. So a question that emerges is what is happening to rural female labourers since the 1990s?

Shankar's (1993) small survey of agricultural labourers in eastern UP is a good starting point. He points out that by the early 1990s, agricultural productivity had increased and so had demand for labour. Declining tenancy, emerging migration and dissolution of old patron–client relations were also observed.[12] Scheduled caste men and women gave up their traditional occupations which for long had been perceived as degrading and a source of their 'polluted' status. But agricultural wage employment continued to be significant and even wages had slightly increased but more as a capitalist tactic to ensure labour supply. Contractual work was on a rise. On the downside though, mechanisation was being introduced and this was adversely affecting labour demand, particularly in ploughing. The high incidence of non-agricultural wages in household incomes led Shankar to conclude that labourers were no longer simply agricultural. Indebtedness was high even in the early 1990s, and credit was largely taken from informal sources. Government policies relating to credit, rural employment and those targeting poverty were making a miniscule difference.

An important observation is that **capitalist agrarian change has gendered effects which differentially influence women depending upon their caste and class position.** According to Sharma (1985), green revolution exacerbated economic differentiation between classes and intensified polarisation between men and women. For example, on the one hand Bhumihar women observe seclusion, even vis-à-vis some male members of own family and are completely engaged in domestic work. At the most, as Sharma observed in a couple of cases, women would recruit labour or fetch water but under the cover of darkness. Their only similarity with Chamar women is that the latter too are responsible for domestic work.

Sharma points out that a rigid observation of socio-cultural customs is not seen among Chamar women, given the tiny areas on which they live, and their poverty meant that women had to undertake wage labour as well. Female Chamar wage labourers received lesser wages than their menfolk. Also, they provide their traditional services as midwives and even perform either unpaid or lowly remunerated forced labour. Unlike Bhumihar women, Chamar women make important contributions to daily household reproduction. An improvement in the economic position of a household is strongly related to the withdrawal of women from the production sphere, that is **men's improved economic position is tied to women's subservience and domination.**

Sharma (1985) makes another point, similar to Kapadia (1995). Though there is differentiation within caste groups and faultlines appear as individuals contest for political power and resources, caste remains the predominant organising principle. Thus, even **labourers' growing consciousness of their exploitation and collective interest are subsumed by the caste identity. Development and articulation of class interests are also limited by the existence of attached labour relations** (Bardhan and Rudra, 1978).

Based on their survey of sixty-five eastern UP villages, Bardhan and Rudra (1978), argued that **interlinked tenant and credit relations are common.** Tenants are advanced loans by the landlords for a variety of purposes or the latter themselves may partly bear production costs. This relationship is not akin to feudal exploitation. Bardhan and Rudra (1978) found the incidence of overlapping tenant–credit relationships to be more in relatively advanced villages where landlords were not primarily into money lending but self-cultivation on the basis of hired labour and they invested high-yield variety seeds and chemical fertilisers on the leased plot. Tenants provided unpaid or lowly remunerated labour services to landlord/employer/creditor, though there was no general pattern to this. Tenants were not prohibited from entering into tenancy arrangements with other landlords. Though rooted in inequality and exploitation, Bardhan and Rudra (1978) concluded that such tied credit–labour relationships were not representative of feudal mode of surplus extraction but seen as serving specific purposes. For the capitalist, it served to secure cheap and reliable labour and for the tenants and labourers, it was a source of food and employment security.

Srivastava (1989) also showed how production relations, accumulation processes of big farmers and reproduction strategies of labourers together provide a basis for labour dependency and exploitation; for instance, through lease arrangements and credit ties. His field evidence from two villages in eastern UP shows that credit ties are likely to exist along lease arrangements, particularly in cases of labourers or poor peasant tenants who are also more likely to provide priority labour services to their creditor/lessors, work for them at low wages or even perform unpaid labour at times. Labourers or poor peasants enter into such lease arrangements for subsistence purposes and take loans to meet production and consumption costs whereas employers not only get a share but also avail of labour at reduced costs or even for nothing. In a few cases where farm servants had leased in small plots of land from their employers, the wives of the former are obligated to work for the employer. The more developed a village is, the more likely it is for these interlocked relations to exist and in fact, they play an important role in securing cheap labour.

Shankar (1996) found evidence also of **debt-based bondage** among the landless Kol tribals. Though Gram Sabha land was redistributed among them, the land is effectively controlled by the landlords. Labourers sought to meet important expenses by becoming a bonded labour. The 'interest' is paid through labour. A small amount of low-quality grain is paid as a wage. The debtor is also given a small plot of land for cultivation. Landlords may provide some production cost and take a percentage of produce or rent out their assets like pumpsets. But unlike the past decades, this relationship was not one of absolute dependence. These labourers could undertake wage labour and where family labour (wives and children) was involved some kind of remuneration, no matter how little, was made. There are instances where earnings from migration and other non-farm employment opportunities have been used to free bonded labourers.

Up till the mid-1980s, the government played an important role in vesting SCs with land, providing subsidies for seeds and fertilisers and provisioning credit (Ruthven and Kumar, 2002).[13] Ruthven and Kumar (2002) identify three major changes in agricultural labour relations in this background. First was the **emergence of piece-rate labour groups**. This became increasingly popular for several reasons. From the perspective of labourers, it was better paid, and they did not have to bear the indignity of supervision. From the perspective of capitalist farmers, it allowed them to secure labour relatively easily according to their requirements and under the piece-rate system, labourers worked faster. Piece-rate work is normally found in paddy transplantation and harvesting. However, labour costs could be influenced by factors such as availability of non-agricultural employment in close proximity or whether the capitalist farmer had access to the labour of his tenants or others dependent on him for social and economic reasons. These performed underpaid and priority services for big farmers.

Second, to economise on rising production costs and reduce their dependence on local labourers, big farmers have resorted to recruiting incoming tribal and scheduled caste migrant labourers from MP. Migrant labourers are preferred because they are better workers, reliable, do not need to be supervised and importantly keep local wages depressed. This is a sore point with the local labour who gets less employment and whose bargaining power is also constrained. Finally, the system of *harvahi* or attached labour has significantly declined. Under this system, the attached labourer and his family provided regular priority services to the big farmer but at market rates. There was no time limit, and it could be passed on from one generation to another. In return, the attached labourer received some advance money, a plot to cultivate for subsistence, a daily wage in kind and the farmer could help with inputs as well. This was even preferred by some labourers because it worked as an insurance against food insecurity and provided some work. *Harvahi* still exists in a modified form but on a much smaller extent because of mechanisation, and labourers now own some land to subsist on and have the option of off-farm work.

Ruthven and Kumar (2002) point out that while the SCs contested *harvahi* under the influence of Dalit activism, tribal labourers initially (1980s) sought to maintain the system. In fact, such ties continue to exist as a part of patron–client relations, particularly in the case of worst-off labourers. In a context of employment scarcity and weak bargaining powers, these labourers or tenants continue to provide regular priority services to their 'patron' at below-market wages in return for food, credit, employment, access to public resources, etc.

Much like Ruthven and Kumar (2002), Lerche (1995, 1999, 2003) also noted the **weakening of traditional bonded labour relations**. As described by Lerche, at the time of independence, the traditional bonded labour relation was one where a Chamar household was attached to a Thakur household. The Chamar worked on the Thakur's fields and tended to livestock. This relationship was not time bound. The Chamar's wife also worked in the field, did cleaning work and even provided services as a midwife. In return, the Chamar household was provided with food, a larger share in the harvest and were given a plot of land to subsist on. This relationship between a Thakur and his *niji* Chamar was marked by debt, physical violence and sexual abuse of women.[14]

Such *niji* arrangements still exist but in a modified form. In Lerche's (1995) field area, it was common till the early 1990s. Though a *niji* Chamar still provides priority services to his Thakur employer, he need not be present at the Thakur's place every day but is contacted as and when his services (which now did not involve tasks like ploughing) are required. The Chamar may be asked by the Thakur to recruit labourers. In several cases, Chamars had borrowed money from Thakurs, and this was an important reason for their continuing in *niji* relation as otherwise they were required to repay debts with interest and provide *begar* (forced labour) till such time. Some were given small plots of land for sharecropping, and they also did *begar*. Like Ruthven and Kumar (2002), Lerche (1995, 1999) also noted some labourers entering such ties because they are a source of credit and work. This was an indication of the general dominance of Thakurs; Chamars performed wage labour for Yadav farmers at market rates, but since these provided less employment, Chamars had to rely on Thakurs and more so in the off-season. This does not mean that Chamars are not aware of their social and economic oppression (Lerche, 1995). Rather, according to Lerche (1995), such relations are buttressed by patron–client ideology in the broader village economy and society.

Also, Lerche (1999) mentions a system where landowners leased out a portion of land for paddy cultivation and met part of the production cost. The labouring household met remaining input costs, worked on it and received one-third of the produce. This arrangement was about as profitable for landlords as cultivation of paddy on wage labour basis. Landowners could avoid the threat that labour conflicts posed to labour supply. Moreover, women of these labouring households did *begar* and provided labour services to the lessor household first. In general, women and other non-migrating household members were expected to participate in sugarcane harvest and weed the fields of landowners. For this, they were allowed to take the leafy part of the sugarcane and access the fields of landowners for grazing their livestock. Srivastava (1999) also described a somewhat similar lease arrangement but one organised on a half–half share basis. He too noted that the big and medium landowners (mostly upper castes) were the primary lessors and land was primarily leased in by SC (mostly landless or small landowners).

An important distinction is made by Lerche (1999) between indebted and non-indebted labourers – but both providing priority labour services – is that the latter can at least refuse working for their employer and limit the scope of *begar*. In both cases, nonetheless, women bear a greater burden of unfree labour relations. Related to this and other unfree labour relations is that the varying extents to which labouring households depend on their 'oppressors' for whatever reasons is often a ground for clashes among labourers, particularly in periods of labour conflicts (Lerche, 2003).

Interlinked land, labour and credit relationships in agricultural labour markets were noted by Rajni also (2007). She observed that most of the labouring households were SC and landless, involved in agricultural casual wage labour in the absence of other opportunities and only a minority leased in land. Most of these labouring households were indebted to large *Bhumihar* farmers. Most of the tenants had also taken credit from landowners on interest and labourers (as well as their wives) provided landowners with under-waged labour services on a priority basis. *Bhumihars* find it convenient to lease out their poor quality and distant small plots of land. A significant number of labourers also take credit on interest against a promise of priority labour service. Such interlinking of land, labour and credit secures *Bhumihars* a ready supply of labour and several such relationships consolidate their positions as socio-economic benefactors of labourers.

As is evident, one implication of agricultural modernisation is that labour demand is concentrated around season time (Lerche, 1995, 1999, 2003; Srivastava, 1999; Diwakar, 2004). Big landowners, who were the major source of demand for labourers, have taken to cultivation themselves and they also do not need as much labour because of subdivision of their holdings over time (Lerche, 1995, 1999, 2003; Srivastava, 1999). Alternative better wage work opportunities are increasingly available (Lerche, 1999; Srivastava, 1999; Diwakar, 2004). Consequently, occupational patterns of agricultural labourers have also changed. The nature of **occupational diversification** is also a reflection of socio-economic status (though there are exceptions): regular salaried employment is significant among upper castes while SCs are at the bottom of the occupational hierarchy concentrated as they are in agriculture (Srivastava, 1999; Lieten and Srivastava, 1999; also see Lerche, 2010). Srivastava (1999) observes that from the perspective of labourers, occupational diversification was a route out of exploitative and oppressive socio-economic relations while for big landowners it was a way out of a complex system of obligation. The latter could continue accessing labour through various forms of attached labour.

This finds mention in Lerche (1995), who pointed out that it is common for members of labouring households to be involved in migrant work and better-paying local non-agricultural employment in nearby towns. The same is seen in Srivastava (1999). He also pointed out that SC labouring households had increasingly turned to petty forms of self-employment in combination with migration and wage labour. But middle castes like Yadavs and Kurmis depended primarily on self-employment and own cultivation. Their women also had mostly withdrawn from casual labour. Another study found labourers to be predominantly engaged in agricultural wage labour and at the same time, most undertook better remunerated local non-agricultural work as in brick kilns or construction (Diwakar, 2004). At the same time, this should not be mistaken as a reduction of labour dependency on big farmers. Labourers continue to work for large farmers for lower wages and as a part of various tied arrangements because the overall context of surplus labour, insubstantial landholdings and stagnating productive employment opportunities has not changed (Diwakar, 2004). Construction, brick kilns, agricultural processing, transportation are some of the sources of non-agricultural employment (Srivastava, 1999).

Migrant work, as an occupational diversification option, has negative consequences for those left behind in the village. According to Paris et al. (2005), migration is primarily male oriented and more among the landless who are completely dependent upon seasonal wage agricultural labour; though it may be undertaken by farmers as well in view of their small land base and lack of local alternative employment.

Paris et al.'s (2005) study of three districts in eastern UP showed that women are left behind to take care of agriculture and household responsibilities. But, in the absence of male family members, they have had to bear an increasing burden of agricultural work themselves and/or hire labour for works traditionally done by men. Most of them cannot afford to pay wages and also face difficulty in recruiting labour or arranging for tractor ploughing during peak seasons. One option is to rely on exchange labour, but this still involves a lot of work. All this is done in addition to their domestic chores. One possible positive outcome of male outmigration is that women may possess greater control over remittances, farming-related decision or daily household decisions. However, Paris et al. (2005) found that in most households, irrespective of migration, men still continued to exercise most authority. Male income was perceived as the primary household income. Additionally, women's limited mobility led her to lease out the land which adversely affects food security of the household.

Lerche (1999) also hinted at gendered consequences of male outmigration when he observed that by the late 1990s, most young men were involved in migrant work and even though they returned in peak season times, their participation in agricultural wage labour was on the decline, except perhaps, in the few better waged tasks. This meant that women and old men who could not migrate bore a greater burden of agricultural wage labour year round.

By now, it is clear from this description that there are elements of change and elements of continuity with regard to rural labour relations in eastern UP, but at the same time there are elements of continuities as well. The few aspects of female labour relations, that the available literature throws light on, show similarities with female labour relations generally. We now know that the upper castes are the dominant class, and the Dalits are at the bottom of the socio-economic hierarchy. Though the power of the former over the latter is not absolute or backed by open violence anymore, unfree labour relations are a common reality and more so in the case of women. Casualisation of labourers and contract work are common. Occupational diversification has occurred, but it is largely male labour that has delinked itself from agriculture. Female labourers are still agrarian, village based and non-migrant. Factors such as caste, class and gender shape and influence labour relations and the impact of capitalist developments more generally. These are also contours for labour fragmentation and inhibit development of labour solidarity.

However, it should be noted that this information is based on a few village-based case studies. While they provide a good background, there remain significant gaps in our knowledge of rural labour relations in eastern UP generally, and specifically, in the case of female members of low caste labouring households. For example, other than a very broad idea, we do not know the dominant forms of labour commodification and how these are combined with self-employment activities or other labour services. On female labour relations, there are gaps in our knowledge on what agricultural tasks female labour is engaged in, the patterns of recruitment and modes of employment, wage relations, whether female labourers combine cultivation and wage labour with some self-employment, whether their labour relations differ depending upon caste and class, their position in the labour market, etc. – these are just some of the questions that remain unanswered.

Caste has figured predominantly in the narrative of rural labour relations in UP. There have also been changes in labour relations as seen earlier, and the social and economic conditions of Dalits have generally improved slightly since the 1990s (Kapur et al., 2010), but there are no structural changes. The evidence presented here indicates the continued dominance of upper caste-class. We saw in the first chapter and here also that gender and caste identities are incorporated in the capitalist logic to facilitate accumulation. In a situation where they have little leeway, can Dalit labourers challenge their oppressors? What form does their political expression take? The issue of labour struggles is not unique to UP (for example, Sinha, 1982; Bhalla, 1999; Wilson, 1999), but what makes this particularly interesting is that in the period between 1995 and 2012, UP has thrice been headed by a low caste government, that is the Bahujan Samaj Party (BSP). Has this regional political phenomenon had any impact on micro-level rural labour relations and on rural labour more generally? And what has changed since 2012, when SP (on the backs of OBC and minority support) came to power and since 2017, when the BJP received a thumping mandate?

The BSP is primarily a regional phenomenon; a political party headed by a Dalit woman, Mayawati, for over a decade now. It is a party that draws overwhelming support from the Dalits. Central to its fight against caste discrimination is capturing political power (Pai, 2007) and the politicisation of Dalits (Lerche, 1999). The BSP has been in power in UP for brief periods in 1995, 1997, 2002–03, and its longest stint has been from 2007 to 2012. Dalits' position in local political structures has improved with the BSP's prominence in the state (Jaoul, 2007). However, as pointed out by Lerche (1999), the party does not have an economic programme or a stand on labour struggles for wages other than labourers' withdrawal from demeaning work and pursuing the 'politics of dignity' (Varshney, 2009).[15] Moreover, since 2012, the party has been losing electoral significance. The concern here is not with BSP per se but what its rise to power has meant for the Dalit agricultural labourers (for an overview of BSP, see Duncan, 1999).

As argued by Lerche (1994), in UP, the mobilisation and organisation of SCs take place at the local and state level, with the electoral arena linking the two. Though aware of their exploitation, caste is the dominant framework within which struggles of agricultural labourers takes place.[16] Dalit labour struggles play out at the level of hamlet or village. Unfree labour relations do not preclude the possibility of labour struggles occurring, but they may be limited by the political dominance of the landed from taking it to district or state level. This has been observed in the case of Jats in west UP (Lerche, 1995). Here, the eastern UP experience is discussed.

Lerche's (1994, 1995) village-based fieldwork showed that caste is the organising principle for the village labour market and space. Thakurs of one hamlet depend upon Chamars of a particular hamlet. This is almost an exclusive relation as far as agricultural work is concerned. Caste and class overlap to a great extent. Thakurs were the prominent landowners and Chamars worked on their fields. The first action by the latter was in the early 1970s against degrading courtyard work done for the Thakurs (in retaliation of Thakurs murdering a Chamar). The Chamars just stopped doing this work and the Thakurs responded by denying them access to their fields and resorting to physical violence. However, the Chamars persisted and after a few weeks, the Thakurs started doing the courtyard work themselves (also, they found it economically more prudent). The Chamar hamlet also has a caste panchayat that came to operate as a labour organisation after the aforementioned incident. As described by Lerche (1994, 1995), the leaders of this panchayat take the demands of labourers to Thakurs. Negotiations take place directly between the two or through a middleman. If no agreement is reached, Chamars may go on strike.

Lerche (1994, 1995) points out that since the first labour conflict, the Chamars have gone on strike every few years, planned around peak season time as this gives them maximum leverage. They have managed to also access local government apparatus in a regional context of the BSP's rise to power and with the help of a local BSP leader. The BSP has initiated various schemes for the development of Dalits, for instance, school scholarships and housing allowance (Jeffery and Lerche, 2000). Importantly, the BSP's political success has instilled a sense of dignity, pride and confidence among the Dalit labourers (Jeffery and Lerche, 2000). The numerical preponderance of Yadav small farmers in the village and their increasing political clout at the regional level also challenged Thakur dominance.[17] There have been times when the village Thakurs have called labour from outside or the indebted and poorer labourers have not participated in the strikes, but this is far and between. Nor has the threat of Thakur violence been completely eliminated.

As argued by Lerche (1994, 1995), Thakur dominance coexists with agricultural labourers' awareness of their exploitation as well as their rights. Also, labourers resort to 'everyday weapons' such as arguing with Thakur employers or gossiping about them in offensive terms. Changing labour relations and occupational diversification have also helped this assertion. At the same time, patron–client relations are also common. Thakurs are expected to defend their Chamar labourers and help them out with credit, employment and any emergencies. Chamars are expected to provide them priority services may be at lower wage rates. According to Lerche (1995), patron–client relations serve a dual purpose: through these the upper caste-classes validate their dominance while appearing yielding to the labourers by making them some 'allowance'.

According to Lerche (1994, 1995), caste–class correspondence is common at a general level and as such, labour conflicts take on a social and economic hue. However, this broad-based awareness of their exploitation has not transformed into collective action that draws on other labourers or even Chamars of other hamlets. Lerche (1994) observed that this was partly because overlapping socio-economic relations are more common between Thakurs and Chamars. Another possible reason could be that these labourers are themselves divided by patron–client relations between Chamars and 'their' Thakurs. Lerche (2003) cites some examples, where these Chamars have been pressured into filing false statements with the police against other Chamars.

Then Chamars themselves are not a homogenous group, but those who are in secure employment or are not completely dependent upon local wage labour are better off than other Chamars (Lerche, 2003). Chamars of different hamlets do not share close socio-cultural ties. Rather, each hamlet faces a different set of constraints, such as being surrounded by Thakur fields or being subjected to particularly brutal forms of suppression, which put them in a worse position (Lerche, 2003). Relations between Chamars and other low castes may also get strained (Lerche, 2003).

In sum, Lerche's works indicate important conclusions: possibility of resistance even in unfree labour relations; significance of local and regional power structures; consciousness of exploitation as labourers, but caste as the more dominant identity which limits the formation of a class for itself; and finally, how rural classes mediate the state institutions to benefit themselves.

Srivastava's (1999) field findings also show similar evidence on labour struggles. Thakur and Brahmin landowners sought to suppress a labour strike for wage hike with force by closing off labourers' access to their fields and by denying them employment. But when the labourers persisted, the landowners had to give in. Another strike followed two years later. But this time there was no physical aggression and employers raised the wages. The reasons for demanding wage increase were the higher wages of public work programmes and increasing garden cultivation where employers paid higher wages to secure timely labour. Availability of better remunerated alternative employment also exerted upward pressure on local wages, particularly during peak season at crucial periods. Like Lerche, Srivastava's findings also point out that these strikes are initiated by those labourers whose houses and fields are not in close proximity of the Thakurs. Srivastava also notes the changing labour attitude, with SCs giving up their traditional occupations – however this – as participation in strikes – is circumscribed by the extent to which one is dependent upon the dominant caste-class.

Srivastava (1999) found caste to be an important axis of labour mobilisation and fragmentation. But unlike Lerche, he concluded that these sporadic labour conflicts were not restricted to any one caste, and the demands raised are indicative of class interests. There is considerable inter-caste economic differentiation within lower castes. On the whole though, class interests are much more sharply organised and articulated among the landed where caste–class divergence is not as strong. These patterns are locally specific, making generalisation difficult.

Evidence is not available on the role of women in Dalit labour struggles or how these impact female labourers, beyond Lerche's (1994, 1995) mention of women not being subjected to sexual harassment as before. On women and resistance, some evidence is available from Jeffery and Jeffery's (1996) work in western UP and though it is not on labour struggles, it shows how women resist and negotiate structures of oppression and exploitation differently. They argue that in the case of women, resistance cannot be understood simply as a public and collective confrontation, for it risks missing out how women create space for themselves (for example, control over household resources, asserting against other controlling family members), without seeking structural change. Such an approach helps to locate how caste and class mediate women's daily lives.

The objective of this chapter was to understand how agrarian neoliberalism has affected low caste rural labourers and particularly the women.

It was established that the current crisis situation in Indian agriculture has much to do with the dominance of agrarian neoliberalism at the global level and its implementation on ground by the GOI. The worst affected are the small and marginal farmers and labourers who are mostly from low or scheduled castes. The continued relevance of the agrarian question of labour found resonance in the worsening position of labouring households under neoliberalism and the current agrarian distress. The same was observed in the case of UP as well. At the level of India and UP, evidence agreed with Bernstein on differentiation amongst petty commodity producers and the ground reality of a fragmented labour.

There on the terrain shifted to rural female labourers from low caste households and how they were implicated in processes associated with agrarian neoliberalism. Here, I established that female labourers belong to low and scheduled castes and still likely to be agricultural. Labour markets tended to be caste and gender segregated. Non-class identities and networks dominate and preclude labour unity and class-based action. Caste and gender are intrinsic to capitalist logic of surplus extraction and accumulation. This is manifest in the feminisation of agriculture (wherein gender wage gap and gendered division of labour are central) and in tied labour arrangements. It is clear that women have not benefitted from new opportunities to the extent that men have. The same was the case in eastern UP, though here we have very little and indirect evidence on female members of low caste labouring households or their labour relations. Issues like forms of labour commodification, position in the labour market, terms and conditions of wage labour, bases of fragmentation or solidarity, evidence on unfree labour relations, etc. for women emerge as some of the big gaps in our knowledge on women of low-caste labouring households in eastern UP. On the theme of labour struggles we know almost nothing about female labourers, but based on Lerche and Srivastava's work primarily, we know that labour struggles do occur and what we need to look for in the fieldwork.

Fieldwork

To recapitulate, the purpose of my research is to study labour relations of Dalit female labourers in eastern UP. But since we do not know who the classes of labour are or what the general labour relations in the region, first these overall trends need to be established. Finally, this research aimed to study the rural political expression and struggles of these women labourers. For several reasons, I chose to undertake village-based qualitative study. This research explores relations between individuals embedded in specific socio-cultural and economic contexts. These relations are part of their everyday lives and not just their 'work'. The purpose was not to merely collect facts but to critically interpret and analyse the change in labour relations over time, to describe what is seen in terms of labour relations and relate these to a broader context. This research engaged with processes, issues of agency, consciousness and resistance which can best be captured and explained in a qualitative framework. A qualitative approach was also expected to be more productive, personalised and therefore less intimidating in working with a 'subject' (Dalit women) not used to being in focus or simply being asked about anything outside of their 'four walls'. Given their gender roles are prescribed so strongly, getting women to interact is not a simple matter of them answering a survey question.

Why a village study? Most studies on rural labour relations in India tend to locate themselves in the tradition of village studies. But apart from this, my reading of relevant literature led me to expect that female labourers were likely to be based in the village or rather, operating from it. A village-level analysis is well suited to a descriptive mapping and comparative analysis of labour relations within and amongst the selected villages while bringing out changes caused by institutions like caste associations, panchayats or in levels of poverty and indebtness (Janakarajan, 1997). At the same time, this 'village' should not be treated as a closed unit. Doing so would risk out on losing how labour action in one village might lead labourers in another village to go on strike or in explaining the varying outcomes of strikes, as observed by Lerche (1999, 2003). Breman (1985a; Breman et al., 1997) has also pointed out that explaining migration patterns or local power relations might require reference to developments at the level of several villages or the regional level. A local-level of analysis has also been chosen because of the close observation and exploration it affords and the possibility of counteracting dominant established facts like the passiveness of women and discovering new trends or 'facts' (Harriss-White and Harriss, 2007). The research problem also required an investigation of the different social relations – within and outside the household – in which women are engaged. This could best be studied through a village approach. Finally, differentiation between hamlets/villages is likely and it was felt that these dimensions would be overlooked in a regional analysis. In addition to the detailed information that could be gathered at this level, it would also be easy to cross-check such information. The strength of village-based studies has to be located in its critical exploration and description which lead to explaining the extent to which observed reality conforms or not to existing theory and literature (Harriss-White and Harriss, 2007).

Different methods were used to gather different types of information and to establish its reliability and validity. Data collection combined a number of methods: case study, village survey, participant observation, oral history and focus group discussions. These methods were used flexibly in varying combinations, as required and depending upon village size and time constraints. Also, I relied on thick description, that is, not just stating what is observed but elucidating its context to make it meaningful, for the same action can mean different things depending upon the setting (Geertz, n.d.). Informal resources like conversations were also relied upon as these help in assessing the impact of changed circumstances on collected data and in the case of women, these are a valuable source of information.

Notes

1 Dalit is a socio-political conceptual invention, literally meaning downtrodden. It was first used by Phule with reference to the (ex) untouchables. The term Dalit is commonly used to refer to Scheduled Castes (Constitution of India), the ex-untouchables.

2 Scheduled Tribes (STs) as per Constitution of India.

3 A GOI initiative, flagged off in 2005–06, guaranteeing a hundred days of work per rural household that demands it. Where it is unable to give work, it provides for unemployment benefit. Also, it makes special provision for women. (See http://nrega.nic.in/rajaswa.pdf for details and for FRA, see https://tribal.nic.in/FRA/data/FRARulesBook.pdf).

4 According to Beteille (1965) castes are found in Hindus, Muslims and Christians. Here the discussion has focussed on the Hindus.

5 Srinivas (1966, 1987) has extended a *jati* and a *varna* interpretation of caste and suggested that the former understanding is more popular. Also see, Mendelsohn and Vicziany (1996, pp. 68–69).

6 See https://ruralindiaonline.org/articles/a-long-march-of-the-dispossessed-to-delhi/ [Accessed 13 April 2020].

7 *Zamindars* referred to landlords. They were responsible for collecting revenue from villages for the state.

8 The *Zamindari* Abolition Act of 1952 and Imposition of Ceilings on Land Holdings Act of 1960.

9 Under land consolidation, fragmented holdings were brought together into a continuous holding. The green revolution referred to increased capital and technological application in farming. *Panchayati raj* refers to rural local self-government.

10 For NCEUS (2008), marginal farmers are defined as owning landholdings of size 0.01–1.00 hectare (ha) and small farmers owning land between 1.01ha and 2.00 ha. There are a few examples where women are engaged in non-agricultural work as in the case of village-based female weavers in Tamil Nadu (De Neve, 2002). This has to be located in the context of rural industrialisation and caste ideology. Heyer's (2001) long-term work in Tamil Nadu indicated that while in the early 1980s, SC labourers were agricultural labourers, by the mid-1990s, there was some evidence of economic diversification. But they still constituted most of the agricultural labour. In the case of women, there was evidence of only one or two being involved in other employment as domestic workers in a school or in construction activity.

11 This seems to be in line with Srivastava's (1989) proposition that forms of attached labour increase as agrarian development proceeds and this is a reflection of capitalist requirements.

12 Bardhan and Rudra (1978) point out that declining tenancy could be due to tenancy evictions, particularly in more advanced villages as landlords increasingly took to self-cultivation with agriculture becoming more remunerative. They and Ruthven and Kumar (2002) point out that small tenants and labourers lost access to land as a result of this.

13 According to Ruthven and Kumar (2002), off-farm employment tapered off after the mid-1980s. Government-sponsored works were replaced by private informal casual jobs, particularly in the construction sector. In view of increasing competition and limited work options, SC labourers could access these only through 'networking'.

14 Lerche (1995) has translated *niji* as 'our own'. Its literal meaning is 'private'. Both imply the same meaning, that is, the exclusive nature of the relation.

15 Politics of dignity refers to, for example, installation of statues of Dalit leaders in public spaces and affirmative action (Varshney, 2009).

16 In western UP, there have been farmers' movements that draw on caste, but these are dominant farmer castes like the Jats. These movements have been concerned with surplus-producing farmers and not agricultural labourers. This is not to deny labour struggles in western UP (Lerche, 1994).

17 The OBC Yadavs mainly ally themselves with the Samajwadi party (SP), which is a significant political phenomenon in the state. In fact, the SP and BSP were political allies in the early 1990s.

3 Are All Peasants Even? Mapping Occupational Patterns and Hierarchies

This chapter shows that village labour markets are segregated on the basis of class, caste and gender. It gives a very detailed and nuanced picture of who does what in today's villages and why? At the top are the upper caste-classes who have successfully diversified outside of agriculture and managed to directly or indirectly access the state and its resources. At the bottom are agricultural labourers, casual labourers, brick kiln workers and those in survivalist self-employment. These are the most stigmatised, tedious and exploitative forms of wage labour and often linked with debt and other forms of unfree labour. As argued by Lerche (2010) and Chen (2008), this hierarchy of jobs is also a social hierarchy. Dalits and more so Dalit women are overwhelmingly concentrated at the bottom of the village labour market. Political economy works such as those of Breman (2007) and Harriss-White (2005) have shown how non-class factors such as socio-religious identity, family networks, access to political power, etc. are important in determining rural labour markets and strategies for accumulation for some and survival for others.

The chapter is organised in the following manner. The first section describes the fieldwork villages. The second section maps the occupational hierarchy along caste and gender lines. The concluding section brings together the main points which frame the background for the next chapter.

Introducing Fieldwork Villages

The fieldwork was conducted during 2009–10 in Kushinagar, a north-eastern district of UP carved out of Deoria district in 1994. Kushinagar is a major Buddhist pilgrimage site, where Buddha died and is said to have attained *parinirvana* (nirvana) (Sengupta, 2007). No gazetteer exists on Kushinagar and there is only one on Deoria from the 1970s (Varun, 1976). The brief description is based on fieldwork and government publications (GoUP, 2008a, 2008b, 2008c) and the district website.

Comprising fourteen blocks, Kushinagar has primarily an agrarian economy. Sugarcane, maize and paddy are main Kharif crops, and pulses, mustard, barley and wheat are the main Rabi crops. Several crops are grown

DOI: 10.4324/9780429321894-3

in one season, though rice and wheat are the main crops. Sugarcane is the main cash crop, though it was noticed in another block that banana was cultivated as well and exported to other regions. In fact, a landowner from the block had even won a medal for the quality of banana. High-yield variety seeds, chemical fertilisers and pesticides are available from government and private outlets. They are used extensively, particularly by the upper caste-classes. Households also grow seasonal fruits and vegetables.

Irrigation agriculture is adopted. The studied area is not dependent on rain completely. But in certain crops like wheat not as much artificial application of water is required as in the case of paddy which requires good irrigation and a good monsoon. However, small and marginal farmers cannot afford to rent in tube wells on the scale required, so a good monsoon is particularly important for them.[1] Canals and private tube wells are the most important sources of irrigation.[2] Agricultural machinery like tractors, harrow and cultivator sets are common. Combine harvesters are used by big farmers. Implements like the spade, hoe, sickle, plough are very common.

Mechanisation depends upon class status and landholding size. Among large landowners, agricultural operations like harvesting and threshing and preparing the field for planting are predominantly mechanised. In a few cases of large landowners, a small area of the field may be manually harvested and threshed because the straw is retained and used as animal fodder or in cases where the land size is uneconomical for mechanisation. Harvesting and threshing are mostly manually undertaken among small and marginal farmers. Socio-economic status and the availability of male family members for operations like ploughing may also influence mechanisation. Upper caste small or marginal farmers are unlikely to cultivate their land. They either lease out land or hire labourers and use a tractor. Dalit small or marginal farmers may be forced to hire labourers or rent a tractor for digging, turning soil, levelling or making rows for plantation in the absence of available male family labour. However, tractor ploughing is now increasingly common even among small and marginal farmers.

A sugarcane research centre is located at Seorahi block. There are several sugar mills and jaggery[3] crushers in the district. The labour market is dominated by agricultural wage labour. Brick kilns are very common. Petty businesses, migrant work and casual wage labour are some other types of employment. Local manufacture of alcohol is another business. Livestock rearing is a common household activity. Village and supra-village labour markets are gender and caste-class segregated. This will become clearer with field findings in the following two chapters.

These economic features are seen across the three villages studied – Sapatganj, Baaspur and Dokhgadh. The first two field villages are small in size and roughly similar in features, located in the same block and they share a panchayat. Comprising just over a 2,000 households, Dokhgadh is located in a different administrative block. Spread over a vast area, it is the second largest village of the block and has its own gram panchayat.

In the following, I describe spatial organisation, caste and religion composition, landownership structure and occupational patterns of the villages. In relevant literature, a common observation is that the physical layout of a village reflects the dominant social relations, clustering of caste groups together, an important axis for formation of work groups, labour arrangements and labour struggles. Therefore, it is useful to see how space is organised in villages and whether or not it is an organising principle in socio-economic and political relations.

It is only by looking at caste and religious composition, land relations and occupational structure together can one answer who does what, who are the classes of labour and what do they do, what is the landholding pattern, who are the dominant castes and classes, is there a caste–class overlap, to what extent does occupational diversification exist, etc. This knowledge constitutes an important background, a necessary means to study rural low-caste and especially Dalit female labour relations; the latter cannot be undertaken without establishing who the classes of labour, their caste and religious composition and what female members of these households do? In sum, this section provides a general overview of the village area and the main aspects of existing social and economic relations amongst the various classes.

Socio-Religious Composition and Spatial Organisation of Settlements in the Selected Villages

First, a brief note on how caste is perceived and closely linked to class status and the pervasiveness of the two together in routine lives of classes of labour.

There is divergence between official terminology on caste and caste as a lived experience.

While all scheduled castes (SCs) are Dalits, not all of them are perceived as equally unclean or untouchable. This is the case in both villages. Caste is understood and expressed as *jati* which frames the everyday understanding and practices. *Jati* is immediately a marker of one's low caste touchable or untouchable status. This then mediates one's engagement in and norms of behaviour in the village society. For example, SC women have a greater freedom of movement and are more outspoken (publicly and within the house), in comparison to Rajput women who are not to be seen or heard. SCs are served in separate utensils and cannot access certain parts of upper caste houses like the kitchen or the hand pump inside the house. Their untouchability limits their work options because they cannot do domestic or any work that would bring them in direct touch with the upper castes. Another example is from the Guptas. The Gupta surname is used by Baniyas, Raunihars and Telis. But Telis in UP are categorised as OBCs. During the village survey, they identified themselves as Telis, that is, a sub-caste or *jati* and not with their surname Gupta. There are *jatis* even amongst the upper caste Baniyas who use the Gupta surname generally. For example,

Raunihars identified themselves with this *jati* name. Most of the rest who used the Gupta surname identified themselves as Baniyas. Gonds are categorised as SCs in UP, but at the time of the survey they mentioned that as in other states in UP also they should be recognised as tribals and this is what they are demanding of the state. In all field villages, *jati* emerged as the most important determinant of social relations, interpersonal behaviour and a medium of political association.

Identification with the government system of caste classifications is limited to the extent of few knowing how their caste is now named in the central OBC or state SC lists. For example, it was pointed out by some respondents that Dusadhs are notified as Paswans, Kamkars as Kharwars in the state SC list, while Koeris are noted as Khushwahas in the Central OBC List. There is no recognition of or association with the term Dalit. Dalits identify themselves as *chutka* (explained later) or *harijan* meaning 'children of God'. It was coined by Gandhi to refer to the untouchables. The government system of caste classification is also overshadowed by the local *badka–chutka* terminology.[4]

However, for convenience sake, I will use the term Dalit rather than SC[5] henceforth and also it is this term that I asked villagers about. Lack of familiarity with political and legal terminology does not mean that Dalits are not aware of the practical implications of their categorisation. For example, women pointed out that the *pradhan*'s seat could be reserved for *chutka* or a woman or could be unreserved. This awareness however is limited. Female labourers explained this as one of the ways in which the government tries to help *chutkas*. Though this is right, there is no understanding of this as an administrative measure consciously designed for their political empowerment or fiscal devolution.

In Sapatganj and Baaspur, caste is also the basic medium of aligning oneself with a political party, irrespective of its ideology. This is particularly the case for women belonging to the classes of labour category. They do not know what BSP is or what is the party's political manifesto, but they are very familiar with the popular BSP leader Mayawati and her administration's pro-Dalit attitude and policies, for example, in accessing police or block officials or provision of school scholarships.

Caste and class correlate to a great extent, but this is not to say that there are no poor upper castes or rich Dalits, that is, the caste–class overlap is not absolute. The upper castes are the most landed and therefore with economic clout, given that they are the most important source of employment for female labourers. They are also politically very well connected which makes them influential in the villages, for example, as a medium of accessing public resources or mediating in a dispute. On the other hand, Dalits are either landless or overwhelmingly marginal landowners, with no economic or political clout and are dependent on the former for employment, mediating bank loans, court cases, accessing public provisions, etc. This is not to say that there is no internal differentiation within castes, but in everyday lives of villagers, no distinction is made between caste and class status. *Badkas* are the upper caste-class and *chutkas* are the lower caste-class. Their expressions and explanations of various phenomena do not recognise the analytical distinction. There is no specific term for OBCs. They are seen as being positioned below the *badkas* and above the *chutkas*. Later, in the caste-wise discussion of occupational patterns, it will be shown that there is a strong correspondence between *badkas* and *chutkas* and Bernstein's categories of petty capitalist and classes of labour respectively.

Henceforth, I have mainly used the local terminology or (upper, middle or lower) caste-class term. However, in explaining the social composition of the villages, I refer to the official categories to bring out the difference between government classification and caste as social reality.

In the following figures, the social composition of the three villages is shown. Since Hindus are predominant in all villages and the few non-Hindu households are all Muslims, a separate figure for each religion was not deemed necessary.

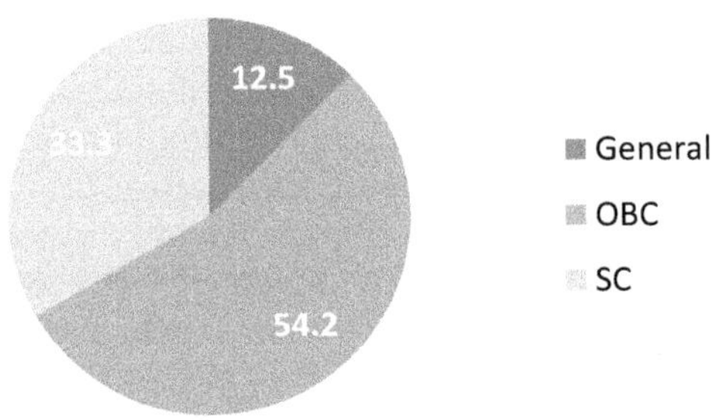

Figure 3.1 Distribution of Households by Caste in Sapatganj, UP

Source: Prepared from field survey data (2009–10).

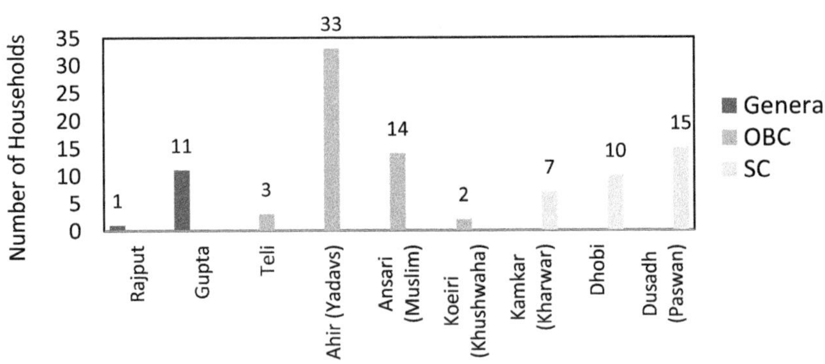

Figure 3.2 Distribution of Households by Sub-Castes in Sapatganj, UP

Source: Prepared from field survey data (2009–10).

Note: Out of a total of 100 households in Sapatganj, 4 refused to participate. Details of 96 households are mentioned here.

In Sapatganj, OBCs, comprising Telis, Ahirs, Ansaris and Koeiris are numerically preponderant. Next are the Dalits – the Kamkars, Dusadhs and Dhobis. Locally, Kamkars are not regarded as unclean as the Dusadhs and Dhobis. This is derived from the fact that Kamkars are employed as domestic workers, for instance, as a cook in the village primary school and washing dishes in the Rajput house. The upper castes –Rajputs and Guptas – are a numerical minority.

In Baaspur, more than half the households are Dalit. Kharwars, Dhobi, Dusadh and Chamars are Dalits. Inside the village, nothing was observed on which basis it can be deciphered whether one caste was less unclean than another. However, more and better examples of petty self-employment are seen in the case of Kharwars, including food preparation (this will become clearer when occupational patterns are discussed). Only one other such example was seen among non-Kharwar Dalit households. So,

Figure 3.3 Distribution of Households by Castes in Baaspur, UP

Source: Prepared from field survey data (2009–10).

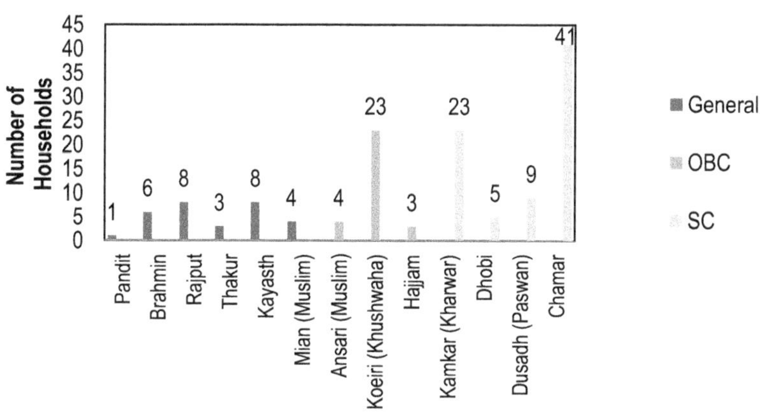

Figure 3.4 Distribution of Households by Sub-Castes in Baaspur, UP

Source: Prepared from field survey data (2009–10).

Note: Generally, the term Mian is used to denote Muslims, but here the households identified their *jati* as Mian.

in all probability it would not be wrong to judge Kharwars as less unclean. There are an equal number of OBC and upper caste households. The former includes Ansari, Koeiri and Hajjams. The upper castes included Pandit, Brahmin, Rajput, Thakur, Kayasth and Mian households.

Overall, Hindus are preponderant. The OBCs are the largest group. OBCs among the Hindus include Teli, Ahir, Giri, Koeiri, Sunar, Prajapati, Gosain, Lohar, Chauhan and Pal castes. Among the Muslim castes, Mansooris, Ansaris, Badhai and one Faqir household are included. Ahirs, Chauhans and Ansaris are the most numerous castes in the OBC group. In Dokhgadh, there was consensus that the Mosahars are the worst off among the Dalits because of their landlessness, they are generally denigrated for their abusive and brash behaviour, very poor living conditions and undertaking the most

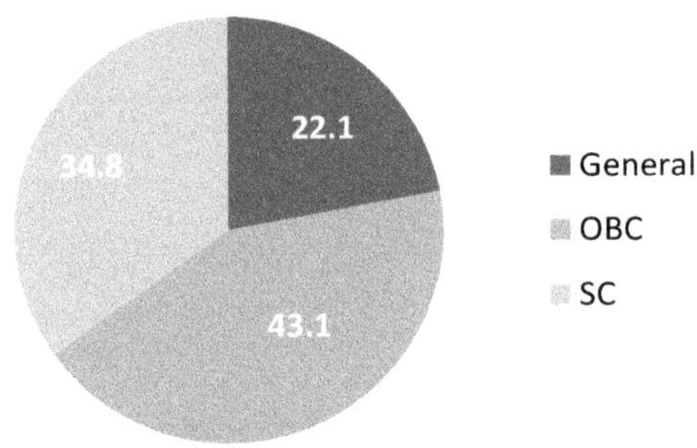

Figure 3.5 Distribution of Households by Castes in Dokhgadh, UP

Source: Prepared from field survey data (2009–10).

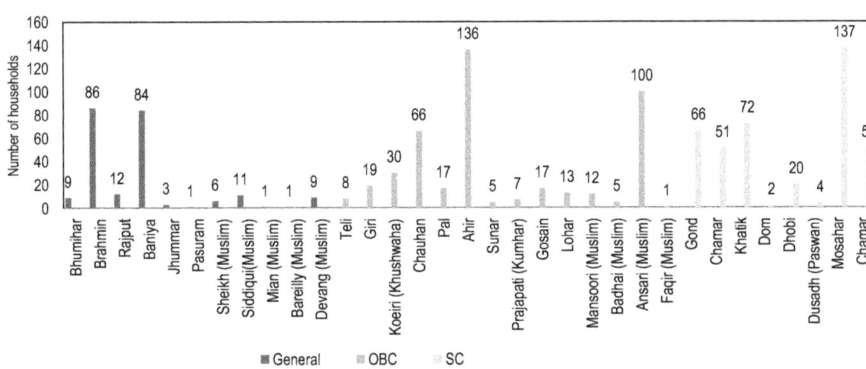

Figure 3.6 Distribution of Households by Sub-Castes in Dhokgadh, UP

Source: Prepared from field survey data (2009–10).

Note: The castes of Jhummar, Pasuram, Bareilly and Devang are not well known in the region. Since they are not listed in the Central OBC list or in the state SC list, they are put under the General category here. Otherwise, not much is known about the local understandings of their caste status.

stigmatised work, that is, brick kiln work. At the same time, Mosahars are begrudged by other Dalits for their success in accessing public resources and schemes. All Dalit groups are Hindus: Gonds, Chamars, Khatiks, Doms, Dhobis, Dusadhs and Mosahars. Within these, Mosahars, Khatiks, Gonds and Chamars make for more than half the Dalit households in Dokhgadh. Upper castes are numerically the smallest group, as was the case in Sapatganj and Baaspur. Hindus are predominant in this group and include Bhumihars, Brahmins, Rajputs and Baniyas. Sheikhs, Siddiquis and one Mian household constitute the Muslim upper caste groups.

Moving on to spatial organisation, all villages are organised along the lines of caste and religion.

Sapatganj does not have physically contiguous boundaries. Actually existing social and economic relations do not follow administrative village boundaries. It is composed of three settlements (hamlets): the main hamlet (*toli*) of the village is located in the centre. It is multi-caste in nature and includes *badka*s, the middle caste-class and *chutkas*, all three clustered separately along different streets; the second hamlet is largely composed of the middle caste- class Ansari households. It is the smallest hamlet, located at one tip of the village; the third hamlet, middle caste-class Ahirs are preponderant. This hamlet is distant from other settlements of the village, separated by fields and a few houses/livestock sheds (ghota) of another village. The Ansari and Ahir *tolis* are not as integrated into the socio-economic relations of the village as the main *toli*. The Ansaris share closer ties with neighbouring village which is inhabited by more and better-off Muslim households. While for Ahirs, the reason is their relative physical isolation from the main village and are more integrated into the socio-economic life of the village just next to their hamlet.

In some cases, there is also a class aspect to this caste- and religion-based spatial organisation. This is indicative of class differences within caste categories. The class differences manifest itself in the household structure, ownership of land and other productive assets and socio-economic behaviour vis-à-vis other caste groups and within castes along gender and age lines. The nuances will be made clear in the section on caste-wise description of the occupational patterns. How these differences are implicated in the spatial organisation is very briefly indicated here. The Rajputs and Guptas are the *badkas*. The former is positioned higher than Gupta households. Both these castes are settled in the main hamlet of the village but not in immediate vicinity. Gupta households are closer to other caste-class households, including Telis. In the Ahir patti (street), the economically better-off are clustered together at one end. The Ansaris do not show much internal differentiation in terms of class, like other *chutkas*. There is only one example of an economically better-off Dalit – Dusadh – household, located at one end of the Dusadh households.

Figure 3.8 shows the map of Baaspur. It is also spatially organised along caste and religious lines. Unlike Sapatganj, it has physically contiguous

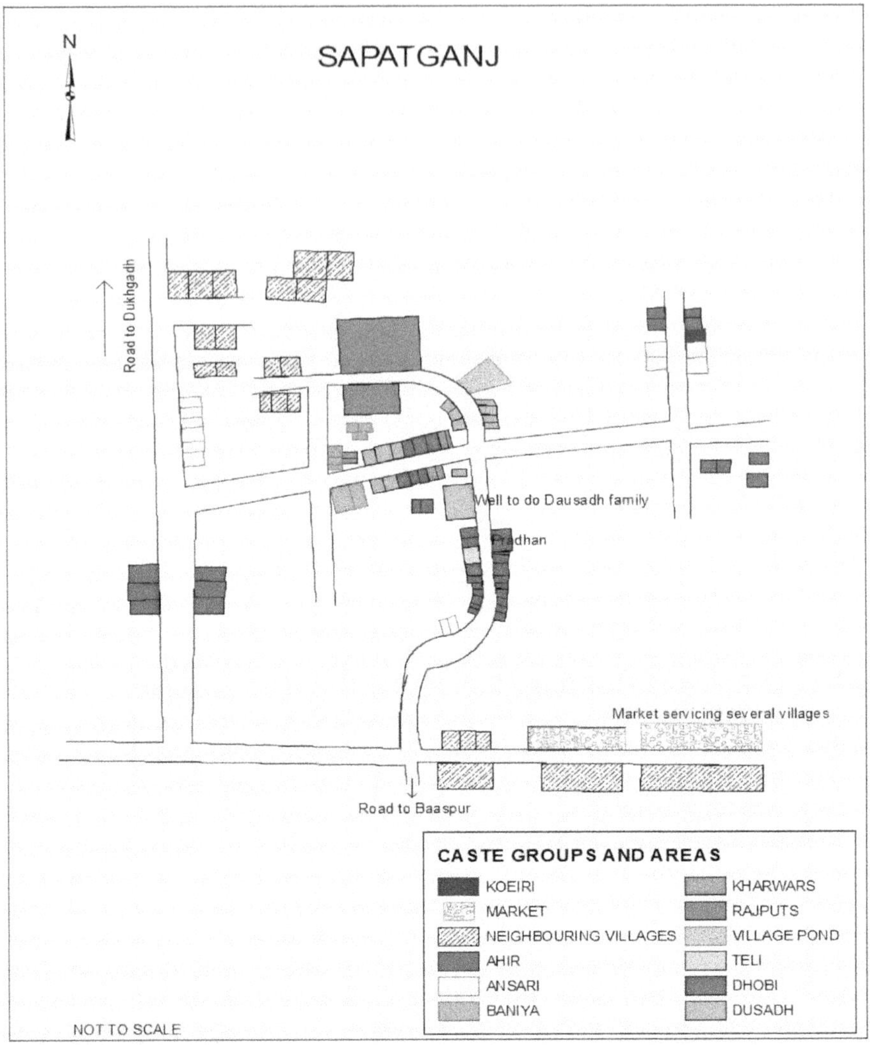

Figure 3.7 Settlement Map of Sapatganj

Source: Prepared from field observations (2009–10).

boundaries, but like Sapatganj, actually existing socio-economic relations do not follow administrative village boundaries.

Baaspur has four settlements. Approaching the village from the main road, the first hamlet one comes across is called the *babu*[6] (upper caste-class men) *tola*. It is the smallest hamlet, includes different castes but so called because the *pradhan* lives in the village, as does another Rajput family.

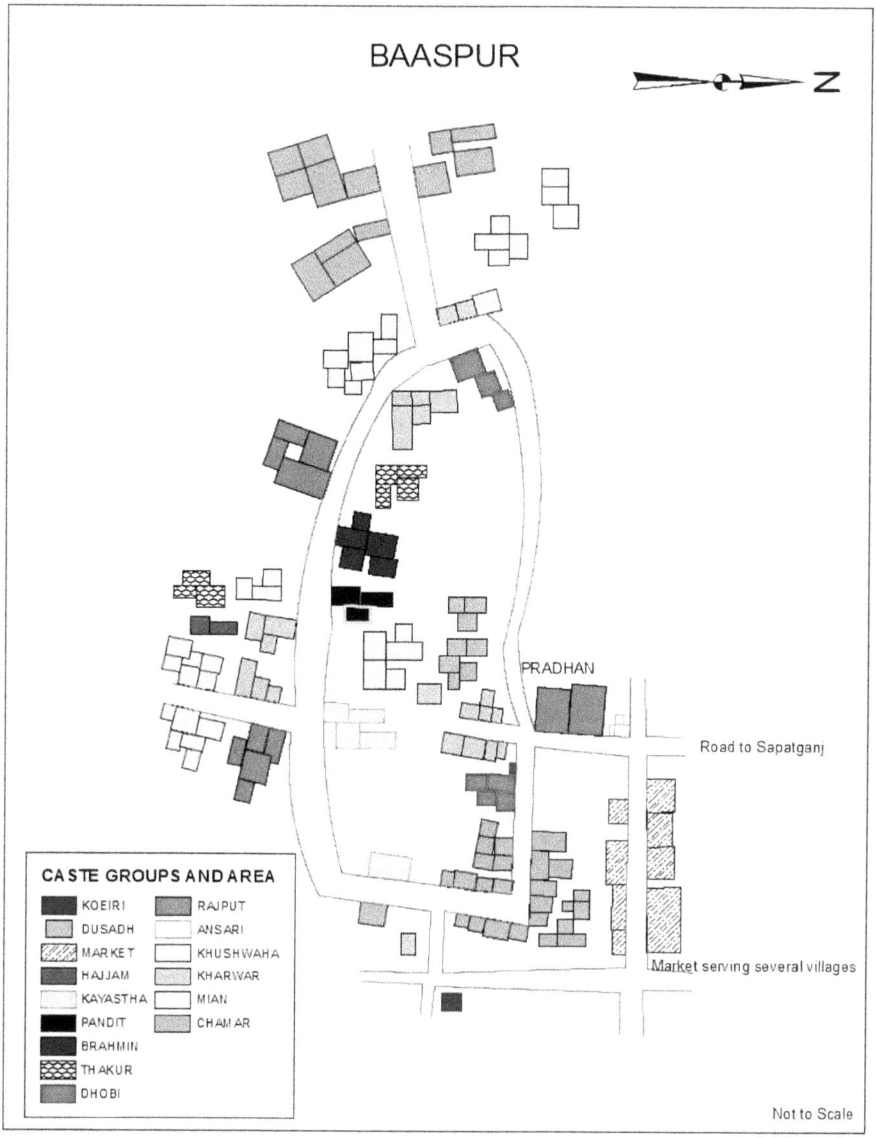

Figure 3.8 Settlement Map of Baaspur

Source: Prepared from field observations (2009–10).

The two are the major employers of agricultural wage labour in the village. Chamar households are concentrated in the second hamlet. The third hamlet is the largest. It has households from different castes. Chamar households are again concentrated in the last hamlet. Geographically, Baaspur is much more compact than Sapatganj. Nonetheless, it shares socio-economic ties with other nearby villages and particularly a neighbouring one as the two together constitute one panchayat. As families expanded or joint families got divided, some residents of Baaspur (the older generation mostly) shifted to the outskirts, near the village with which it shares a panchayat. Contractors from the same village recruit villagers from Baaspur for migrant work. Residents of the fourth hamlet share deeper socio-economic ties with another village closer to their settlement. This shows also a peripheral nature of habitation and contiguity with similar castes located in adjacent peripheries.

At the level of hamlets, there is a further caste, class and religious aspect to this spatial structure. In the first hamlet, middle caste-class Ansaris live along one side of the village approach road. The *badkas*, that is Rajput houses, are situated at the centre of the hamlet, separated from other households in the hamlet by a wide expanse of land and flanked by fields at the front and the back. Situated at the end of the hamlet are the *chutkas*, the Dhobis and Kharwars. In the second hamlet, the better-off Chamars live in *pucca* (concrete) houses, slightly set apart from the neighbouring huts. One Koeiri household is located outside the village perimeter, within their field and a single Kharwar household is located separately from the cluster of Chamar households. However, there is not much difference in the class position of most Chamar households, the Kharwar and Koeiri households, even though they are settled separately. Majority of the households in this hamlet are *chutkas*. In the third hamlet as well, the *badkas* including the Brahmins, Rajputs and Kayasths are clustered together, as are the middle caste-class Khushwahas and Hajjams and the *chutkas*, that is Kharwar, Dusadhs and Dhobis. The class aspect is not evident in the last hamlet, but all Muslim houses are clustered together.

In Dokhgadh as well, spatial organisation is along caste lines.

Dokhgadh does not have contiguous boundaries. As in Sapatganj and Baaspur, caste, religion and class aspects (building, assets, social conduct of women, landownership) are evident at the hamlet level and existing socio-economic relations do not coincide with the census village. In the first hamlet, the few Rajput, Brahmin and Baniya households are located in one side; the Giris in the centre of the hamlet and at the other tip (at some distance from the Giris) are the Gonds. The second hamlet is dominated by Koeiris and Ahirs to a lesser extent. The only other castes are Chamar and Gonds. The Dalits live at two ends of the hamlet, separated from the main part of the hamlet where Koeiris and Ahirs reside.

The third hamlet is centrally located, multi-caste in nature and the largest hamlet. It is the hub of political and economic power as the *pradhan* and several prominent *badka*s reside here. The panchayat bhawan (building) is in this hamlet. Brahmins and Baniyas live in the centre of the hamlet but are separately clustered. Among the Brahmins, the *pradhan* and the next most powerful household are situated next (though not closely because they are built on big plots and surrounded by empty expanse of

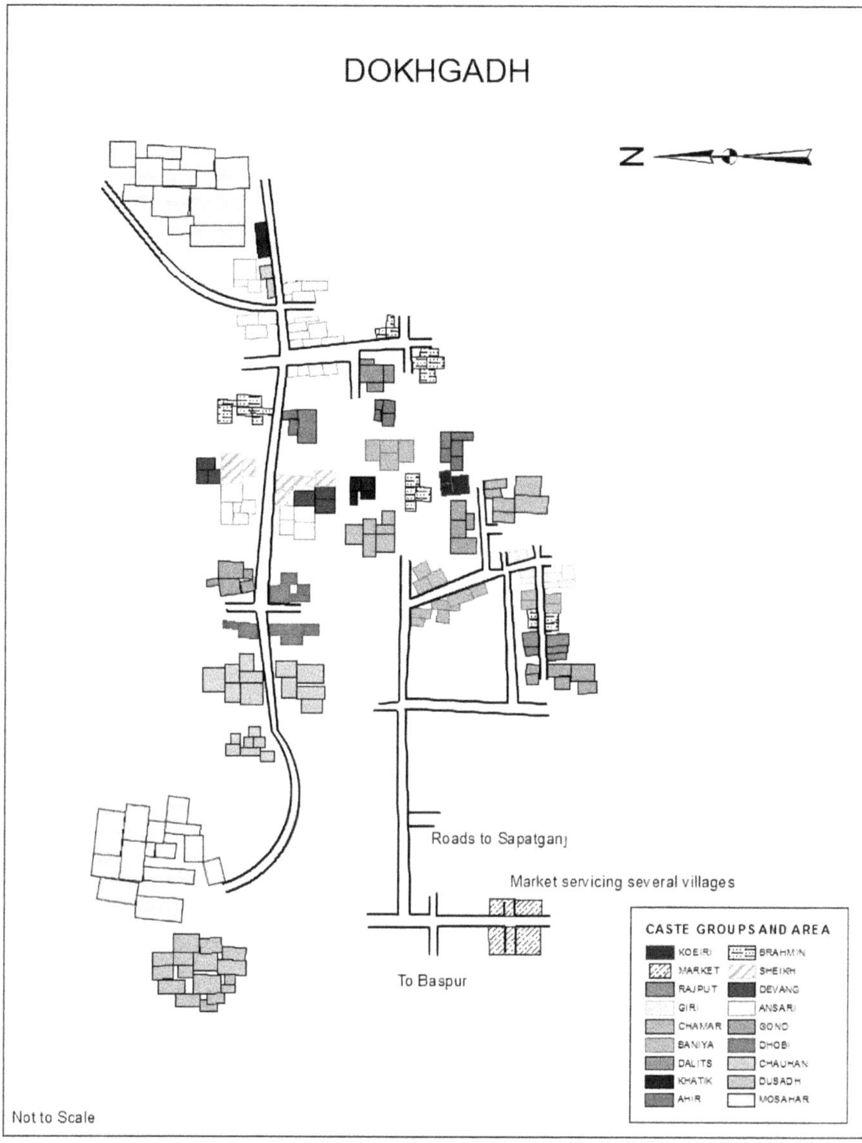

Figure 3.9 Settlement Map of Dokhgadh

Source: Prepared from field observations (2009–10).

land) to each other, away from the other Brahmin households. The OBCs – Koeiri, Sunar, Ahir, Prajapati, Mansoori, Ansari and Faqir households – are scattered towards the end of where Baniyas live. Dalit households include those of Chamars, Khatiks, Doms, Dhobis, Gonds and Dusadhs.

Most of these are situated on the outskirts of the village and households of each caste are arranged together. The one Pasuram caste household is also located in this hamlet.

The fourth hamlet is the second largest hamlet. The Ahirs, who are the better-off in the hamlet, live along the two main streets. Gosains live together. Dalits comprising Khatiks and Gonds are settled at the end of the hamlet. The next hamlet comprises only Brahmins. Class differences are not evident. In the sixth hamlet, households are located on both sides of a major road. The few upper caste households – Brahmins and Baniyas – are located together. Irrespective of caste, Muslim households are clustered together. The Dalit households – Gonds, Pals and Khatiks – are situated apart from the main hamlet on the way to the next hamlet. The one Bareilly household is also located in this hamlet. The seventh hamlet is located very far from other Dokhgadh hamlets. It is a very small hamlet, comprising only Mosahars. In class terms, they are a homogenous group. These households were originally a part of the last hamlet of Dokhgadh. But given the high population density in a very small area, some of these were resettled on *abaadi* land (the new hamlet) years ago. In the next three hamlets, it is the case that upper castes are clustered apart from the other castes. The Muslims, irrespective of caste, are settled very close to each other. The Dalits are all located apart from the other caste households, usually along a different street at the outskirts. Irrespective of caste, class or religion, the class differences are not stark in these hamlets.

The next hamlet is important in the sense that outside of the third hamlet, it has the largest employers of agricultural wage labour. One of the families is the most landed in the three villages and my impression is that this is the case for the region. The class aspect is also significant to the caste-based spatial organisation in the hamlet. The upper castes comprising the Bhumihars, Brahmins and Guptas live at the centre of the hamlet, each caste grouped together. The Chauhans (OBC) and the Dalit households, comprising Gond and Dhobi households are located at the end of the hamlet, at some distance from the centre. The last hamlet is a sizeable one. With the exception of two Dusadh households, all others are Mosahars. The Dusadhs are better off and located right at the tip of the hamlet but not distant from the Mosahar households. Economic differentiation within Mosahars is insignificant. The hamlet has a small panchayat bhawan also.

Land Relations

Land base is an important but not necessarily the only indicator of one's economic status. One Chamar male labourer attributed Chamars' poverty to expanding family size and small landholdings (Fieldnotes, 12 April 2010). A male Dhobi labourer associated landownership with a sense of pride, self-worth and social status. As he put it,'*what is a man without land?*' (Fieldnotes, 11 April 2010).[7]

The current social base of landownership (as it exists on the ground and not as per legal titling; actual operational holding, in other words) and landlessness is detailed in the following.[8] Here, I will use official caste categories in the tables so as to leave the class aspect out of the equation for the time being. I will then describe the tables, highlighting any emerging correspondence between caste status and land position (as a marker of economic status). After this, I will discuss the local categories to bring out the underlying logic of *badka–chutka* terminology. However, it should be noted that land by itself is not a sufficient condition for labelling upper castes as *badkas*. It was indicated earlier that a broad economic power and political influence also matters. These nuances will become clearer in the caste-wise description of occupational patterns.

In line with the regional trends, landlessness is limited and not caste specific. The majority of the holdings are marginal and small, followed by semi-medium and medium. There is a complete absence of large holdings. Among the upper castes, half of the holdings are small, and a quarter are marginal. There is only one case of a medium holding. In the OBC category, more than half are marginal holdings. Just under one-tenth of the holdings are small. The remaining few are semi-medium. In the case of SCs, almost all the holdings are marginal. There is only one case each of semi-medium and medium holdings. The land status of the lower castes is the worst. The trend of family nuclearisation is particularly strong among them and is an important reason for the increasing fragmentation and marginalisation of landholdings among them.

In Sapatganj, the largest landowner is the Rajput family, the biggest source of agricultural employment and wields considerable economic influence. They are also a source of credit, help labourers access loans and ration

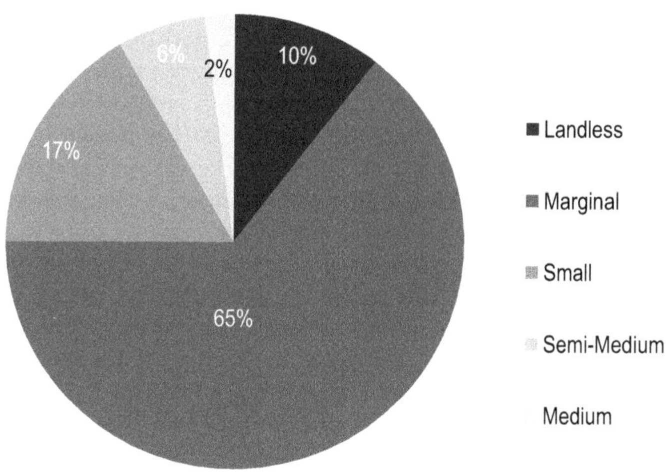

Figure 3.10 Distribution of Households in Sapatganj by Size of Landholdings

Source: Prepared from field survey data (2009–10).

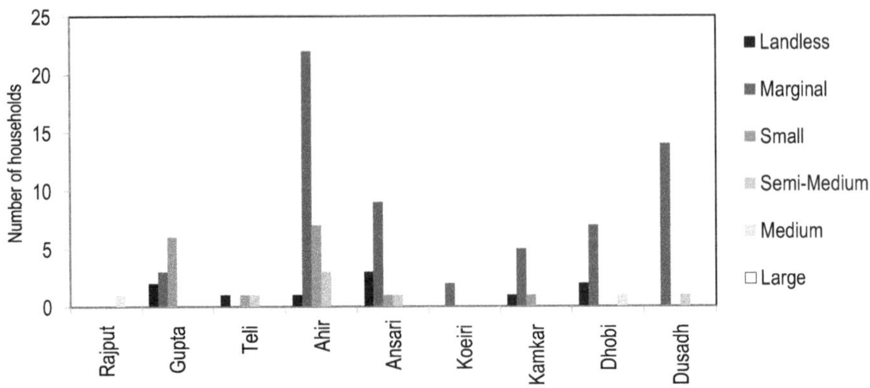

Figure 3.11 Distribution of Households in Sapatganj by Size of Landholdings and Sub-Castes

Source: Prepared from field data (2009–10).

cards, they rent out their tractor and tube well, allow labourers to use the hand pump outside their house, etc. Also, the family is well connected with the local bureaucracy. Though it can access political power through its networks, the Rajput family actively seeks political position either directly or indirectly by supporting a proxy figure. Political power is aspired because it gives knowledge of and access to development funds, other financial resources, public schemes and power to make crucial decisions like on which land should a school come up or redistribution of Gram Sabha land. These are controlled and channelled to augment one's social, economic and political authority. Social status and economic and political influence are undoubtedly the sources of *badkas'* prestige and dominance in the region.[9]

On the other hand, OBCs employ labourers on a smaller extent. Their middle caste status means that they are not revered like the Rajput family. These households are not a major source of credit for the villagers and do not wield political influence. The one exception is the *pradhan*'s house. It is actually the wife of the male head of the household who is the *pradhan*, but she is merely a proxy. The *pradhan* is a comparatively larger employer of agricultural labourers and is known to favour Ahir labourers (who also live near his house) in accessing NREGA work, BPL ration cards and IAY[10] money. Unlike, Rajputs, here the male family members are directly involved in cultivation and the wife of the male head of the household supervises the labourers. The SCs neither have land base which can be a source of economic influence nor do they have or can access political power. Their caste is also of the lowest status. Therefore, they are *chutkas*. However, there are two exceptions of slightly well-to-do Dalit households. This is indicative of class differentiation within caste. Their economic influence is restricted to extending small loans.

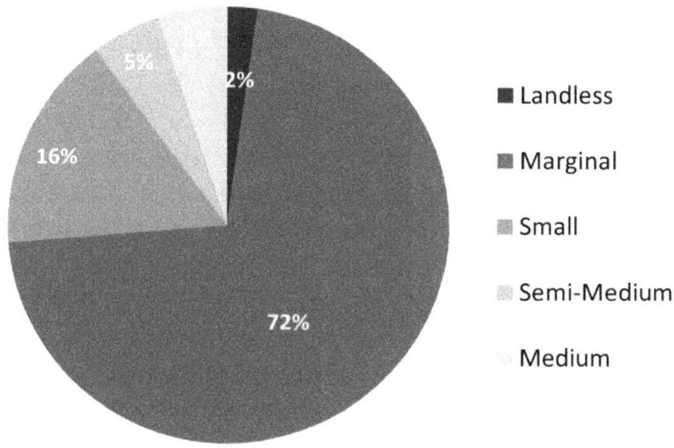

Figure 3.12 Distribution of Households in Baaspur by Size of Landholdings

Source: Prepared from field survey data (2009–10).

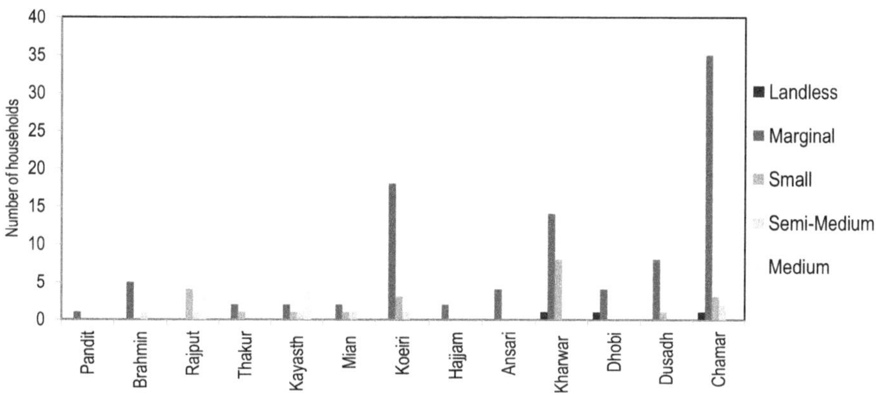

Figure 3.13 Distribution of Households in Baaspur by Size of Landholdings and Sub-Castes

Source: Prepared from field survey data (2009–10).

Like Sapatganj, Baaspur also has a low incidence of landlessness, a prevalence of marginal holdings and the complete absence of large landholdings. Upper castes are the largest landowners in the village. All medium holdings and over half the semi-medium holdings are found in this group, concentrated among Rajputs and Kayasths. Most of the OBC and SC households are marginal holders, with isolated cases of semi-medium holdings. Nuclear families are common in case of SCs and an important factor for subdivision of holdings.

As in Sapatganj, in Baaspur also there is absence of complete overlap of social and economic status. But it is clear that Rajputs are the dominant caste-class: the biggest landowners, employers of agricultural labour and a source of credit. In Baaspur, the post of *pradhan* is occupied by a Rajput who is serving his second consecutive term. In recent history, another Rajput and a Chamar have been *pradhans*. But the Dalit labourers openly criticise the latter for being controlled by the upper caste-class people. Rajputs have a well-developed network of connections vis-à-vis block officials, police and other local administrative structures. Kayasths are also big landowners. Though upper caste-class, their social status is inferior to that of Rajputs, and they do not have the political authority associated with Rajputs. Both, Rajputs and Kayasths are referred to as *badkas*, but villagers are aware that Rajputs' superior caste, economic influence and political authority make them more dominant and powerful. Similarly, villagers view Brahmins and Pandits as *badkas*, but mostly in terms of caste status only. This is indicative of economic differentiation within caste categories. As in Sapatganj, OBCs and SCs of Baaspur, neither have the land base to be seen as important employers of agricultural labour nor do they have any political clout. In terms of caste status, SCs are the worst off. Therefore, they are *chutkas*. But again, here too there are a few cases of better-off households within castes.

Land relations could not be historically traced. Nonetheless, a common observation made by many households, from different caste backgrounds, was the loss of land under land consolidation. According to several labouring households, their ancestors were allocated smaller or poor quality plots. In a few cases, parts of fields were acquired by the government for road construction, but the affected households were not compensated. With increasing population pressure, the older generation of many households has moved to livestock shelters on the village fringes while some live on *aabadi* land, that is land allotted to Dalit households by Gram Sabha. Inability to keep up with repayments of loans taken against land is a common cause for land loss.

Leasing is not a common phenomenon in either village. One Chamar female labourer, from Baaspur, attributed the low incidence of leasing to increased farming costs, subdivision of holdings across caste-class which means not many have substantial holdings to lease out some part and finally, now most people own some land and are not completely dependent on leased land. Leases were informal. There was no definite time period of leases which could be revoked anytime provided there was no standing crop on the leased land. The lease system operates on 50:50 share basis with respect to the produce. The investments and decisions were independently made by the lessee. However, with a few exceptions, sugarcane was not cultivated on leased land. Primarily, food crops are cultivated on leased land. According to villagers, landowners do not like it if they grow sugarcane because it will 'profit' villagers. One male Dhobi labourer, from Baaspur, mocked that it will catch *badkas*' evil eye.[11] It is inferred that since landowners cultivate sugarcane on their own land, they would benefit more from a share in food crops which can be used in their households.

From the existing lease arrangements, it is clear that land is basically leased in to supplement own agricultural production for household consumption. As such, land is seen as a crucial buffer against food insecurity. Land may be leased out for several reasons. One is that entire families migrate or unavailability of family labour due to reasons such as old age or disability. One example is that of Hajjam household in Baaspur: the male household head is an alcoholic and abusive man. His mother is blind and often has to resort to begging to support the family. His wife cannot afford farming costs. What little income she scrapes together is used for essential household expenses. She is responsible for their young children, and this limits her participation in wage labour. For her it makes most sense to lease out her land, for this would at least entitle her to some produce without incurring any expense.

Lease arrangements may exist as a part of patron–client relations. For example, the Rajput household in Sapatganj had leased out a small plot of land to a labouring household that lived near it. The male member of the labouring household guarded the crop on another nearby field of Rajputs. He was seen as a loyal supporter and worker. Land could be leased out to avoid the costs of improving land quality and making it suitable for cultivation again. According to a landless Chamar male labourer from Baaspur, whose lease was revoked after only two years, people lease out land to labouring households who work hard on it to restore/improve the quality of land by investing in fertilisers, irrigation, ploughing and tilling, to prepare it for cultivation. But labourers get to harvest only one crop before it is taken back by the owner.

In Dokhgadh too, villagers take land to be not only an indicator of economic worth but also a source of pride. The social base of landownership in Dokhgadh is presented in the below Figure 3.15. It is representative of the ground situation rather than formal title ownership. Various arrangements regarding distribution and cultivation of land and the sharing of yield exist. However, there are some households to which neither of the aforementioned case applies but nonetheless, receives some share of the yield from the parent house. This is observed where the male head of the new household is a migrant worker, completely involved in local non-agricultural wage employment or self-employment. His young wife is required to adhere to socio-cultural practices restricting her mobility and wage labour participation. But since, both the parent and the new household come across as independent socio-economic units in all other respects, their landholding status is accordingly tabulated. Households which do not cultivate jointly or independently and do not receive any part of the yield are classified as landless.

Just above half of the landholdings are marginal. Around 14 per cent are small. Semi-medium and medium holdings constitute just over 10 per cent of all landholdings and less than 1 per cent are large holdings. The rest

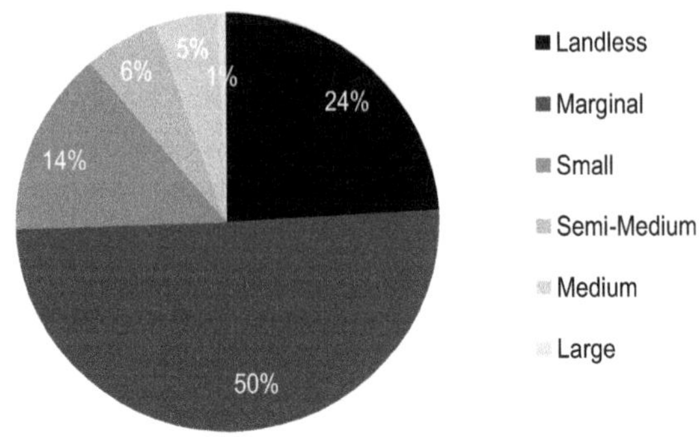

Figure 3.14 Distribution of Households in Dokgadh by Size of Landholdings

Source: Prepared from field survey data (2009–10).

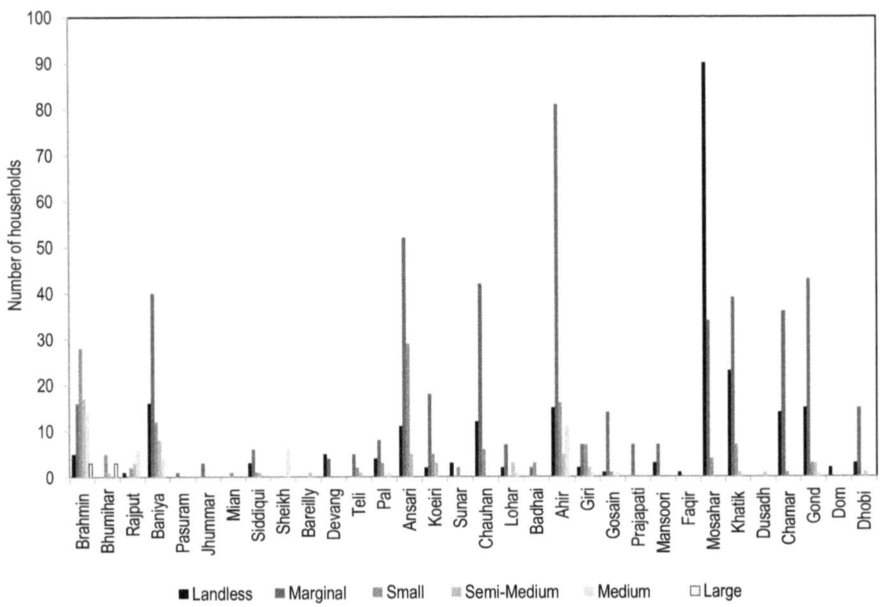

Figure 3.15 Distribution of Households in Dokhgadh by Size of Landholdings and Sub-Castes

Source: Prepared from field data (2009–10).

Note: Overall, details of forty-six households (less than 5% of the total households), from various caste groups are unknown. This is because of several reasons. For example, male members of the household were unavailable or are migrant workers and the women respondents were very young and involved in domestic chores only. Land and other details are not shared with them and neither do they ask. A few households refused to provide land or any other information. In these cases, some basic information about the caste and occupation of the household members could be gathered from neighbours but not land details other than knowing whether they are landless or not.

are landless. Like Sapatganj and Baaspur, marginal and small holdings are preponderant. This is also in line with regional trends. But Dokhgadh is different as here landlessness is significant (just under 25%) and 63 per cent of the landless households are Dalits. About 24 per cent of the OBCs and 13 per cent upper caste households are landless. All large landholdings and majority of the medium- and semi-medium-sized holdings are found among upper castes. Some instances of semi-medium and medium holdings can be found among the OBCs as well, but very few in the case of Dalits. Marginal and small holdings are predominant among the OBCs and Dalits. As such, a direct correlation is found between caste status and land base.

As in Sapatganj and Baaspur, a substantial land base is an important determinant of the *badkas'* clout because this makes them large employers of agricultural wage labour. This is buttressed by political connections and their superior social status.

The upper castes are *badka*s. In comparison to Sapatganj and Baaspur, politically the most powerful in Dokhgadh are Brahmins and not Rajputs. Political power is concentrated in the hands of two Brahmin families from the third hamlet. They are big but not the largest landowners in the village. One of them is a previous *pradhan* (two consecutive terms) and the present de facto *pradhan*. The second is a distant relative. No one from the second household occupies a political position, but a male member worked as a contractor for a government authority. The two are economic and political rivals. Villagers spoke out in favour of either of these households, of how they had helped them get job cards, BPL ration cards, extended credit in times of need, sponsored religious functions in the village, provided vehicles for transportation in health emergencies, mediated with other bureaucratic structures and the police and various other acts of patronage. There are other Brahmin and Rajput families who exercise significant economic and political influence but not of the same stature as the other two households. In either case, the economic and political command of these various households is augmented by the high social status of their caste.

A further related point deals with the issue of how different the petty capitalists are from big capitalists. Based on NSS criteria, there are very few large landowners in this village. However, as will be evident from the occupational profiling, these do not show unique features that would distinguish them from petty capitalist producers' economic or social outlook and have been described as such. They could be seen as emergent capitalists, following Bernstein. However, a blanket generalisation is not possible. In a neighbouring block, cash crop cultivation was diverse and more extensive (banana, litchi, turmeric, sugarcane). These big capitalists exported also to regional markets. One of them had even been nationally awarded for their farming methods and crop quality. This dynamism was lacking in field villages.

On the other hand, the *chutkas* are either landless or marginal and small landowners, with mostly no independent access to corridors of power. It appears that even when in position of power, *chutkas* are used as pawns. For example, the present *pradhan* of Dokhgadh is actually a Chamar. However, all powers associated with the post and privileges and influence thereof are commandeered by the previous Brahmin *pradhan* referred to earlier. The latter was identified as the *pradhan* by the villagers, as he is in practice. According to some accounts, the Chamar *pradhan* worked as a labourer for this Brahmin household. He was learning to drive (so that he could operate the jeep of the Brahmin as a taxi acquired under a government scheme), when in an accident, he injured another person. The Brahmin bribed the appropriate authorities to ensure that no charges were brought against the Chamar. In the next *pradhan* election, when the seat was reserved for an SC candidate, the Brahmin filed papers in the name of his Chamar 'servant'. Now, the former operates as the de facto *pradhan* and the actual Chamar *pradhan* is employed by him at ₹100 per day, he signs all papers, etc. Villagers scoffed that he sells bananas.

The caste–class overlap will become clearer in the subsequent discussion on occupational patterns. This has been mentioned earlier, though the overlap is not perfect.

Leasing is more common in Dokhgadh than Sapatganj and Baaspur. The reasons for leasing in or leasing out land are similar to those mentioned in the previous chapter. There were two other reasons in Dokhgadh, not seen in the other two villages. One is that land consolidation has not yet taken place here. Therefore, land fragmentation is high. A common observation made by villagers was the fragmented nature of their holdings and a parcel of their land being located in another village. This makes it difficult for them to travel everyday for cultivation purposes and look after the crop (and more so in the case of family labour involving female members of the house). In many such cases, villagers have leased out that parcel of land to locals from that area and leased in roughly the same area of land in an area nearer to them. The second reason for leasing out land was seen in the few upper caste households not having access to family labour, unable to afford hiring in labour, they did not undertake manual labour and therefore could not rely on exchange labour as well. Overall, upper castes (Brahmins primarily) are the net lessors and OBCs (Ahirs primarily) are the net lessees of land.

In majority of the lease arrangements, the nature of lease and its terms were similar to those in Sapatganj and Baaspur. In Dokhgadh, it was more common for landowners to lease out land after sugarcane harvest (generally three years or so when the land needs to be prepared for cultivation again before sugarcane can be planted) and reclaim it after one crop is harvested. This is the case, where landowners are not based in the village for most of the year. A different trend from other two villages is that in some cases lessors make half the investments and decide what is to be cultivated. For example, some landowners ask lessees to grow fruits and vegetables, in addition to other subsistence crops. Fruits and vegetables are taken by the landowners who then sell them in area markets. Like Sapatganj and

Baaspur, in Dokhgadh as well, leasing relations may follow socio-economic ties: land may be leased out to a labouring household which does regular wage labour for the landowning household.

Other than through leasing, households have also come into land as creditors. This land is called *rehan*. In these cases, the creditors retain the right to cultivate land till the time the debt is cleared. They can cultivate any crop and the produce is not shared with the owner of mortgaged land, that is, debtor. This is also an oral arrangement and largely found in cases where households have access to cash and family labour but little land. The most common reasons for mortgaging land were health and wedding expenditures. This is true even in the case of upper castes like Rajputs who do not participate in local wage labour given their social status. *Rehan* land relations appeared in Sapatganj and Baaspur also but on a very small extent. In these two villages also, the terms are the same for *rehan* land relations.

When this micro picture is compared with the national picture in recent years, a similar story is seen as mentioned in the previous chapter. The main point of consideration here is the high degree of landlessness, near landlessness and marginal holdings among the Dalit labouring households. This would imply a preponderance of Dalits in casual labour. According to the India Exclusion Report 2016, even where Dalits own land, they are mostly marginal and small farmers, and their land is of very poor quality. It reports that about 56 per cent of woman-headed households were landless – indicating multiple layers of exclusion. More recent field-based studies show a similar trend – that there is a strong overlap between caste position and not just land but also asset and wealth ownership (Ramachandran et al., 2010; Swaminathan and Rawal, 2015; Kumar, 2017; Swaminathan and Das, 2017). Anecdotal evidence from my fieldwork pointed to landownership being almost completely concentrated in male hands with isolated examples. This picture of high incidence of landlessness among women in general is true even today for the country. According to an Oxfam report, about 85 per cent of rural women in India are engaged in agriculture, but only 13 per cent of them owned land (Oxfam, 2018). In the case of Dalits, landlessness is high and given patriarchal norms and cultural bias, it is possible that landownership among Dalit women would be even worse. During my own filedwork, with the exception of isolated cases, no woman claimed landownership and read alongside the evidence on Dalit women's labour relations presented in this book leads us to a conclusion similar to Bina Agarwal's (1994) that landownership is crucial of women's empowerment.

Rural Labour Market in Village India: Class, Caste and Gender

Neoliberal globalisation has influenced rural classes in different ways and to varying extents. In the literature on agrarian political economy, the changing role of agriculture in household reproduction and occupational diversification emerges as common features of rural classes. Small and marginal farmers combine cultivation with a range of wage labour, self-employment activities and forms of labour[12] that are not monetarily remunerated but important for household reproduction. As little is known about village-level occupational structure in the context of eastern UP till date, particularly in terms of caste and gender disaggregated data, a detailed description of the same is made in this section. This is then related to the class position of the social groups in terms of Bernstein's three-fold classification of petty capitalists, petty producers and 'classes of labour'. This type of a mapping exercise is necessary to first establish what the local rural labour market is like and then to understand labour relations.

But first I remind the reader how Bernstein's class categories are operationalised.

Bernstein (2010) defined petty capitalists as farmers who reproduce themselves as capital, diversify economic activities and accumulate over a long time frame. They are the emerging rich capitalist farmers. Petty producers can reproduce themselves but not accumulate in the process. They combine family and wage labour. Petty producers can hire in labour or hire out their labour as and when needed. They may lease in or lease out land. These are middle farmers. Classes of labour find it difficult to reproduce themselves as labour. Their daily survival is dependent on the ability to sell their labour power. These are poor farmers who engage in different types of irregular and exploitative informal casual work and self-employment activities.

Lerche (2010) has used Bernstein's concept of classes of labour in the context of the Indian informal economy to identify who are the labourers. He proposes a hierarchy of types of wage labour and self-employment activities. In wage labour, formal occupations are at the top and casual agricultural labourers and bonded labour at the bottom. He mentions some other types of employment as well. Self-employment activities that show a substantive asset base and/or employ workers are at the top and those indicative of survival mode or draw on unpaid family labour are at the bottom. Those situated towards the bottom of the occupational hierarchy are the labour classes. According to Lerche, these occupations correspond with low income and power base. Dalits and scheduled tribes are concentrated in these. Though Lerche does not comment on the gender aspect, he cites and draws on Chen (2008), who argued that women are generally preponderant at the bottom of the informal economy (including agriculture) in low-wage work.

This comes across clearly in Table 3.1 which presents gender disaggregated occupational and wage data from Sapatganj and Baaspur villages.

Several things stand out in Table 3.1; the village labour market is gendered and within agriculture, there is a sexual division of labour; occupational diversification has occurred to a greater extent among men; male occupations are better paid and female occupations least well paid; public employment is well paid in comparison to agricultural and other local

Table 3.1 Gendered Patterns of Labour Commodification and Wage Structure in Sapatganj and Baaspur, UP[13]

Village	*Ocupation/Task*	*Wage (in Rupees)*	*Gender*
Sapatganj	Sowing (i) Rice (ii) Sugarcane	(i) 25 per *bhoja* (bundle)[14] (ii) 5–15 depending upon age or even just sweets	(i) Female (ii) Children
Baaspur		(i) Similar (ii) Similar	(i) Similar (ii) Similar
Sapatganj	Weeding	15 per day (for about eight hours of work and half of this for work done till afternoon.)	Female
Baaspur		20 per day (for about eight hours of work and half of this for work done till afternoon.)	Female
Sapatganj	Harvesting (i) Rice/Wheat (ii) Cutting sugarcane leaves (iii) Cutting sugarcane stalks	(i) 20 per day or payment in kind i.e. one bundle of rice/wheat for every ten bundles harvested, threshed and delivered at the employer's house. (ii) 15 per day (iii) 50 per day	(i) Female (ii) Female (iii) Male
Baaspur		(i) One bundle of rice/wheat for every ten bundles harvested, threshed and delivered at the employer's house. (ii) Similar (iii) Similar	(i) Similar (ii) Similar (iii) Similar
Baaspur	Ploughing using oxen and a wooden plough	15 per *katha*	Male
Sapatganj Baaspur	Various types of spade work (digging, mud filling, preparing the field)	50–80 per day Similar	Male Similar
Sapatganj	Loading/unloading	60–70 per day	Male
Sapatganj	Repairing or laying of new thatched roofs	100 per day	Male
Sapatganj Baaspur	Unskilled construction work (carrying headloads, making concrete mixture, watering)	100 per day Similar	Male Similar

(*Continued*)

Table 3.1 (Continued)

Village	*Ocupation/Task*	*Wage (in Rupees)*	*Gender*
Sapatganj	Moulding bricks in kilns	200 per 1000 bricks (takes two to three days to mould thousand bricks)	Male
Sapatganj	Domestic worker (dish washer)	She washed dishes twice a day and sometimes mopped the floor in the mornings. She was given dinner everyday and a lump sum of 300 every month	Female
Baaspur		200–300 per month and a meal everyday	Female
Sapatganj	Sale of curd/milk	20–25 per kg	Male and Female
Baaspur	Carpenter	75 per day	Male
Baaspur	Painter	125 per day	Male
Baaspur	Skilled construction work (brick laying)	200 per day	Male
Baaspur	General store owner	7000 per month	Male
Baaspur	Chemist shop owner	4000–5000 per month	Male
Baaspur	Rickshaw driver	50 per day	Male
Baaspur	Tractor driver	1500 per month. He is also given accommodation, food and old clothes	Male
Sapatganj	Tending to livestock	500 per month. Also, she is given two meals per day	Female
Baaspur		1300 per month. He is also given accommodation, food and old clothes[15]	Male
Baaspur	*Anganwadi* worker[16]	1700 per month	Female
Baaspur	Woodcutter	100 per day	Male
Baaspur	Primary school teacher (public employment)	3500 per month	Female
Baaspur	**Doctor (public employment)**	**22,000–30,000 per month**	Male

Source: Field survey (2009–10).

Table 3.2 Dokhgadh: Gendered Patterns of Labour Commodification and Wage Structure

Occupation/Task	*Wage (in Rupees)*	*Gender*
Sowing of rice/wheat	(i) 35–40 per *bhoja*	(i) Female
Weeding	30–35 per day (for about eight hours of work and half of this for work done till afternoon.)	Female
Harvesting (i) Rice/wheat (manual) (ii) Small tractor-operated thresher (process is called 'dauri') (iii) Cutting sugarcane leaves (iv) Cutting sugarcane stalks	(i) One bundle of rice/wheat for every ten or twelve bundles harvested, threshed and delivered at the employer's house or in rare cases 35 per *katha* (ii) Payment in cash or kind; the tractor/thresher owner retained the chaff as fodder (iii) 30 per day (iv) 50 per day	(i) Female (ii) Male (iii) Female (iv) Male
Ploughing using oxen and a wooden plough (usually owned by the ploughman)	20 per *katha*	Male
Various types of spade work (digging, mud filling, preparing the field)	100 per day or 30 per katha	Male
Unskilled casual labour (roofing, construction)	100 per day	Male
Skilled labour (roofing, construction)	150–200 per day	Male
Moulding and carrying head loads of bricks	200 approximately per 1000 bricks and towards the end of the season this may go up to 300. It usually takes two to three days to mould thousand bricks, but if other family members are involved, then it can be done sooner	Male and female (as attached unpaid family labour)
Carpenter	100 per day	Male
Tractor driver	1100 per month, 1500–2500 per month. May be given food and clothes as well	Male
School/college teacher	800 per month; 850–1500 per month; 2000 per month	Male
Watchman	1000 per month	Male

(*Continued*)

Table 3.2 (Continued)

Occupation/Task	*Wage (in Rupees)*	*Gender*
Tending to livestock	100 per day; 1500 per month	Male
Tailor	1000 per month	Male
Shop assistant	100 per day	Male
Security guard	140 per month 4200 per day	Male
Taxi driver	50–100 per day; 2500–3000 per month	Male
Insurance agent	2000–2500 per month	Male
Sale of milk	15–20 per litre	Male and female
Fertiliser shop	200–400 on good days and 0–50 on bad days	Male, his mother helps out occasionally
Cycle repair shop	50–60 per day	Male
Home-based general store (mobile cart)	100–200 per day	Male, senior female members may help out
Peddlers	0–150 per day	Male
Quack doctor	2000 per month	Male
Sale of milk, curd, cream	15–25 per kg	Male (milk) and female (milk, curd, cream)
Madrasa[17] teacher	850 per month	Male
Head clerk	**5000 per month**	Male

Source: Field survey (2009–10).

casual labour, even in non-regularised services like *anganwadi* workers. The wage structure was more or less fixed with respect to different types of work, but nevertheless it could change depending upon individual labour relations or work location. For example, labourers in unfree relations with dominant employers were likely to be paid less than the going wage rate and wage labour outside the village is remunerated at a higher rate. Regarding self-employment, it is difficult to establish a general pattern given the few instances of it. On this there is more evidence from Dokhgadh. Overall, the local rural labour markets are organised on the basis of caste and gender much along the lines of Lerche's work.

Dokhgadh also shows similar trends as in Sapatganj and Baaspur: the gendered nature of village labour markets, sexual division of labour within agriculture, only male labourers reflect movement out of agriculture, gendered wage gap in agriculture and more generally, higher rates of remuneration for male occupations. It is notable that wage rates in Dokhgadh are slightly higher than in the other two villages, in agriculture and a few other occupations (tending to livestock, tractor driver). Additionally, it is possible that certain agricultural tasks like harvesting and ploughing may be given on piece-rate basis as contractual work. This was not the case in Sapatganj and Baaspur. Wage rates vary slightly owing to work location, individual labour relations or caste of employers. I will return to this point later.

Caste and Gender-Based Mapping of Occupational Patterns

I now move to caste-wise description of occupational patterns and some subsequently in the chapter. Non-labouring caste households are described very briefly. This mapping exercise describes castes from top to bottom. Only the main caste groups have been discussed in detail here.

Bhumihar: All Bhumihar households are in Dokhgadh and best understood as petty producers. Cultivation of sugarcane is combined with food crops. The extent of mechanisation is low, in most cases limited to ploughing operations. They own assets like tractors and tube wells which may be rented out to villagers. In all cases, agriculture is based on hired labour and male family labour in supervisory capacity. In fact, a labourer present at the time of survey in one house quipped that the Brahmins had never even seen their land. Where men are migrant workers, elderly women of the household hire agricultural labour. The only two instances of local non-agricultural employment are those of a man working as a teacher in a private inter-college and a woman employed as a *shiksha mitra*.[18] The only example of public employment is of a man serving in the army. Male members of three households are involved in casual migrant work as a clothes vendor, an electrician (Dubai), a welder (Saudi Arabia, with family) and as casual labourers. Women of these households bear similar domestic responsibilities and subscribe to similar socio-cultural norms as described in the previous chapter, in the case of female members of upper caste petty capitalist households.

Labour commodification in this caste category reflects some level of education and a regular job and salary. Given their upper caste status, these households are not involved in local agricultural or unskilled casual wage jobs seen as the preserve of Dalit labourers. Caste status is a limiting factor for these landowning households lacking capital. They resort to migrant work or even mortgage part of their land to meet living expenditures. For example, one household owning a medium-sized landholding had mortgaged part of it to meet health expenditures and for '*naukri*', implying that debt incurred against land was 'invested' to obtain public service or regular employment for a male member. In these households, reproduction is ensured through either and/or combining small surplus generating agriculture, non-agricultural employment and remittances.

Brahmin: All six Brahmin households are from Baaspur. One is a petty capitalist, and the others are petty producers. The petty capitalist Brahmin household combines own cultivation with local non-agricultural self-employment and migrant work. They are a semi-medium landowning household. Commercial farming is practised on a relatively large scale and is almost completely dependent on hired labour.[19] Male members, and sometimes the wife of the male household head, are mostly involved in a supervisory capacity. The male household head owns a homeopathic pharmaceutical store in a public hospital in Lucknow. The eldest son owns a medicine shop in a local market. The middle son is in the military. In this household, local self-employment is symbolic of a non-agrarian base, resource endowment and a comparatively regular and better income source. Migrant work shows higher education level, economic progress and employment and income security, particularly when linked to public employment. Within the household, gendered relations and women's position in relation to life-cycle changes circumscribe the mobility, visibility and behaviour of female members of the family. With the exception of the eldest female member, all other women of the household practise seclusion. Women are involved in domestic work.[20] Being a surplus-generating, accumulating household that is involved in diverse economic activities which are secure, better paid and show a significant asset base, this Brahmin household is a petty capitalist household.

The petty producer Brahmin households are mostly self-employed. They are marginal landowners. Agriculture is largely a subsistence activity, drawing on male and female family labour and is combined with small-scale sugarcane cultivation. The degree of mechanisation is low.[21] Livestock rearing is a commercial activity drawing on male and female family labour.[22] Non-agricultural self-employment is seen in three households. Men from these households work as carpenters (home based). They usually get orders to make or repair agricultural implements and this demand is high around season time. Furniture orders are few and inputs may be supplied by the customer. One carpenter also operated a clock/watch repair shop in a neighbouring block on rented ground. According to his wife, there was no income from this shop. Such instances of self-employment are irregular and low-paying, but nonetheless, a sign of skill-based occupational diversification and a minimum level of productive asset base. The few instances of labour commodification were as local agricultural (male and female) and casual wage labour (male). In neighbourhood exchanges, in cutting grass for fodder or as wage labourers, these women are more mobile, visible and show a degree of autonomy.

In Dokhgadh, there are 86 Brahmin households. They are a large group. More than half of these households are petty capitalists, just over one-fourth of them are petty producers and an even smaller number come across as labour classes. Petty capitalist Brahmins are semi-medium, medium and large landowners. Commercial farming is undertaken on a comparatively large scale. Agriculture is mechanised and substantially draws on hired labour as well (weeding, transplanting paddy, harvesting and threshing on a small scale). Male family labour may be involved in a supervisory capacity. In isolated one or two cases, where male members are not available, land may be leased out or elder women or daughters of the household hire labour and give out wages. A source of income is renting out tractors and tube wells. Part mortgage of land to meet health, wedding and house repair/construction expenditures is not uncommon. Livestock rearing is a small-scale commercial activity.

Self-employment is found only among men. Examples include home-based taxi service, trust-run school, owner–operator of a JCB, manager/principal of own school, flour mill owners and wood contractors. Some of these self-employment activities are indicative of a strong asset base and employment of other workers. A few also showed connections with and access to public officials and resources. For example, the brother of the JCB owner worked as a contractor for the Public Works Department (this is one of the two most powerful Brahmin families). Another (the de facto *pradhan*) has a jeep (under a government disability scheme) which is operated as a taxi by the driver employed (according to some villagers, he employs three drivers who ply the van as taxi). Men work as teachers. There was one example of a journalist. A woman was employed as a nursery teacher. These forms of labour commodification show a non-agrarian base, most exemplify regular employment, educational skills and better remuneration. High social status is attached to most of these self-employment activities and forms of labour commodification.

Migrant work is uncommon. Very few households extended details about migrant work, destination and remittances. One was a reader and his family was based with him. Two others were based in Oman with their families. One man did business in steel, one worked in a medical shop and two others worked for a private security company. It was noticed that where migrant work involved casual labour at the lower ends of the urban informal economy, family members in the village tended to evade saying so. The shame associated with admitting a Brahmin doing such labour was evident in a Brahmin woman whose husband is a migrant worker in Dubai, who told me that she did not ask her husband for details. She (and by extension, her husband) feels embarrassed and humiliated as he has not studied much.

Types of male public employment included an upper *zilla krishi adhikari* (district agricultural officer), a constable at the local police station, one in CRPF, two in the army and one as a compounder in the government nearby hospital. A woman worked as an *anganwadi* worker. Like women from upper caste petty capitalist households, interpersonal relations of Brahmin women and their domestic role show similar characteristics.

Petty producer Brahmins are mostly semi-medium and medium landowners. Sugarcane is cultivated as cash crop, though on a much smaller scale than the petty capitalist Brahmins. Mechanisation is low. Agriculture is organised on a mix of family and hired labour. In family labour, both men and women (to a much lesser extent and generally middle aged or elder women) are engaged in supervision and/or manual labour. Female labour is particularly hired in paddy transplantation and where weeding is extensively required. Livestock rearing is a commercial activity. A significant proportion of these households has mortgaged substantive land area in the absence of any other income sources. Health and wedding expenditures, low or infected yields, high labour costs and lack of alternative regular income sources and family labour are common reasons for mortgaging land. A home-based male tractor mechanic was the only example of non-agricultural self-employment. A petrol pump attendant and a teacher, both men, were the only examples of local labour commodification. As salaried government employees, one man was in the army and the other employed in a district development office.

A few young men were engaged in migrant work such as welding, casual labour, shop assistant, dye master and as casual workers in a hotel and steel factory. In only one instance was migration family based. To a limited extent, migration reflects a failure to turn education into productive employment. I was told by a Brahmin man that his son had an MA degree but could not find any respectable and productive employment and consequently migrated. Migrant work appears to be an alternative to local wage labour. A woman lamented that she was given such a caste by God that she cannot do *banihari* (wage labour) for others. She was embarrassed doing agriculture on her own, but it had to be done and there was no other option. If a needy person comes to her for old clothes, she gives her own clothes so that the '*izzat*' (honour and respect) of a Brahmin is not violated. When another woman was asked about wage labour, she felt insulted and asserted that a Tewari (Brahmin) will ask for '*bhiksha*' (food, grain, etc. obtained by asking for alms, charity) but not do *banihari*. Women of these households followed the usual socio-cultural sanctions but not as rigidly as in the case of Brahmin petty capitalists.

The few Brahmin households which at best can be understood as labour classes either are landless, or their entire landholding has been mortgaged since many years. Where land had not been mortgaged, both men and women were involved in own cultivation and rarely hired labour. Livestock rearing is undertaken as a commercial activity. In the one case of self-employment observed, a widow had recently opened a small general store at her home. The only case of local labour commodification is a female agricultural wage labourer. Her marginal landholding is mortgaged, her husband has mental illness, and she has six children to support. Migrant work, undertaken by young men, is an important source of income for these households. Examples included skilled construction labour (and in the village when at home), dyeing work, private security, brick kiln work and casual labour.

When queried as to how they sustain in the absence of agricultural or other income, one woman said they do '*Brahmin ka dhanda*' (the work of Brahmins) that is, they perform marriages and other religious functions or perhaps, as previously indicated, they are involved in '*bhiksha*'.

These can be perceived as non-income generating activities that contribute to household reproduction. As classes of labour, these Brahmins may be materially as worse off as Dalit classes of labour, but they are not treated with contempt or subjected to exploitation or oppression which is typical of agricultural wage labour. They project an attitude of helplessness and pity. Socio-cultural restrictions on mobility and interaction were not observed to any significant extent in elderly or middle-aged women (as were the women owning a store and one undertaking wage labour), but the young married women were involved in domestic chores only. But even they did not practise seclusion to any noticeable extent.

Rajput: The one Rajput household in Sapatganj and eight in Baaspur are all petty capitalists. All are surplus-producing farming households undertaking extensive sugarcane cultivation. In both villages, Rajputs are the dominant landowners and main employers of agricultural labour. They rent in combine harvesters and hire out own tractors.[23] Men may plough fields with tractors, but otherwise they and the older women of the households are involved in agriculture in supervisory capacity only (with one exception, where men and women did manual labour, but irregularly). Livestock rearing is not a commercial activity. Migrant work is linked to public employment and non-agricultural self-employment. With the exception of a woman primary school teacher, all other instances of public employment are found in the case of men – an engineer, a doctor and a policeman. Another person is a compounder in a government hospital in Meerut, though it is not clear if he is a regular employee or not. Two, a dentist and a lawyer, are based in Lucknow. These types of employment are associated with high educational qualifications, stability and security, strong resource base and higher status. The responsibilities, mobility and social conduct of Rajput women are similar to the women of the petty capitalist Brahmin household. The dominant economic and social standing of Rajputs is bolstered by the fact that they are the key political players in the villages.

However, this does not mean that there is no differentiation within the caste. Differentiation can be seen in the quantity and types of assets owned, the extent to which commercial agriculture is practised, the political and economic influence commanded. For instance, the serving Rajput *Pradhan* of Baaspur wields greater power and influence than other Rajputs in the village. He is the largest employer of agricultural labour in the village and more crucially many labouring households can access their land only via the *pradhan*'s fields which is a major cause of dependence and subservience.

Dokhgadh has twelve Rajput households. Just under half of them are petty capitalists, half are petty producers, and one belongs to the labour classes. The petty capitalists are the bigger landowners among Rajputs. Commercial and subsistence agriculture are combined. Ploughing functions are mechanised. With the exception of two households wherein family labour (male and elder female members) may undertake manual labour in own cultivation, agriculture is dependent on hired labour and male family labour in supervisory capacity. Livestock rearing is a commercial activity. Male members of two households are migrant workers. Migration is family based. In one household, one male member worked in a sugar mill during season and another as a computer manager. In the other household, the male member is involved in electrical work. Three were government employees; one in Central Public Works Department, one worked with the Delhi electricity department and the third was a *Krishi Adhikari* (agricultural development officer). Migrant work comes across as dignified and salaried and based on skill and educational qualification. Women's economic responsibilities and social conduct are typical reflection of upper caste petty capitalist women.

Petty producer Rajputs are small and medium landowners, a fact most of them were embarrassed to tell me. Sugarcane is cultivated as a cash crop on different scales. Ploughing functions are mechanised. Agriculture is based on family (primarily male and in a few cases, elder female members) and hired labour. The component of hired labour is less. Livestock rearing is a commercial activity. There are no instances of local labour commodification or migrant work. Two men were regular government employees: one is in coal service and the other in New Delhi Municipal Council. In these two cases, migration was family based. Women from these households were engaged in domestic chores and observed socio-cultural restrictions as well.

The only Rajput labouring household is landless. It is involved in livestock rearing for commercial purposes. The male household head is a migrant worker and at the time of the survey was engaged in cloth weaving in Mumbai. His young wife is responsible for domestic care and reproductive economy.

Gupta: All eleven Gupta families live in Sapatganj and are marginal and small petty producer households. Sugarcane is cultivated on a small scale. Mechanisation is low. Agriculture draws on family (male and female) and hired labour, though family labour is only an occasional feature in most cases and usually takes the form of labour control, that is working alongside labour as a method of supervision. While the extent of hired labour is relatively small in comparison to the Rajput household, overall Guptas are net hirers of labourers. Livestock rearing is a commercial activity. Two instances of non-agricultural self-employment are seen in case of men – a wedding music band and a small tent house operation. These petty businesses are home based and depending upon the scale of work, labourers may be hired. The only instance of female non-agricultural self-employment is a home-based small *kirana* (general store), stocked with stationery, tobacco, food items, etc. These forms of self-employment activities underline a better-off resource base, ownership of productive assets and possible employment of others. At the same time, these do not show substantial educational attainment or vocational skills. Though irregular, they are better paid than agricultural and local casual wage labour and are in keeping with the high social status attached to their own local caste perception.

Agricultural wage labour is the only form of local male and female labour commodification, and this too was seen only in the case of two households; one was landless, and the other had mortgaged land. According to one Gupta woman, agricultural wage labour was not her *jati's* occupation. According to one male migrant worker, agricultural work and casual labour is associated with humiliation and embarrassment, particularly in the case of returning migrant workers. There is also the added dimension that local wage labour would put upper caste Guptas in a subordinate position vis-à-vis other upper caste employers. On the other hand, it would be shameful to be employed by those inferior in social status. This assertion, however, was challenged by the local 'classes of labour' who pointed out that Guptas lie since it is embarrassing for an upper caste to admit doing such wage labour. Later, some Gupta women admitted to taking up wage labour under extreme economic duress. A man in the military is the only example of public employment. Migration is an important source of income for most Gupta households. Only men migrate and nearly three quarters of the households reported one or more migrant members at the time of the survey. As migrants, they are involved in petty trades and casual labour. Examples include an electrician, a labour contractor, vegetable vendors, weavers, construction labourers and selling clothes door to door. Migrants reflect relative stability and regularity in terms of destinations and the type of work undertaken. Migration is a much-preferred alternative to the oppressive and exploitative local labour relations. It is a source of irregular but substantial income. Migration is associated with a sense of pride and achievement.

The social conduct of Gupta women is similarly prescribed by gender and life-cycle changes but not as strictly as in the case of petty capitalist Brahmin and Rajput women, given their weaker economic position. For example, of the two female labourers, one was elderly, and her mobility and interaction were not restricted or subjected to societal monitoring as is for a Rajput woman. The other female labourer was young, but her participation in wage labour was 'justified' on the grounds that her husband was a migrant and there was no other family member to ensure daily household reproduction. The woman operating the general store was also elderly. As such, these women show relative freedom of movement and autonomy.

In Dokhdagh, the *jati* name Baniya was used for identification. There are 84 Baniya households. Majority of Baniyas portray petty producer characteristics and some classes of labour. Depending upon landholding size, petty producer Baniyas combine subsistence and commercial agriculture on different scales. Mechanisation is low. Agriculture is mainly organised on family (manual and supervision only) and hired labour. Women are involved in agriculture to a much lesser extent than men and particularly young married women, unless there are no elder female or male members in the house. The extent of hired labour depends upon individual economic circumstances, availability of family labour or as claimed in some cases, it is just that they (Baniyas) do not do such work. A tiny number drew on exchange labour as well from among neighbours or extended family members. Some of them own tractors, bullock-carts, diesel pumpsets and pipes which are rented out to villagers for primarily agrarian purposes. Livestock rearing is an important source of income. Tractor owners may themselves plough fields of others for a price and bullock-cart owners, owning a plough as well, may operate as ploughmen.

Baniyas are traditionally traders, and they show strong continuity on this front. Male members of more than half the petty producer Baniya households are into self-employment as petty traders and in several cases, a household is into more than one self-employment activity. Some are vegetable vendors in various local markets.[24] They operate from alongside roads, as peddlers from their cycles or in a few cases, from own land located near a market or some rent a tiny room nearby to store vegetables. Many own small mobile general stores that stock tobacco products, warm food and other snacks. These may be located either outside their homes, elsewhere in the village or in prominent market junctions. In the latter cases, these are mostly located on rented ground. Where they are home or village based, (elder) female labour may help out. In one case, the store doubled as a flour mill. There was another instance of a rice mill located on own land.

Several others are peddlers selling wool, cosmetics, wrapping paper, clothes and ice cream. One's cycle was even equipped with a stove on which he made *jalebi* (a sweet). One operated a fertiliser shop in a nearby market. The fertiliser was bought on the black market and then sold to villagers. This man's mother helped him out in the shop. Several ran fixed shops located in various markets, selling cloth, rope and other roofing material and sand and cement. A quack doctor worked out of one such shop in addition to travelling around villages.[25] One bought and sold medicines from home. There were only two instances of female self-employment. Both these women owned sewing machines and worked as tailors out of their home.

The income from these sources widely fluctuates, but they are nonetheless crucial for daily household reproduction. These are also in keeping with the social status of the Baniya caste and indicate a non-agricultural base, ownership of productive assets and some minimal resource base. For example, the earnings from the fertiliser shop ranged from ₹200–₹400 on a good day and on bad days ₹50 or even nothing. Income would increase during season. But the female head of this household stressed that they did not do *banihari*. Her husband is mentally ill and when her sons were young, she had mortgaged a part of her land to support the family rather than taking to wage labour. According to another, there is no '*laaj*' (shame, humiliation) in doing own business, but there is '*laaj*' in working in another's field.

Villagers attribute the low and volatile earnings from these self-employment activities to a small consumer base, depressed rates and the poverty of the consumer. These factors are likely to have a differential impact on fixed shops in major market locations and cycle vendors. Shops in prime locations have attendant benefits like broad customer base, higher prices, timely payment, etc. Compare this to a scarcely stocked home or village-based shop. It appears that caste is an important factor even where businesses are home based. Though there were only two instances of female self-employment, it is possible that women are more affected by the aforementioned factors (see later, the case of female self-employment in labouring Baniyas).

Members of only five households were involved in local labour commodification. Men and women from these households did agricultural wage labour. Usually, older female members did wage labour and young married women undertook wage labour only in the absence of other family members capable of supporting the household or precarious economic circumstances. Male members from three of these households also did non-agricultural casual labour. Migration is not a very important phenomenon. Young men were involved in migrant work as welders, clothes/vegetable vendors, casual labourers, as a watchman, a casual worker in a hotel, potter, petrol pump attendant, crane driver, and carpenter, in sari work and in a ply factory. In some cases, migration is stable in terms of income and destination and remittances are relatively high. Women of these households are engaged in domestic economy and do not observe the restrictive socio-cultural traditions to any significant extent.

More than half the Baniya classes of labour households are landless. Agriculture is mostly a subsistence activity, and mechanisation is low. It is organised on the basis of family and exchange labour. Both men and women (excluding young married women) are involved in it. Two of these households mentioned hiring in labour as well. Livestock rearing for commercial purposes exists to a very small extent. Men from a little over half of these households are into self-employment activities. Operating from alongside roads in various local markets or as peddlers, they sell vegetables, fruits, utensils or sweets. One runs a general store, one a small mobile cycle repair shop and one other sells eggs, all located in a market. One has a tea stall in the market. The wife of the man helps out in the stall and their young son sells eggs at the stall.

The only instance of female self-employment is a woman owning sewing machine and sew clothes. However, this is not symbolic of any challenge to repressive traditions or economic empowerment. Her young age and married status limit her mobility. Her mother-in-law gets orders and delivers finished products. Her clients are the villagers who themselves are unable to afford the going market rate. On top of it, they are often unable to pay the full amount at the time of delivery. Those who can pay more prefer going to established shops in major market areas. Often, it is the case that caste, kin, social relations dominate the economic relation, and the woman has to accept whatever amount she is paid.

Nonetheless, these self-employed workers do own a minimum of productive assets like cycles and stitching machine.

Local labour commodification is not common. Agricultural wage labour is undertaken by men and women. In the latter case it is limited in extent, found only in the case of middle-aged and older women and dependent on other factors. For example, one woman had been deserted by her husband. She is the sole earner of the household. But she does wage labour only within the hamlet because of '*sharm*'. Also, she provides unpaid labour activities like scooping to *badka*s of the hamlet. Another said that she did wage labour when '*garj pade, jab garib tab jaayenge hi*' (Fieldwork Notes, July 2010), meaning when economic needs demand it because when one is poor, one has to do wage labour. Her husband works in a brick kiln and when she was asked if she also worked there, the husband immediately shot back '*aurat kis liye jaayegi chimney par, hum kis liye hai*?', meaning *why will the woman go to the chimney? What am I for?* This is an indication of how strongly the breadwinner notion is attached to the man and the movement and interaction of women controlled to reflect the household's honour and socio-economic status. Men were engaged in casual labour, brick kiln work, and one works as a roofer. Out of three brick kiln workers, one took advance from the kiln in the off-season. An *Asha Kiran*[26] worker was the only example of non-agricultural female labour commodification.

Young men are involved in migrant work. They work as peddlers selling clothes, as vegetable vendors, one did embroidery, one worked as a weaver and several others as casual labourers. Women from Baniya classes of labour households did not observe seclusion. They are more mobile and visible as wage labourers.

Kayasth: All eight Kayasth households are from Baaspur. They are all petty producers, though lines between Kayasth marginal and small landowners and classes of labour are blurred. In other words, Kayasth petty producers are not a homogenous group. Commercial and subsistence agriculture are combined to various extents in the case of Kayasths, depending upon the landholding size. Mechanisation is low; in very few cases harvesting may be mechanised but ploughing operations are largely undertaken by hiring tractors. Agriculture is based on family and hired labour. In family labour, it is largely men who are involved, mostly in supervisory capacity or sometimes even undertake manual labour. Female members of only two or three households occasionally do agricultural work in own field and these are either older women or daughters. The component of hired labour is small in comparison to petty capitalists. Livestock rearing is undertaken as a commercial activity.

Much like the Guptas, Kayasths do not participate in local wage labour. Their upper caste status is a 'limitation'. An elderly Kayasth woman asserted that Kayasths who have even passed class eight do not do wage labour for others but live on their income from own cultivation. Another middle-aged Kayasth woman remarked that an upper caste man will not work in others' houses.[27] One Kayasth woman mocked that

> Srivastavas do not have the stamina to do farming themselves. They fall sick if they go to the field for two minutes. Kayasths will employ

labour even if they have only two katha land. They may go to the field to supervise.

The one example of non-agricultural self-employment is of a man owning a medical store in a local market on rented ground. One man is a primary school teacher in a nearby village. This is the only example of local labour commodification. One or more male members of three households are migrant workers and in one of these instances, the entire family migrated. In all cases, migration is stable. Two male members of one household are in public employment (Indian Railways) and their families are based with them. Women do not practise seclusion but are still restricted to the domestic economy.

Ahir: All thirty-three Ahir[28] households are from Sapatganj. They are all petty producers. Agriculture is mainly subsistence oriented and dependent upon family labour (male and female). Very few households reported hiring in labour. Tractor ploughing is common. Men and women are involved in livestock rearing. In line with their traditional occupation, selling of milk and curd is common. Curd is made and sold by women in the village or to nearby shops (in this case, either shopkeepers fetch the product or male members of the households deliver to them, not women).[29] Men and women from roughly half the households do agricultural wage labour. Non-agricultural labour is undertaken by male labour of a few households only. This includes jobs such as casual labour in construction, sugar mills (loading/unloading trucks), brick kilns, as a shop assistant, watchman, peon in a private school and tractor driver.[30] Migrant work, as a risk spreading and coping mechanism, is common among young men. They work as weavers, electrical workers, casual labourers, tailors, agricultural labourers, drivers and factory workers. Women's participation in the domestic economy and wider socio-economic conduct is influenced by the gendered household relations and how they are positioned vis-à-vis other women in terms of changing life cycle. Social interaction or movement is not rigidly constrained, at least in households where women undertake wage labour. A few households undertake livelihood activities. Women primarily do these, and men may be involved in sugarcane harvesting on a *geda* basis.[31]

Dokhgadh had 136 Ahir households which is quite a large number compared to the other villages. One Ahir household is a petty capitalist, a little less than half of the remaining Ahir households are petty producers, and the rest are classes of labour. A ten-hectare landholding family, the petty capitalist Ahir household's agriculture comprises substantial sugarcane cultivation and is completely based on hired labour. The male head of the household may be involved in a supervisory capacity. He retired as an officer from the Indian Airforce and then went on to work in the Bihar Excise Department. His eldest son is a Judge and the son's wife is a doctor. The middle son recently became a sub-inspector of police. It is difficult to comment on the socialisation and mobility of female members of this household. I interacted with only the male head of the household, though it was noticed that unlike in other houses, the female members were not visible outside the house, or it could be that they were not in the village at that time (as is usually the case). In any case, these women would not be involved in any wage labour or even in own agriculture in any capacity. Unlike the upper caste petty capitalists, this household showed no linking of economic and political power in the village.

A small number of petty producer Ahirs are semi-medium and medium landholders. Most of them are marginal holders. Boundaries between these and Ahir classes of labour are fuzzy, and they do not show much difference in terms of how agriculture is organised or wage labour participation. A couple of the larger landowners had mortgaged parts of their land and therefore, their operating land area was much smaller. Depending upon owned landholding size (as sugarcane cultivation on leased land is rare), petty producer Ahir households combine subsistence agriculture with sugarcane cultivation. Agriculture is mostly based on family (men and women) labour. In comparison to upper caste petty producers, more number of young, married Ahir women are involved in own cultivation. Exchange labour is also common and takes place among fellow caste people and neighbours. They seldom hire in labour, except in peak season time. Exchange labour is less significant and the component of hired labour more in the case of medium and semi-medium landowners.

Livestock rearing for commercial purposes is common. In Ahirs, the sale of curd and milk is a more important source of income than in other castes. This is also their traditional occupation. Several of them owned one or two bullocks and a cart and/or plough. Where the plough is provided by the employers, wage rates are less (₹10 instead of ₹15 per *katha*). Those owning ploughs work as ploughmen and those with carts use them to transport sugarcane, people, material and/or carry brick loads at kilns. Non-agricultural self-employment is rare. One man owned a medical shop in a major local market, and another owned a grocery-cum-general store in the same market. One is a veterinarian at the block. Just over half the households have one or more male and female members (to a much lesser extent) undertaking local wage labour. With the exception of two *anganwadi* workers, women are into only agricultural wage labour. Apart from agricultural wage labour, men work as casual labourers, they mould or carry head loads of bricks at kilns and even take advance in off-season, work as skilled construction labourers and as watchmen.

As one moves down the petty producer hierarchy, it is noticed that despite economic distress, several Ahir women do not undertake wage labour at all or do it only within their hamlet. This is because of *sharm* and *laaj*. One said that she did wage labour in only other villages. These feelings can possibly be attributed to either one of the following reasons: that in terms of caste status, they are not worst off; that as *gvalas* (milkmen), agricultural wage labour is not their main occupation; and finally, that wage labour is associated more with *majoora jaat*, that is labouring castes (*chutkas*, Dalits). Given the concentration of Ahirs in this hamlet, the employers of agricultural labour are also mostly Ahirs, and this works both ways. Either women are shy to work outside the village for other caste employers in view of their own caste status or would rather do wage labour in own village for same caste employers.

The extent of migrant work is even less. Only young men are involved in migrant work as skilled or unskilled construction labourer, casual labourers, welder, electrician, driver, painter, one did electrical wiring work, one worked in a chemical factory, one was involved in carpet weaving and another in cloth weaving. A casual labourer simply said he did 'private work' and that he did not wish to elaborate because of the presence of many other fellow caste villagers. In isolated cases, migration is stable and income comparatively higher. Five men are in public employment: two in government coal companies, details of one were not clear other than he worked in 'cane union' (as told by his relatives) and the last refused to give details for fear that I would send the CBI after him! In these cases, migration is family based.

Most of the Ahir labour class households are marginal holders, and a few are landless. A significant proportion has leased in land and since many years. As the operational landholding size is actually large, in rare cases, these households may hire in one or two labourers for paddy transplantation or if family labour is unavailable. Agriculture is mostly a subsistence activity. It is based on male and female family labour and exchange labour with neighbours and relatives. Young married women are seldom engaged in own cultivation. Livestock rearing is common and an important source of income. One man operates as a milkman, that is he buys milk from villagers and sells it in a local market. He buys milk at ₹16 or ₹17 per kilogram and sells it in the market for a rupee or so more. Non-agricultural self-employment is rare. A couple runs a small tobacco stall at their house. According to them, earnings are insubstantial. Two of their sons are involved in migrant work. No member does local wage labour. As the male head of the household puts it, '*abhi samay theek chalta*', meaning they are doing fine and do not need to undertake wage labour at this time (Fieldwork Notes, July 2010). The only other example is of a tiny grocery stall in the village, run by a *sadhu* (hermit) who also asks for *bhiksha* in nearby villages.

All households have one or more male and/or female members in local wage labour. Women (usual provisos regarding age and availability of supporting family members apply) are involved in only agricultural wage labour. Men did agricultural and non-agricultural casual labour. Those engaged in brick kiln work moulded or carried head loads of bricks. They took advance in the off-season. In a couple of cases, women were involved as unpaid attached family labour. Brick kiln work is remunerated on a piece-rate basis and therefore, output is important. When women took lunch to their husbands, they helped out in moulding bricks (watering new bricks, laying out bricks, carrying head loads), while the husband ate. One family cultivated only vegetables in their field and the male head sold these in weekly bazaars. Two men worked as taxi drivers. One was a dancer cum singer as a part of 'orchestra' that performed on weddings. The group may earn ₹1,500 per performance and this is split among five to seven members of the group.

Fewer than half of the households have one or more migrant male members. Types of migrant work includes skilled construction work, carpet weaving, welding, shuttering, cloth weaving, washing bottles, casual labour and one worked as an electrician. Migrant workers from one household are usually involved in the same work and in the same place. Livelihood activities other than sugarcane harvesting on *geda* basis by men were not observed. Women do not observe socio-cultural restriction to any significant extent, with the exception of young married women who are restricted to the house.

Chauhans: All 66 of these households were in Dokhgadh. Some Chauhans are lower-end petty producers and the rest belong to the classes of labour. Amongst petty producers, agriculture combines subsistence production and sugarcane cultivation to different extents. It is primarily based on family (including women with the usual provisos applying) and exchange labour. In rare cases, labourers are hired in peak season. Mechanisation is low. In a few households, livestock rearing is undertaken as a commercial activity. Male members of only two households were involved in non-agricultural self-employment – as a fisherman and the other household combines this with a small general store at their house. Mostly men are involved in local labour commodification. Only two women did wage labour. Both are middle-aged and one of them only occasionally did wage labour. As put by the wife of a skilled construction labourer, her husband would not allow her to do wage labour even if he had to resort to begging. One man worked as a tractor driver. One owned a small thresher operated through their tractor and a male member used this for 'dauri', that is threshing. Members of two households worked as insurance agents. Some others did casual labour, and two men were involved in brick kiln work.

Half the households have one or more migrant men. In most cases, respondents were unable to provide details other than that the migrants were involved in casual labour. It is common to see long-term migration to where one family member has been based for a considerable time or is in service. Regarding public employment, one man worked with the Military Engineer Service, three households had members in government coal companies (one household had three members in it, including a woman who was given the job on her husband's death). Government service is linked to family-based migration. Though women from Chauhan petty producer households do not strictly observe the traditions and customs as do some others, they are not involved in wage labour. They may undertake livelihood activities and men may be involved in sugarcane harvesting on *geda* basis.

In Chauhan classes of labour, agriculture is mostly subsistence-oriented and sugarcane cultivation is minimal. It draws heavily on family labour of men and women (with usual provisos). Exchange labour is less common. Livestock rearing is a commercial activity. There are only three instances of non-agricultural self-employment: a woman home-based tailor, a widow operating a small grocery/tobacco store from home and the third household had a flour mill in which the female member also helped out. Almost all households have one or more members engaged in local wage labour. More men than women are involved in local wage labour. The latter do only agricultural wage labour. Men do this and non-agricultural casual labour. A common type is brick kiln work where they are involved in moulding, carrying head loads of bricks or carrying them on cycles and rickshaws supplied by kilns. These labourers often borrow money from kilns in the off-season and women may be involved as unpaid attached labour. Most male migrant workers are into casual labour, while skilled construction work and welding are the only migrant works requiring some skill. Many show stable migration patterns in the type of migrant work undertaken and their destination. Again, relatives often migrate to the same place. Remittances are rather low and irregular.

Though as many household members as possible pursue occupational multiplicity, young married women are restricted to the domestic economy. Women are involved in livelihood activities, and men harvest sugarcane on *geda* basis.

Koeiri: Of the twenty-five Koeiri households, two are in Sapatganj and the rest are in Baaspur. All are petty producers. Sugarcane is cultivated on a small scale. At the most, tractors are used for ploughing. Agriculture is mainly based on family labour (men and women). Livestock rearing is a commercial activity. Non-agricultural self-employment is uncommon. All six instances of it are in Baaspur. Male members of three households own general stores; two of these are located in the market and one in the village. In the latter case, the young wife also helps out. One man owns two speakers which are rented out for various functions at ₹100 per day. Male members of another house run a tobacco and a mobile phone repairing shop in a local market. In both cases, the start-up money was taken from an SHG located in a nearby block. One of them had taken ₹10,000 from the SHG and has to deposit ₹250 per week. He earns about ₹1000 per week.

These forms of self-employment are indicative of a non-agrarian base, ability to access resources like credit through SHG, possession of some resource base or productive assets and shops are located in relatively prime location with their attendant benefits like a broader customer base, market rates and timely payment.

Very few Koeiris undertake agricultural wage labour. Most of the female labourers are middle-aged or elderly and in the case of young married women, it was noticed that they are from nuclear households with no senior family members to depend upon. According to one woman, Koeiris do not work in others' fields. Non-agricultural forms of labour commodification are found in the case of men only. Examples include coolie work, skilled construction work, as a painter, operating the village PDS outlet and one instance of teacher in a private nursery school. Although not extensive, migration is an important source of income for a little less than half of the households. Mostly young men are migrant workers, but in a few of these, migration is family based. Types of migrant work include skilled and unskilled construction work in Lucknow, as weavers in Surat, embroiderer in Delhi, as a welder in Meerut and as casual labourers. Three men were in public employment: one was in police service; one was in some kind of agricultural job (spraying pesticide) and details of the third were not known as the entire family had migrated and villagers did not know the details.

Here also, women are responsible for all household chores, and they are highly likely to be engaged in livelihood activities, while men harvest sugarcane on *geda* basis. Seclusion is not observed in the case of Khushwaha women in relation to their relatives or neighbours. With the exception of young married women, their mobility is not restricted as in the case of upper caste petty capitalists.

Ansari: There are a total of eighteen Ansari households, four in Basspur and the remaining in Sapatganj. All are petty producers. Largely subsistence farmers, both men and women are involved in agriculture. Tractor ploughing is the only form of mechanisation. Livestock rearing is undertaken as a commercial activity. There are only two examples of non-agricultural self-employment work. One man owned a motorcycle repair shop and the other a cycle repair shop, both in a local market. According to the latter, income fluctuated widely; in one day he could make anything up to ₹100. One of the households had a jeep, which previously was operated as a taxi. Another household had a (broken down) wheat-grinding machine. A female member of the household operated it when it worked. The family planned to sell it and were waiting for scrap iron and steel prices to rise.

Men and women from very few households do agricultural wage labour which is the only form of local labour commodification.[32] The four Baaspur Ansari households are located next to the *pradhan*'s house. Women from three of these households did agricultural wage labour for the *pradhan* primarily, but they stopped doing so since the last few years. This is associated with upward economic mobility owing to stable migration and high remittances and domestic responsibilities. According to one Ansari woman, they are 'untouchables' and therefore cannot do paid domestic labour or other such work in the houses of *badkas*. One man in the police service was the only example of public employment.

Migration is an extensive and enduring trend. In Sapatganj, most households have migrating members and migration can be traced back to the 1970s at least. Its early appearance among the Ansaris (as also their absence in local non-agricultural self-employment activities and patterns of labour commodification) has to be understood in view of their segregation from the village-based socio-economic relations. Because of this they faced greater vulnerability and insecurity in relation to other groups and were forced to seek alternative sources of livelihood. Only young men migrate. They work as scrap dealers, as weavers, welders, tailors, truck drivers and various other forms of casual labour. In terms of destination and work type, they reflect considerable stability.

In Baaspur, male members of three households are involved in migrant work. They are brothers. The eldest has been working in Saudi Arabia since the last six years. In addition to working in a cloth and tailoring shop, he undertakes other casual work also such as construction labour, tiling, painting, etc. The middle brother had migrated to Saudi Arabia two years ago. He works as a truck driver and does casual labour such as electrical work. Remittances are high and comparatively regular (approximately ₹10,000–₹16,000 every two to three months). The youngest brother went to Saudi Arabia only about two months earlier and does casual labour.

Surprisingly, socio-cultural restrictions are not seen in the case of Ansari women to any significant extent. Even though they do not participate in wage labour, they do not wear veil and move freely in their hamlet. This is seen even in the case of upwardly mobile Baaspur Ansari households. Ansari women too are anchored to the responsibilities of domestic chores and care and reproductive responsibilities. Women from Baaspur Ansari households do unpaid labour for the *pradhan* because they can access their fields only through the *pradhan*'s fields. They are also indebted to the *pradhan*. The incidence of unpaid labour has decreased over time, however. They are able to meet debt payments through remittances. Also, their withdrawal from agricultural wage labour has reduced their dependency on the *pradhan*, who is the major employer of agricultural labour. At times, women from these households try to evade these 'tied' labour services through procrastination and making excuses. This should not however be taken to mean that there are no more grounds for dependency (for example, accessing fields for grazing). These women observed that they are constantly subjected to pressure by the *pradhan*'s household. Most households undertake livelihood activities, done mostly by women. Men may be involved in sugarcane harvesting on a *geda* basis.

Dokhgadh has 100 Ansari households. The majority of the Ansari households are petty producers and the rest belong to the classes of labour households. Most of the petty producer Ansari households are small or marginal farmers. Agriculture is primarily subsistence oriented. Ploughing operations are mechanised. Otherwise, agriculture is based on family (only senior women) and hired labour mostly, with a few households engaging in exchange labour as well. As is typical of petty producers, the extent of hired labour is small and depends on the availability of able family labour. Labour is hired mainly for paddy transplantation. Male members from two households are ploughmen. Livestock rearing is a commercial activity.

Several men run petty businesses or trades from local markets, for example, shops selling footwear, readymade garments, electronic goods, medicines, cycle repair workshop, tailoring shop and general stores. There are a few instances of general stores and one flour mill being located within the village where senior female members of the household help out. One man was a vegetable vendor. These self-employment activities reflect occupational diversification, resource base and are more respectable in comparison to Baniyas selling vegetables on the roadside and likely to better pay. Two women owned stitching machines but only occasionally stitched clothes. Agricultural wage labour is undertaken by a few households and mostly by men. Two women said that they did wage labour within the hamlet and among relatives only. One man did wage labour only when needed. Male members of these households may also undertake other casual labour. Men were employed as car and tractor drivers, teachers, skilled construction labour, insurance agent and carpenter.

Migrant work is a relatively important source of income. About half the households have one or more men engaged in migrant work like cloth weaving or stitching, carpentry, welding, skilled and unskilled construction work, wiring and one worked as a clerk. There are only two instances of family based migration, where one is a teacher and the other a civil foreman. As seen elsewhere, members of one household are often found in same type of work in the same city. The one example of public employment is of a male teacher in a government junior school. With the exception of young married women, their mobility and visibility were not rigidly controlled. For instance, they could be seen outside their houses, tending to livestock or interacting with neighbours unlike the Brahmin or Rajput women. Their movement beyond the hamlet is as circumscribed as in the case of women generally. They may be involved in livelihood activities. Men harvest sugarcane on *geda* basis.

Ansari classes of labour are either landless or marginal farmers. Agriculture is primarily a subsistence activity and based on family (with usual provisos) and exchange labour. Livestock rearing is undertaken as a commercial activity. The two cases of female non-agricultural self-employment activity were of home-based tailors. One charged ₹15 for blouses and ₹50 approximately for suits. Her husband added that there are no fixed rates in village and people pay randomly. Men are into agricultural and other casual labour. Female members of fewer households are into agricultural wage labour. In two landless households, young married women also undertook wage labour. Migrant work is significant. Male migrant workers are involved in cloth weaving or sewing, starching saris, skilled construction work, leatherwork, pipeline and iron work and car repair work. Social conduct of women is similar to those of women from petty producer Ansari households. Women are involved in livelihood activities and men in sugarcane harvesting on *geda* basis.

Kharwar: All 30 Kharwar households are classified as classes of labour. Seven of these are in Sapatganj and the rest in Baaspur. Almost all Kharwars are marginal holders. Agriculture is largely undertaken as a subsistence activity and some households cultivate sugarcane on a small scale. Agriculture is family based. Exchange labour is very less.[33] Rarely in one or two cases, due to unavailability of family labour, one or two labourers may be hired in peak season. Both men and women are involved in own cultivation. Tractor ploughing may or may not be a mechanised operation. While livestock (cattle and goats) is sold, Kharwars may or may not sell milk, depending on need, consumption and availability of surplus. Households not owning livestock sell the straw/chaff (after harvest) to livestock owners. By one estimate, this usually brings in ₹150–₹250 or a maximum amount of ₹300.

Only four examples of non-agricultural self-employment were found, all undertaken by men. In the case of a home-based general store, women helped out. One owned a sweet shop in a local market and according to his wife, income from the shop varied between ₹1,000 and ₹2,000 per month. Their son ran a separate snack shop in the same market. His wife helped out at the shop when she brought him lunch. Another ran a general store in the same local market and his sons assisted in the shop. Shops in the market are located on rented space.

In comparison to petty producers, Kharwars are involved more in local wage labour. Agricultural wage labour is an important form of male and female labour commodification. However, in a few cases of joint families, where the elders are still involved in wage labour, the young daughters-in-law do not participate in agricultural wage labour. Examples of non-agricultural employment among men include jobs as drivers, construction labourers, coolies, hotel workers (these were children who were paid ₹300 per month), carrying head loads of bricks at a kiln, tending to livestock and a watchman. A woman did domestic work for the Sapatganj Rajput family and was an occasional cook at the village school. During the course of fieldwork, several women pointed out that Kharwar women could do work that could bring them in touch with non-Dalits because they are locally perceived as less unclean than other Dalits. In Baaspur, a widow did casual labour under NREGA. She is landless and has five children to support. There are no other adult members in the household.[34] There was only one example of public employment, that of a man in Indian Railways.

Most of the Kharwar households in Sapatganj had male migrant workers, but in Baaspur, migration was uncommon. Types of migrant work included tailoring, painting, casual labour, a tractor driver, scrap dealer, cloth weaving and as a carpenter. Livelihood activities are more common in Sapatganj. In both villages, these are undertaken by mostly women and children. Men are involved in harvesting sugarcane *geda*. In times of need, to cover any shortfall in food or such requirement, Kharwars show a high dependency on upper caste-class. This is possibly because, among classes of labour, others are less likely to be able to provide any help.

What is common across castes and classes so far is that the role of women is strongly gendered and embedded in the domestic economy. However, significant differences exist in terms of socio-economic behaviour of women from petty capitalist and petty producer households and Dalits, an overwhelming number of whom belong to the category of labour classes. While women belonging to the classes of labour are still subjected to socio-cultural controls and monitoring, in certain aspects they show greater autonomy and agency. For example, whether or not they participate in wage labour is still circumscribed by factors like age and availability of other household members being able to productively contribute to its reproduction. However, economic needs and absence through most of the year of migrant male members mean that women start moving out of the house for wage labour at a relatively early age. These women show initiative, organisational skills and independence in accepting wage labour, organising labour groups and religious functions, negotiating their wages and work conditions. They travel to other villages for work, social, religious, health and such reasons, alone or in the company of other villagers. They travel only when there is a 'justifiable' cause and avoid interaction with unknown men.

For example, Dalit women from the labour classes organise big religious ceremonies that last through the night and provide food. These are attended by women from all over the area. While their social behaviour and etiquette (with whom do they mingle, where they go, how they are dressed, etc.) are closely monitored in the village, on special occasions, they can let themselves loose, dress up, dance, etc. They show organisational skills and decision-making powers. The neighbourhood women contribute to the organisation, purchase of food materials, hiring of loudspeakers, the main organiser approaches a *badka* to rent his tractor-trolley to purchase things from the market (women do not go to the market, so they send some men from the village or tell the tractor driver what has to be bought) and to ferry people. However, on the other hand, there are cases where in doing so women have faced the wrath and suspicions of their husbands (and in some instances physical abuse) and the taunts of even the upper castes and classes for indulging in 'loose behaviour', for being out the whole night, for dressing up, etc.

Nonetheless, women belonging to the Dalit labouring households do not meekly accept or submit to male authority. Low caste women are very vocal, and they express their anger, discontent, rebellion indirectly; for example, by not performing essential chores like cooking or feeding the livestock, refusing food, frequent domestic fights, verbal diatribes, etc. They may win their conflicts in this way. However, there may also be adverse consequences such as wife-beating. At the same time, female classes of labour blame their rowdy behaviour on their *chutka* status and contrast it to *badka*s. As one female *dusadh* labourer put it,

> *[B]adkas* do not fight amongst themselves and even if they do, no one comes to know, unlike in the case of *chutka*s who are loud, brash and

the entire village comes to know of it. *Badka*s possess '*buddhi*' (implying knowledge and intelligence).

A sense of low esteem and self-blame is evident among the *chutkas* vis-à-vis their position and status.

Dhobi: There are ten Dhobi households in Sapatganj and four in Baaspur. All belong to the labour classes. Agriculture is again subsistence oriented, with minimal sugarcane cultivation, but their subsistence is commodified. Agriculture is mechanised to a limited extent, if at all. It is based on a combination of family (male and female, and the participation of young daughter-in-laws depends on economic needs and availability of other family labour) and exchange labour relations. In isolated one or two cases, households may hire in labour at peak agricultural season. This is not necessarily a sign of economic prosperity. For instance, in one case, the male member of the house was a migrant worker and in view of his young wife's restricted mobility, they had to hire labour. Livestock rearing is a commercial activity.

Non-agricultural self-employment activities are common and typically evidenced only in the case of men. These include giving tuitions, roofing, digging water boreholes and plying donkeys carrying brick loads in kilns in dry season, running a cycle-repair- cum-snack shop on rented ground in the local market which fetched anything between ₹50 and ₹100 in a day or even nothing. The wife of another cycle repair shop owner mentioned earnings between ₹50 and ₹100 per day. A man owned a large battery-operated music speaker which was rented out on special occasions for ₹50 per hour. The male head of one household ran a rice mill from the cowshed adjacent to the house. Male and female members helped out with this. His son runs an omelette stall in a local market, located on space rented at ₹80 per month. He buys a box of eggs for ₹500 and sells one omelette for ₹4. Egg trays are collected and sold to a scrap dealer for ₹4 per kg. According to his wife there is no profit but, it is a source of a little income crucial to their survival. His younger brother ran a cycle repair shop in the same market on space rented at a similar rate. These types of self-employment activities are of survival mode.

Agricultural wage labour is common and undertaken by both men and women (involvement of young daughter-in-laws depended on availability of other family labour). Non-agricultural forms of labour commodification are confined to male labour. Examples include unskilled construction labour, tractor driving (year-round or only during sugarcane harvesting to transport sugarcane to the mill) and ironing clothes in someone's shop in the village market. Migrant work figures prominently in Sapatganj Dhobis' occupational patterns. Only young men migrate. Types of migrant work include tailoring, embroidery, welding, plumbing and working in a packaging factory.

Livelihood activities are extensively undertaken and here men only harvest sugarcane on *geda* basis. Unpaid labour services like scooping, sweeping or tending livestock are provided by Dhobi women to *badka*s. These often overlap with debt relations, neo-bondage or are undertaken in view of a household's history with a particular *badka*. These may or may not be willingly undertaken. An indebted household (particularly one situated near the creditor household) is not in a position to decline to do this work, while a non-indebted household may provide unpaid labour services as insurance against unforeseen needs or emergencies. In the latter sense, the recipient household is perceived as a source of food security, a medium of accessing resources, a source of credit and more generally as benevolent 'protectors' who would help out in times of need. Underlying such self-exploitation is an awareness of the social and economic divide between *badka*s and *chutka*s and the dependency of the latter on the former. Irrespective of the circumstances under which a household provides unpaid labour, refusal to do such work can be subtly expressed in the form of procrastination. In comparison to livelihood activities, 'benefits' of doing unpaid labour are not immediate or direct. But both are crucial to the survival of local classes of labour. The socio-economic behaviour of Dhobi women is similar to that of Kharwar women.

Dusadh:[35] The fifteen Dusadh households in Sapatganj and nine in Baaspur, all belong to the category of classes of labour. Almost all Dusadh households are marginal landowners. As is typical of classes of labour, agriculture is subsistence oriented and, in some cases, combined with minimal sugarcane cultivation. Cultivation draws on men and women (with rare exceptions of young married women) and also exchange labour. In isolated cases, households may hire in labourers for a day or two during peak agricultural seasons because of individual household circumstances. For example, one woman's husband was a migrant worker. She had a very young child to take care of. Though relatively young, her mobility and wage labour participation were not restricted by socio-cultural reasons. Nonetheless, she had to hire a few children to sow sugarcane in her field. She worked alongside them, while her elder daughter, who had skipped school that day, took care of her young sister. Only ploughing operations may be mechanised. Livestock rearing is a commercial activity.

Non-agricultural self-employment activities are not common. Only men engaged in these. Examples include digging water boreholes, plying a push-cart in a neighbouring block on which load is transported, cycle/puncture repair workshop, *dholak* (musical instrument) player, wood cutter, a quack doctor or compounder and a teacher who gave private tuitions. Self-employment appears as a survival activity, an irregular source of income from mostly low status and lowly paid work. Agricultural wage labour is the most predominant form of male and female labour commodification. Men undertake non-agricultural wage labour as well. They worked as casual labourers engaged in digging, mud-filling, carrying head loads, loading/unloading; as unskilled construction labour; in brick kiln work and in a sugar factory. A woman from Baaspur is an *anganwadi* worker. Though this is not regularised government service, it is secure work, better and timely remunerated, indicative of education, does not involve the drudgery of agricultural wage labour and is not perceived as degrading work.

Overall, migration is an important source of income, but the decision to migrate is shaped by the availability of other family members to support the household in the absence of migrants. Securing daily survival in the face of economic vulnerability requires all members to be productively employed and particularly men as male forms of local wage labour are more remunerative. This was certainly the case with Sapatganj Dusadhs where a little less than half the households had migrant male members, while in Baaspur, more than half the households had migrant workers. Unlike in the case of Ansari petty producers, migration has not contributed substantially to the household income and has not decreased th ereliance on local wage labour for Dusadhs. Only young men migrate. They worked as welders, rickshaw pullers, cloth weavers, hawkers, painters, scrap dealers and did other low-paying and low-status informal casual labour. In terms of destination, duration and type of work, Dusadh migrant workers are more unstable than Ansari migrants. Remittances from Dusadh migrants are lower than those fromAnsaris. In some cases, Dusadhs were involved in debt-based migration and reported receiving delayed and low payment at the destination.

Regarding livelihood activities, social conduct of women and unpaid labour services, Dusadhs are similar to other local classes of labour.

Chamar: All forty-one Chamar households are in Baaspur. With the exception of four households which are characterised as petty producers, all other households belong to labour classes. Petty producer households are engaged in a mix of subsistence and commercial (on a small scale) agriculture. Only ploughing operations are mechanised. Agriculture is based on family labour, including men and women. Two of these four households undertake livestock rearing as a commercial activity. There are no examples of non-agricultural self-employment, local wage labour or migrant work. Petty producer Chamar households either had or have a member in public employment who has had an important bearing on their comparatively better economic status vis-à-vis Chamars belonging to the labour classes. For example, in one household, the retired male household head receives a pension of ₹3,000 per month. His son works as a teacher. In another household, the mother-in-law and daughter-in-law are widows. The latter is an *anganwadi* (not a regular, pensioned government service, but a better alternative as explained previously) worker (the job was 'got' through her brother-in-law who himself was in public employment) and receives ₹1,700 per month. In the third household, the male household head is in the Central Reserve Police Force (CRPF henceforth). In the fourth household, a male member is in police service.

It is usually the case that irrespective of caste, upward economic mobility is associated with social seclusion of women. This is true of these households as well, but it is influenced by other factors. For example, the two widows are involved in own cultivation, but not the wife of the former CRPF man. So, the availability of male family labour is a determinant of female labour participation. The widowed *anganwadi* worker cannot afford to live in seclusion. However, the economic vulnerability is not as extreme as in the case of Chamar female labourers who are extensively involved in agricultural wage labour. With the exception of one household (the one whose male head was in the CRPF), female members of others freely move about and interact in the hamlet. These households are unlikely to undertake livelihood activities. They reflect greater investment in education and land. For example, a sixteen-year old daughter in one household was still in school, children in another household went to private schools and in one other case the household had purchased land in the past. These are not accumulating households who have managed to consolidate their position, but they have managed to maintain and provide for the household on a simple basis and therefore can be understood as petty producers.

Among Chamar households belonging to classes of labour, agriculture is subsistence oriented and combined with small-scale sugarcane cultivation in a few cases. One household had sown carrots which would be bought by a Baniya from a neighbouring village who would sell them. Agriculture is organised on family and exchange labour. Both men and women (young women work only where other family labour is unavailable) are involved in it, as they are in livestock rearing for commercial purposes. One household owned a plough and oxen and a male member worked as a ploughman.

Non-agricultural self-employment is rare. One man is a rickshaw puller, another a cobbler (earning ₹10–₹15 per day) and one is a tailor (₹100–₹150 per day) who works from a rented shop in a local market. Only one girl was involved in non-agricultural self-employment as a home-based tailor. She had recently learnt tailoring and could do only simple designs. Rather than as source of income, the skill was acquired for personal use; stitching and embroidery are skills usually taught to young girls of marriageable age. The girl's mother complained that now people own machines and either stitch at home or prefer to give clothes for stitching in the market.

Local labour commodification is extensive. Agricultural wage labour is the most common type of female and male labour commodification. Even young married women undertake agricultural wage labour, except in rare cases where there are other family members to support the household. Men undertake non-agricultural casual labour, in construction, assisting roofers or in a shop or loading/unloading sugarcane during harvest season. There were one or two isolated and irregular cases of men working in brick kilns during season. They carry head loads of bricks for ₹4–₹5 per head load. A man was an apprentice with a compounder (his work profile was explained as taking medicines to different places) and he was paid ₹1,000–₹,2000 per month. There were two examples, where men were learning tailoring at different shops in a market, and they were either paid a petty amount or were given some snacks every few days.

Two older Chamar women are engaged in their traditional occupation, in addition to wage labour. They assist in childbirth and travel considerable distances to do so. They may be remunerated with clothes, grains, token amount and at times with a goat or a nose-ring or anklet. On special occasions like wedding, some Chamar women are called upon to sing at functions and they may be paid a token amount and/or are served food and sweets. They are not only important sources of income and food but an integrated part of the fabric of village life. Women pointed out that they undertake these activities because of '*vyvhar*' (literally meaning behaviour and implying general social relations here), referring to the common community bond and as wage labourers.

Over half of the Chamar labouring households had male members in migrant work. They were mostly involved in casual labour, some in weaving, welding, sewing, agriculture (in sugarcane farms, tending to livestock), one worked in a soap factory and one in an iron rolling mill. As is the case generally, these migrants started off with villagers or relatives and in a few cases with contractors from nearby areas. Like the Dusadh migrants, migration in Chamars is not stable. It is a survival activity and workers take up whatever work they can get. Several of them spoke of overhead expenses like room rent, low-paid overtime work, living with many others in small accommodation, long work shifts, etc.

Regarding livelihood activities, social conduct of women and unpaid labour services, Chamars are similar to other local classes of labour.

Dokhgadh has 51 Chamar households. Very few Chamar households are petty producers, the rest are labouring households. The few petty producer households are marginal farmers, and one is a small landholder. Sugarcane is cultivated in small quantities. Agriculture is based on family (including younger women) and exchange labour. Two of these households mentioned hiring in labour for paddy transplantation if exchange labour could not be availed of. The only case of self-employment is of a male peddler selling bananas. Two women undertake agricultural wage labour, and two men are into this and other casual labour. There is one case of migration of a casual male labourer.

Chamar labouring households are mostly marginal landholders, and some are landless. Agriculture is mainly a subsistence activity, based on family labour. Relatively younger married women are more involved in own cultivation. Exchange labour is less common and organised among relatives and hamlet residents. Livestock rearing is a common commercial activity and in many cases, it is *batiya*. One man is a ploughman. Also, he has a cart to transport material. The one example of non-agricultural self-employment is of a male peddler selling fruits and vegetables. Agricultural wage labour is very common. Only women do this. Men are involved in agriculture and other casual wage labour. A male labourer is learning to sew for ₹50 per day. Another works as a rickshaw puller for a disabled man, who owns the rickshaw. When the rickshaw is being used by the owner, the labourer plies it in markets. Skilled construction work is another example. Though there are more men engaged in brick kiln work than Khatiks and Gonds, they are much less than the Mosahars. Migrant work is less. Migrant men are mostly into casual labour, two are in carpet weaving and one is a cobbler. In two cases, migration is family based. These migrant workers undertake local wage labour when they are in their villages.

Chamar women from petty producer and labouring households are engaged in livelihood activities and men in sugarcane harvesting on *geda* basis. Socio-cultural traditions limiting female mobility and interactions with own family and others is not seen to any significant extent.

Khatiks: All 72 households are in Dokhgadh. They are lower-end petty producers and labouring households. Most petty producers are marginal households, a few are small. Sugarcane is cultivated in small quantities. Agriculture is based on family labour (including relatively younger women). Exchange labour among extended family is common. In rare cases, labour is hired because able family labour is not available. Livestock rearing is a commercial activity. Less than half the households are into non-agricultural self-employment. Many men sell seasonal vegetables and fruits, which according to them is their caste occupation. They usually operate as peddlers or from along side roads. One had a fixed shop in the local market and earned approximately ₹5,000–₹10,000 per month. The only other example of self-employment is that of a rickshaw driver.

Fewer households are involved in agricultural and other casual wage labour. Participation of women is even less in agricultural wage labour, may be limited to own village and undertaken occasionally. Non-agricultural employment is found only among men as security guards, head clerk in a private college, tractor and taxi driver. The taxi driver worked for the *pradhan*. He had recently joined and according to his wife, he drove in '*vyvhar*' (social relations) and was given one to two quintal grains by the *pradhan* from the PDS quota. Migrant work is undertaken by young men who are usually into casual labour, for example, as coolies, potter, welder, truck driver, etc. Only two cases of public employment existed. One was with the Provincial Armed Constabulary (PAC) and the other in a sugar mill.

Khatik labouring households are either landless or marginal landholders. In this case too, agriculture is mainly a subsistence activity and based on family labour, including younger women. Livestock rearing is also undertaken for commercial purposes. Male members of a few households are involved in other self-employment activities, primarily as seasonal vegetable and fruit hawkers. The only other examples are that of a fisherman and a rickshaw driver. More than half the households are engaged in local wage labour. Agricultural wage labour is the only form of female labour commodification. In very few cases, even younger married women do wage labour because of their precarious economic situation and lack of other family members. Men are involved in non-agricultural casual labour as well. There is one example of a tractor driver and men from a few households undertake advance-based brick kiln work. Half the households have male migrant members. Mostly, they are casual labourers. In one case, it was family based. When in their village, these migrant workers undertake local wage labour.

As classes of labour, these Khatik households depend on the sale of their labour power for daily reproduction. There are isolated cases where they may own minimal productive assets as in the case of the rickshaw driver and fisherman. But mostly they undertake types of local wage labour perceived as demeaning and are lowly paid. Among Khatik petty producers and classes of labour, women (with rare exceptions of newly married women) do not observe seclusion or other restrictive practices. They are involved in livelihood activities. Men do sugarcane harvesting on *geda* basis. Practice of socio-cultural traditions inhibiting free movement and social interaction is not seen among women.

Gonds: All 66 households are in Dokhgadh. They are also lower-end petty producers and classes of labour. A little less than half the Gond households are petty producers. Most of these are marginal farmers. Agriculture and livestock rearing show similar patterns as witnessed in the case of Khatik petty producers. In addition, three men are ploughmen and one of them has also a cart which is used to ferry men and material. There are a few instances of leasing and in a couple of these cases land leased in is comparatively substantial. Male and female occupational patterns are also very similar. Two men are vegetable vendors. A household owned two generators and fancy lights which were rented out. Women do only agricultural wage labour. In certain cases they do wage labour only within the nearby hamlet (also because their hamlet has employers unlike some other hamlets) or only where they share close interdependent socio-economic ties with employers. Men are into agricultural and non-agricultural casual labour. Brick kiln work is rare. Other instances include an insurance agent, a teacher and one learnt welding for a token amount per day.

Fewer men do migrant work like construction work, painting, skilled construction work, welding and other casual labour. In the two cases where migration was stable and family based, these brothers had another brother in public employment in the same place. Migratory trends are influenced by changing family structure. The few men in government service worked with government coal companies, Delhi electricity department, PAC and in two cases, the service details were unknown. In three cases, public employment is linked to family migration.

Gond labouring households are landless or marginal primarily subsistence farmers. Agriculture and livestock rearing patterns are similar to those observed previously among Khatik classes of labour. Agricultural wage labour for women and agricultural and other casual labour for men are the predominant types of labour commodification. Brick kiln work is found on a small scale, is advance based and may involve unpaid attached family labour. Migrant work is an important source of income. Only young men are involved in it. Types of migrant work undertaken are casual jobs like driving, dish washing, hawking, welding, starching saris, cloth weaving, skilled and unskilled construction work, coolie work, etc. Women from Gond petty producer and labour class households are involved in livelihood activities and do not show any signs of inhibited mobility or circumscribed social interactions. Men undertake sugarcane harvesting on *geda* basis.

Mosahars: All 137 of Mosahars households are in Dokhgadh and belong to labour classes. The majority of these are landless and the rest are marginal and small landowners. Unlike the Ahirs and Ansaris, Mosahars do not resort to leasing because they can hardly afford farming costs and even if they can the uncertainty of leasing is a big drawback. In cases of landowners, agriculture is mostly subsistence oriented, organised on family (male and female, including comparatively younger women) labour. A few draw on exchange labour with relatives and neighbours as well. One man works as a ploughman. Livestock is a commercial activity and Mosahars reflect more instances of *batiya* livestock than other castes.[36]

There are four cases of self-employment. A disabled man, who learnt sewing in a local market, was provided a sewing machine by the district administration as part of Mosahar development efforts. Though he has to pay for it in future, he earns more than he did at the shop. However, payments are often delayed and lower than market rates. Another man had taken credit from a *samuh* (micro-credit society or SHG) and used it to open a small general store in the hamlet. However, it hardly gets any business and the owner, whose land is mortgaged, has no money to buy any stock also. The third instance is also that of a man operating a general store from his home. The fourth, a fisherman, sells his catch alongside the road in the local market.

Among the Mosahars there is very limited occupational diversification. Generally, it is seen that even where diversification has occurred, caste is a major drawback. In the village, a Brahmin or Rajput is unlikely to go to a Dalit's hut, which is likely to be located away from the main settlement area, to purchase tobacco or *bidi* (hand-rolled cigarette). According to several Dalits in the village, demand for milk sold by them is less because *badkas* do not want to drink milk that comes from their households (Kapadia in 1995 makes a similar point). Also, any sub-caste is highly unlikely to take up self-employment activities which are not traditionally associated with them. For example, during the course of fieldwork it was observed that only Ahir women, made curd which was sold by their male relatives. Chamar women assisted in child-birth. Though women from various sub-castes wove baskets, hand fans and mats at home, most would not market these because this is not what members of their sub-caste did.

Almost all households are involved in local wage labour commodification. Mosahar women undertake agricultural wage labour. Households seek to maximise wage-earners and income sources. Even young married women and older women do wage labour, despite there being other productive family members available. There are a few households that do not undertake wage labour due to old age or health reasons. Men undertake agricultural, other casual and/or brick kiln work. Brick kiln work is fundamental to their survival. Attached unpaid family labour is common. Many incur debt from kilns in the off-season. Other than this, there are very few examples of non-agricultural employment – a *tanga* (horse-drawn carriage) driver and two tractor drivers.

Male outmigration is not as common as one would expect in their case. Mosahars explained this with reference to their landlessness and the absence of even a minimum buffer against food security. This means that they have to be resident in the village to provide for the household on a daily basis. More so because men undertake non-agricultural labour which is more readily available and pays more. This has to be read in conjunction with the nuclear family trend. Another reason is that there is perhaps enough work for them to survive on, owing to a relatively large number of landowners dependent on hired labour, in the village and locally. An important reason for low migration is that many of these households are also indebted to the area kilns and cannot migrate in the dry season. In the wet season, agricultural work is available in the village. Poor networking is another handicap. There is a contractor from nearby who recruits some Mosahars for tomato farming in Nainital. A few other male migrant workers work as casual labourers elsewhere. Unlike other returning male migrant workers, Mosahar migrants extensively undertake local wage labour when in their village.

Mosahar classes of labour depend directly or indirectly on the sale of their labour power for their daily reproduction and are engaged in the most demeaning and debt-based oppressive forms of wage labour. Their living conditions are the worst. The hamlet is located on a low-lying ground and in monsoon certain areas are flooded, causing damage to crops and houses. Their huts are tiny and low. Other than agricultural implements, productive assets are hardly seen (also see, Dhuru, 2008). Livelihood activities are common. Socio-cultural traditions circumscribing women's interpersonal relations and inhibiting their mobility are not seen.

Concluding Remarks

Several conclusions can be drawn from the aforementioned mapping exercise, which will be discussed in the following paragraphs.

First, of course, what does a village labour market look like? In the field villages, the labour market as a physical space of competitive bargaining, like the daily urban labour markets at their micro-level, is absent. In fact, women labourers do not actively search for work even in the peak season. This is the case for men also, but their mobility and visibility in public spaces make them more approachable for employers. Women remain based in their villages and work within only a small radius (mostly). In such a relatively intimate setting who does what job is common knowledge. Importantly, it is considered highly inappropriate for women (of all castes) to be actively looking for work – because this is seen as not in keeping with women's gendered image as dependent entities, wholly reliant on male breadwinners. This norm is very strong in the highly patriarchal rural UP setting of my research villages.

Accessing stable, productive and well-paying jobs through the labour market is an important avenue out of poverty. My fieldwork showed how valued *naukri* (government job or implying a regular salaried job) was by villagers economically and socially. UP, however, has failed to produce good jobs (Srivastava and Jain, 2016). Even where Dalits are in salaried employment, their income is much less compared to that of salaried upper castes (Foundation of Agrarian Studies, 2015). This scenario is complicated by the fact that village labour markets are segregated on the basis of class, caste and gender. The discussion in this chapter brings this out clearly by providing a very detailed and nuanced picture of who does what in today's village and why. At the top are the accumulating upper caste-classes who have successfully diversified outside of agriculture and have managed to directly or indirectly access the state and its resources. At the bottom are agricultural labourers, casual labourers, brick kiln workers and those in survivalist self-employment. These are the most stigmatised, tedious and exploitative forms of wage labour and often linked with debt and other forms of unfree labour. India's pursuit of capitalist modernity is based on the exploitation of traditional hierarchies, where women and especially Dalit women from labouring households fare the worst. Along similar lines, scholars have argued that capital accumulation and more so contemporary neoliberal times is built on 'conjugated oppression', that is class relations along other forms of social oppression (Bourgois, 1988; Lerche and Shah, 2018).

UP is still primarily an agricultural state given its low diversification away from agriculture; this means that an overwhelming number of people are still in agriculture (Srivastava and Jain, 2016). At the village level, whether or not the role of agriculture in rural livelihoods is decreasing needs to be further nuanced. Even in the case of *badkas* their source of surplus and dominance is not restricted to agriculture but also their closeness to state, their economic power derived from other commercial activities, etc. At the bottom, for households where men do not migrate, the non-farm sector is an important source of income. While agriculture itself is not sufficient in securing household reproduction, it is a crucial minimum buffer against absolute poverty and starvation. For women labourers, however, irrespective of whether their male relatives migrate or not, the link between rural and agriculture continues to be strong. This is in line with the national-level scenario where 75 per cent of rural women are still engaged in agriculture (Mondal et al., 2018).

Occupational multiplicity and income diversification are common trends in village India today. However, as my fieldwork shows, this needs to be disaggregated and nuanced along the lines of caste and gender specifically. *Badka* households have members in agriculture and related activities, professional jobs and business. For them, diversification is a matter of more surplus in general and accumulation and better lifestyles, employment and educational opportunities for their younger generation. Women, of course, are restricted to the private domain. *Chutka* households have members diversifying to ensure their daily survival and also because this affords the men a sense of dignity and pride by freeing them from exploitative agricultural relations. However, as indicated earlier, this diversification is more the case for men as women are confined to agricultural wage labour. Is there any relation between size of landholdings and diversification? *Badka* households own the most land (even though in my area there are very few large or even medium holdings overall) and *chutka* households of course own very small plots of land and therefore cannot survive on just crop income. Diversification is seen in both types of households though it is not distress driven amongst the *badkas* (see Trivedi et al., 2016).

In general, this occupational mapping is also a mapping of classes. It identifies the classes that exist and the nature of these classes in the context of neoliberal capitalism. What also starts to emerge is the nature of the state and the state–class nexus – more on this in subsequent chapters. The lived reality of small farmers presented in this chapter questions the relevance of using the theoretical framework of peasantry as is still the dominant practice in agrarian political economy. In the context of neoliberal capitalism, conditions of peasantness (subsistence oriented) do not hold ground. Conceptualisations like peasantry are not very useful in capturing the ground reality.

Moreover, there is no one representative smallholder farmer. Rather, there is a high degree of social and economic differentiation. Though there is some economic variation within castes, caste and class overlap to a great extent. So, the upper castes are still socially, politically and economically dominant whereas the Dalits are at the bottom of the village social and economic hierarchy and mostly without any political clout by themselves.

Migration comes across as a complex phenomenon. The opportunity of migrant work elsewhere is completely closed not only to local women of all castes because of their gender and patriarchal ideology but also to the 'lowest of the low' (castes), like the Mosahars, who can neither afford it and nor have the necessary social capital/networks to access it. The structural parallel between the socio-political positions of local women and Mosahars is strikingly obvious – both of these highly exploited groups are marginalised and subordinated by those who have power over them – namely by men and the higher castes respectively.

In sum, in rural labour markets, who can access what jobs and on what terms and conditions depends not just on economic factors but perhaps more on one's gender, religion, asset base, social capital, family structure, age, etc. (Mehrotra, 2017, 2019). As such, the inclusion of women in labour markets has taken place under very adverse conditions. Socio-cultural and political structures hold them captive in the village economy with all its attendant forms of oppression. Even within the villages, they are ghettoised in least paying and demeaning work often featuring unfree labour. Their unfreedom actually facilitates male capitalist accumulation.

Building on this, the next chapter describes how rural employment relations have to be understood against the backdrop of wider village-based social, economic and political relations of dominance and subjugation. So, the very institution of labour market that is supposed to be a possible way out of poverty and humiliation ends up reiterating these inequalities. This is particularly true for Dalits in general and Dalit women more so.

Notes

1 Some have boreholes in their field and rent in only a pump set and pipe. Others have to rent the use of tube wells. The most common source is the upper caste classes.
2 Canal water is directed in the fields through irrigation channels. Water reaches those who are closer to canal and on plain areas. Those with holding in higher land do not get benefit.
3 Jaggery is unrefined sugar.
4 At the first instance, the difference can easily be seen externally. At the top, the *badkas* live in big, planned, concrete houses with proper fixtures and flooring, amenities like electricity, in-house toilets, cooking gas, washing machines. They own cars, tractors, tube wells and wear good quality clothes. Even their livestock shelters are proper concrete constructions akin to small houses. At the bottom, *chutkas* live in bamboo and mud huts with thatched roofs and/or covered with plastic or tin sheets. In some cases, there have been a few IAY-financed brick construction. Their granaries are mostly constructed of mud and covered with straw. Other than their land and livestock, they own a few agricultural implements like hoes and sickle. Cycles are common but not motorcycles. Some households have television, radio, a light bulb and other such small utilities.
5 A few well-to-do Dalits identified themselves as SCs and not *harijans*. This is indicative of their better educational standards and political consciousness.
6 The word *babu* has a dual meaning. At a general level, it is a term used to refer to sons or young men. The sense in which it is used here refers to the upper caste-class men (or households). In both connotations, the word is used with an attitude of respect and deference towards the addressee.
7 To quote the male Dhobi labourer, '*be khet ka aadmi kauno aadmi hain?*'
8 Independnet kitchen was taken as the identification of one household unit. The landholding classification is from the NSS. The local unit used for land sizes is *katha* and the figures recorded have been converted into hectares unit using the following calculation: 4 decimal=1*katha,* 20*katha*=1*beegha* (*pakka*), 1/4th*beegha*=1acre and 1acre=0.4ha. In very few instances, where the respondent was not sure of actual size, an estimate was taken. Here, the landownership as it exists on ground has been mentioned. For example, where three households (all brothers) jointly cultivate 4.8ha, landholding of each is taken to be 1.6ha.
9 The Rajput family has set up a non-governmental organisation in the village (however, for the entire duration of the fieldwork, it was not observed to be actually functioning on ground). Sometimes, family members expressed a desire to build a school in the village in future and at times they held functions to mark special occasions (I was shown a paper clip attesting to this). Such initiatives serve to assert their socio-political largesse and dominance.

10 Under the Indira Awaas Yojna (IAY), now known as the *Pradhan* Mantri Gramin Awaas Yojna, the government provides a house and toilet construction allowance in the name of a woman or in joint name.
11 As he put it, '*aankh lagi*'.
12 The term labour is used to refer to those non-income generating activities which nonetheless generate value and contribute to survival and subsistence. For example, collecting sugarcane roots to be used as firewood, cutting grass or sugarcane leaves to be used as fodder or making cow dung cakes which are also used as firewood and fertiliser. They can be seen as livelihood or in kind remunerated activities.
13 Some occupations were found in one village only. Where occupation details are same for both villages, these are mentioned in detail in one village only and in the other, it is stated that details are similar.
14 One bundle is made of forty stalks. One bundle of seedlings is transplanted/sown over an area of one *katha*. It is claimed by labourers that one person is able to sow only one *katha* in one day. However, a few other labourers and employers claim otherwise. Seedlings are separately grown in a 'nursery' (on small area of field) and these are then transplanted in the field. First, labourers uproot these seedlings and make bundles of forty stalks each. Before these can be transplanted, the field has to be watered. In the time that it takes the field to be watered, labourers go to another field and uproot seedlings and bundle them. They then go back and transplant seedlings in the first field, while the second field is being watered. In this manner, labourers may sow two to four *bhojas* per day.
15 However, in the household survey, the respondent from this household said that the person was paid only ₹200 or ₹300 per month. The wage mentioned earlier was quoted by the employer (*pradhan*).
16 Started in the 1970s, as a part of the GOI's Integrated Child Development Services Programme, *Anganwadi* centres and workers provide health and nutrition guidance to new mothers, administer polio vaccine, arrange pre-school activities, etc. They are not permanent government workers. The respondent claimed that their salaries are paid by the World Bank.
17 A school where Islamic teaching takes place.
18 *Shiksha Mitra* refers to para teachers who are teachers hired on a contract basis in government schools.
19 Commercial farming implies sugarcane cultivation primarily. In the case of big landowners, surplus rice or wheat may also be sold.
20 Including caring for the elderly and children.
21 Mechanisation refers to use of combine harvester (seen only in the case of big landowners) and tractors which are usually rented in by the petty producers and classes of labour to varying extents and depending upon social factors.
22 Livestock involves cows, buffaloes, goats and in the case of Muslims, chickens as well. By livestock rearing as a commercial activity is meant that these animals are either sold and/or surplus milk/curd is sold. A few households own oxen and a plough. Male members of these households undertake wage labour as ploughmen. A gendered division of labour is implicit in livestock rearing. Women involve in grazing goats. Women or children cut grass for fodder every evening. Women make cow dung cakes. Women, children or men (if at home) tend to livestock at home. Decisions regarding sale of milk or livestock can be made jointly, or just by women if men are migrant workers. But how this money is spent is mainly decided by the men.
23 The tractors were rented out to villagers for ploughing. Tractors with attachable trolleys were rented out for ferrying people, transporting material, etc.

24 Vegetables are bought from the local *mandi*, that is the main market where vegetables are likely to be sold on wholesale rates.
25 These shops were mostly located on rented land. Depending upon size and location, rents varied between ₹50 and ₹500 per month. In one case it was ₹1,000 per month.
26 A GOI initiative, it trains women to disseminate advice on hospital deliveries, birth control and other related health information. The respondent denied any remuneration, though the programme stipulates a pittance amount on a case-by-case basis.
27 To quote her, '*ab aap jaante hain, bada aadmi kha jaayega kisi ke ghar mein kaam karne*'.
28 The *pradhan*'s (Ahir) household is not considered. This is because of lack of access (see p. 125). But my sense, from participant observation and drawing on conversations with villagers is that it would be classified as a petty capitalist household positioned below the Rajput household (at least socially and economically, for the political domain is consistently competitive and changing). This household hires combine harvestors. The male members of the household may do manual work in their fields. The wife of the male head of the household also comes to the field, located at some distance from the house to supervise labour. Ahir households in the main part of the village are located in the same lane as the *pradhan*'s household and access to them was also very limited, particularly in the context of collecting oral histories.
29 Practice of caste-based occupation was seen in some other (albeit a few) cases during the course of fieldwork in the region. For example, the Dom caste reared pigs and made baskets and hand fans; Bhedyads (shepherds) reared sheep, Chamar as cobbler; Koeiris grew and sold vegetables, some Muslim women travelled from village to village selling bangles, clothes, bindi, *sindoor*, etc. Largely, these would be middle-aged women. Other caste women may also weave baskets or make curd but only for household consumption. One Ahir woman pointed out that while Muslim women sold clothes and cosmetics door to door in villages, men from any caste could do this. It would follow from this that unlike women it is easier for men to diversify but women are expected to stay within prescribed caste norms.
30 Where labour from any of the three field sites worked in brick kilns, they were involved only in moulding bricks. The chimney work is solely the reserve of incoming migrant labour from Ranchi.
31 In sugarcane harvesting, men cut the stalk and women cut the leaf tops. Labour is not employed for sugarcane harvesting usually. Men travel in groups around villages to cut sugarcane. They take the leaf tops and use them as fodder and leave the sugarcane in the field. Women cut leaf tops in their own village.
32 There are examples of members of a few more households who did agricultural wage labour in the past or worked as a tailor or a vegetable vendor but not since male members from these households took to migrant work.
33 To save on labour costs, the *chutkas* often work on each other's fields on an exchange basis. These exchange relations follow caste and neighbourhood ties. Exchange labour can take place only between households owning land and having access to family labour. Labour is exchanged primarily in paddy transplantation, a female task. As such, male labour is involved in exchange labour relations to a much less extent.
34 This woman also mentioned that she was unable to do the physically demanding work (carrying head loads) on a regular basis. She had worked only under NREGA once for a few days. Two things can be inferred from the fact that she had never done non-agricultural wage labour outside of NREGA: first, only a

government-sponsored scheme can effectively challenge the gendered division of labour and second, this example indicates that this type of wage labour participation is a survival mechanism, not a preferred choice and therefore, it is questionable if the woman would undertake similar work had there been a male member in the house.

35 Access to one Dusadh household in Sapatganj was severely limited. Only survey details could be collected for this household. From observations, survey data and conversations with villagers, this household would be categorised as a petty capitalist below the Rajput family and the *pradhan*'s household or as a comparatively well-off petty producer household. This was the only Dusadh household which had a male member in public employment (now retired). This is an important factor in explaining its relatively better resource endowment and land position (semi-medium). During the course of fieldwork, it was observed that the same household opened a tiny general-cum-*paan* (betel leaf, tobacco) store in front of their house which was operated by the male members. In the village it is only engaged in own agriculture and petty self-employment activity. This is combined with male migrant work where they undertake casual labour as well. The women of this household practise seclusion and this is reflective of a widely held view that across all groups and strata upward economic mobility is associated with withdrawal of women from social and economic activities.

36 *Batiya* means shared. For example, an animal is given to another for rearing and when it gives birth, one off-spring is given to the original owner and the other is completely owned by the latter.

4 Subsidising Patriarchal Capitalism

Labour Relations of Dalit Women

Labour markets, especially rural labour markets, are arenas of social relations where unequal power relations are a norm. Labour relations are based on a political economy of difference – of caste, gender, religion, region, asset base, capabilities, etc. These influence who can access what type of jobs, under what terms and conditions and with what labour market outcomes. This chapter shows how labour relations are best understood as a part of wider village-based social, economic and political relations of dominance and subjugation and are shaped by class, caste and gender identities. It shows that rural female labour is agrarian. Dalit female labourers are concentrated in the least-paying and low-status tasks that often feature unfree labour relations. It argues that with male outmigration, women have been pushed into unfree labour relations, which may even be willingly chosen, because they operate as insurance/safety net. Patron–client relations are still associated with many benefits and at the same time they function to keep labourers divided and facilitate male capitalist domination.

I begin with a discussion on the wider social relations by way of highlighting overlapping socio-economic relations in agriculture and more generally in the village, the rationale behind delivering unpaid labour services, impact of male outmigration and finally, how the idea of labour market is approached in a village setting. With this background, I will then go on to discuss the specifics of labour relations of Dalit women – forms of female wage labour commodification and the wage structure, how recruitment is organised and aspects of labour relations that serve as forms of labour control and how unfree labour relations manifest and underscore labour relations is looked into. Intra-labour relations are described, and the role of caste, class, gender and locality reflected upon. Overall, we will see that it is actually Dalit women labourers' confinement to villages and their unfreedom that enables the men to pursue jobs that bring more income and which are regarded as more prestigious. On a more general level, these primordial identities and traditional norms and values which are very much patriarchal in nature are deliberately deployed and exploited to ensure modern capitalist accumulation which is owned and/or controlled by men (see also Shah et al., 2018).

DOI: 10.4324/9780429321894-4

General Social Relations: An Overview

In agriculture and generally in villages, socio-economic relations (employer–labourer, credit, food security, patron–client relations) overlap. Socio-cultural, religious, economic, political relationships which one forms and experiences in their daily lives are influenced by factors like location, proximity, tied labour arrangements, caste, familiarity and shared history and socio-cultural restrictions circumscribing the participation of female labour. These relations do not follow village administrative or physical boundaries.

In Sapatganj, for example, the labouring households of the Ansari hamlet mostly did wage labour in a village bordering their hamlet. Dalit and Ahir classes of labour households in the main hamlet worked for the petty capitalists and petty producers of their own village and a few from nearby villages for whom they had been working for years. Labouring households of the Ahir hamlet worked in a village neighbouring their hamlet. In Baaspur, petty capitalists and petty producers, who are the main employers of agricultural wage labour, are concentrated in two hamlets. Employers from the first hamlet call upon the Dhobis and Kharwars of their hamlet and the Chamars of the nearby second hamlet. Employers from the other hamlet depend on the Dusadhs and Kharwars of their hamlet, Chamars from the second and to a lesser extent, Chamars from the fourth hamlet. The latter are largely involved in wage labour in another village closer to their hamlet. It should be noted that during peak agricultural season, factors like a stand-off with local labour on wage rates temporarily influence these established routes as the employer may call upon outside labour on different terms and conditions.

In Dokhgadh as well, socio-economic and even political relations coincide. These ties cut across village geographical boundaries, closely following established routes of labour demand and supply. For example, the Gonds of the first hamlet do wage labour for other caste households in their own hamlet, other nearby hamlets and neighbouring villages. The Chamars and Gonds of the second hamlet do wage labour for the first and the third hamlet primarily. The Brahmins of the fifth hamlet largely depend upon the labouring households of a neighbouring village. The Mosahars do wage labour for the prominent *badkas* in three village hamlets, apart from other villages bordering their hamlet.

Labouring households and 'their' employer households are usually located in close proximity. Over the years, labourers have been engaged in various social relations with them for purposes such as credit, food security, land leasing, enabling access to public resources like MGNREGA, bank credit under special schemes or mediation with other government structures. For *badkas*, who are also politically dominant and therefore in a position to control access and distribution of scarce resources and 'benefits', these relations are a means to ensure an easily accessible, cheap and reliable workforce. Caste is important to the extent that labouring households from the

OBC group tend to avoid working for lower caste labour-employing households or even work outside their 'own village'. This is their way of avoiding social disgrace and embarrassment, retaining a sense of modesty and social honour. These factors were seen across field villages.

In Baaspur, an additional factor reinforcing overlapping socio-economic relations of dependency is the control of space by the *badkas*. In many cases, *badkas*' fields surround those of classes of labour. In one instance, the *pradhan* unlawfully acquired a dirt road through which a few labouring households approached their fields. He cultivates sugarcane on the encroached land. The affected labourers are dependent upon him for access to their fields and this severely limits their bargaining power vis-à-vis the *pradhan*. This *pradhan* is also a major employer in the village which contributes to his upper hand in all negotiations.

Similarly, in Dokhgadh, for most labouring households, employment relations were village based or at most, extended to neighbouring villages. However, it was noted that labourers from other castes in the area, Mosahars take up wage labour in quite distant locations as well; though for food and credit, they largely depended upon employers nearer to their hamlet. So, while their employment relations were more widespread, they remained economically more dependent on and socially more integrated with employers from own village or nearby areas. Politically, they had largely bypassed the village political structure. I will return to this point in the next chapter. Conversely, it was observed that though the village is 'geographically dispersed' over a large area, with a few hamlets physically isolated from the main settlement, and economic relations were accordingly arranged, the political dominance of the Brahmins in the main settlement had permeated even these farther away hamlets of Dokhgadh.

The concentration of political power in the hands of the two most prominent Brahmin families of Dokhgadh was mentioned earlier. Political and economic rivalry between these two households is much pronounced, while such 'competition' in the case of other petty capitalists was not observed (but it was not absent altogether). A male member in each of these two households (the de facto *pradhan* and the contractor for a district government authority) has access to political power and resources. This access is used to distribute 'patronage' (MGNREGA job cards and accessing work, BPL ration cards, old age/widow pensions, other government schemes and mediation with bureaucratic authorities) with a view to cultivating a benevolent image vis-à-vis labourers cum voters, establishing their authority and spheres of influence. The daughter of a former Ahir *pradhan* described her father as a social worker. Also, she mentioned that they possessed a BPL ration card but gave the procured food to the needy. While the image portrayed is one of a benevolent benefactor, this household appeared sidelined from the 'mainstream' village politics unlike the earlier.

Across the three villages, divisiveness among the petty capitalists is a limiting factor on labour unity (by providing indirect benefits which privilege some over others) and dissidence. But this lack of horizontal solidarity at hamlet or village level does not translate into fragmentation of the upper caste-class alliance at the level of several villages or block. Petty 'power-games' are never directly played out in confrontation between them (except in contesting elections perhaps). In Dokhgadh, village petty capitalists disagreed with each other or expressed dissatisfaction with the *pradhan*, but none of them openly aligned themselves with either of these two Brahmin households, as the labourers did explicitly. At the level of villages or block, *badkas* tend to close ranks. Here, caste plays an important unifying role. As a male member of my host family in Sapatganj said, they have to politically support each other because they are of the same *biradri* (community). To some extent, the Mosahars have successfully challenged the Brahmin dominance or at least put them on a back foot but without fundamentally upsetting the established power relations. This will be explained later.

Another example of general social relations comes from how routine, or a fact of everyday life, corruption is and how the politically powerful resort to corrupt practices as a source of income and accumulation. In fact, it is the most dominant theme in labour's analysis and critique of local politics and is perceived as all pervasive, irrespective of party affiliation or whether the *pradhan* is a *badka* or *chutka*. As put by a female dhobi labourer (Baaspur),

> *[B]ribery*[1] *is a common practice. Irrespective of their castes, pradhans are motivated by self-interest only. The pradhan before the present one was a chutka. He was allocating abaadi land to the poor, but he was pressured by the badkas who opposed his decision.*
>
> (Fieldwork notes, April 2010)

In both villages, it is common for villagers to grease the *pradhan*'s palms with petty amounts for allocation of red BPL cards, MGNREGA job cards or IAY benefits. Nepotism is rife in accessing provisions like free tube well/hand pump boring for SCs or old age and widow pensions which anyway are intermittently disbursed. Less than the stipulated ration is distributed under PDS, and this ration may later be sold on the black market for a higher amount. A percentage of the IAY allowance was retained by the *pradhan* prior to disbursement to the beneficiary. Payment for work done under MGNREGA is often delayed and there is discrepancy between the number of days worked and wages received.

In recent years, MGNREGA has become a major ground for labour dependency and subservience in both villages. The fact that the job cards are often with the *pradhan* is a ground for manipulation and corruption. Even where labourers were paid wages in their own account, they are not aware of when the payment is made unless notified by the *pradhan*. As survival is dependent on the sale of their labour power daily, they cannot afford to waste both time and money in visiting banks which are located at some distance from the villages. Uncertainty over payments is exacerbated by the fact that payments are much delayed as first the entire work has to be completed and measured. Then there are other practical issues at hand which act as hindrance like, a very limited awareness of their rights, labourers are not entertained by the bank staff, inability to do the paperwork by themselves and being charged a hefty amount to open accounts which they cannot afford, though the accounts for these purposes are supposed to be opened free of charge. According to the Baaspur *pradhan*, since the banks have to meet predetermined targets, they are reluctant to open accounts free of charge as this is not profitable and also labourers usually withdraw the entire amount (which is not much) at one time, rather than keeping a deposit with the bank.

One Dusadh female labourer (Sapatganj) elaborated:

> *The present pradhan does not take hundred rupees per day wage of one who has worked in a MGNREGA job. Instead he goes to the bank with them, once in five or six months and gets the villagers to withdraw the entire unemployment benefit.*[2] *He keeps this money which could be between seven thousand to eight thousand rupees. The pradhan gives a token amount to the account holder/beneficiary to buy alcohol. The bank personnel also side with the pradhan.*
>
> (Fieldwork Notes, November 2009)

At the time of fieldwork, in Baaspur, some beneficiaries still did not have bank accounts, and wages were received and disbursed by the *pradhan*, a major cause of labour dependency. This simultaneously provides the *pradhan* with a channel to divert the funds. Labourers in Baaspur pointed out that it is possible that only a small part of the project (usually digging, paving a road) involved manual labour while the remaining was completed with the use of machines and fake entries made in job cards.

MGNREGA has had some indirect benefits though. The Baaspur *pradhan* pointed out that now labourers refused to do wage labour for less than ₹100 per day. Respondents from both villages remarked that the government minimum wage has pushed up the wages of casual male wage labour. However, MGNREGA has not made much of a difference where female labour is concerned, either in terms of wage labour participation or indirect impacts. In terms of the types of work available under it, MGNREGA has special provisions for female labour, but women are not aware of this (or other provisions for that matter). They are also unwilling to challenge the established gendered roles. Caste is another limitation as poor upper and middle castes are unwilling to take up work associated with Dalit male labourers.

There are other examples of how corruption pervades socio-economic relations. According to another Dusadh female labourer (Sapatganj), under IAY,

> *[S]he received an instalment of eighteen thousand of which she had to give three thousand and six hundred rupees to the pradhan. The*

> *remaining money will be received when a further two thousand rupees is paid. She was told by the pradhan that he would help her in getting Awaas money, if she paid him. He has to work hard to get the money-travelling and approaching authorities takes time and money and possibly there is some bribe involved.*[3] *People from rich caste groups like Rajputs, Guptas or Ahirs have got Awaas money, but from her caste group few have got. When they approach the pradhan, he tells them that will not be given Awaas money because they did not vote for him.*
>
> (Fieldwork Notes, November 2009)

In Baaspur, the ration for mid-day school meal was not stored at the primary school but distributed among the *pradhan*, aaganwadi workers and a few others. School meals were provided only once or twice a week. A lavish feast at the *pradhan*'s house, attended by block-level officers and gram sabha members, was immediately followed by the extension of the *pradhan*'s tenure and postponement of panchayat elections. In both Sapatganj and Baaspur, villagers spoke of distribution of alcohol and clothes before elections as a means to purchase votes.

In view of the aforementioned grounds of dependency and the failure of male outmigration to substantively counteract the economic vulnerability of labouring households, delivering unpaid labour services to petty capitalists is crucial to classes of labour seeking access to resources, security and protection against socio-economic adversity and mitigate the omnipresent threat and fear of sanctions. These labour services are mostly provided by Dalit women and include scooping, washing and drying grain, tending to livestock, making cow dung cakes, sweeping the front courtyard, etc. In a few instances, women may be served food or just tea in return, and if it is a ceremonial occasion then grain is given, or a token amount is paid.

These standard practices provide security at a high cost. For example, in Sapatganj, a Dusadh migrant labour fell out with his contractor who is also from the same village. The labourer returned without his due wages and subsequently he was paid less than the due amount. In his absence, his wife (on his advice) had borrowed money from the Rajput family to meet household and agricultural expenses. They were expecting to pay this through the remittance money. When this did not work out, both, the husband and wife did wage labour for them on a priority basis and at reduced wage rates. The wife also performed unpaid labour within their house. In Baaspur, a Chamar woman explained that though her family had repaid the debt they had incurred from a Rajput, they continued to provide wage labour to them on a priority basis and on less-than-the market wage rates. They fear that if they stopped doing this, the Rajput family would not help them in times of need in future. Another Chamar woman (Baaspur) complained that she and another woman had cleaned seven sacks of mustard at the *pradhan*'s house, but instead of being given lentils which they could eat, they were given a measly ₹20 each.

The fieldwork showed that there is an ongoing process of feminisation of agriculture in both villages. Feminisation of agriculture is limited to certain operations only (at least in the labour market; this is elaborated subsequently) and is linked to male outmigration. This is moreover reflected in Jassal's (2012) research in Jaunpur on folk songs sung by women. For example, when women in her field say that women and children constitute a large part of the labour force. One reason for this was the cheap labour argument and the other that the men preferred to work outside agriculture. Similar findings emerged from my fieldwork, as shown in this chapter. My fieldwork also showed that returning migrants are unwilling to take up agricultural work because it is demeaning, involved delayed wage payment or part payment, and doing agricultural wage labour for *badkas* is a constant reminder of their inferior status. Returning migrants who are Dalits might still resort to non-agricultural casual labour in and around their villages because they simply cannot afford to not earn even for a day. Non-agricultural male tasks (whether migrant or local work) are better paid than agricultural wage labour and owner-cultivation activities. Income from these is crucial in ensuring household reproduction. Female labour also cited the lure of city life and the hold of consumerism.[4] Spread of literacy is another reason. This has imbued a sense of confidence and self-esteem among the younger male generation of classes of labour. They do not want to be associated with humiliating and exploitative agrarian work or even to be seen taking livestock for grazing. A Chamar woman from Baaspur implicitly linked migration with masculinity. She commented that if her sons did wage labour in the village, they would be the subject of public rebuke: that as young and able men, they are doing wage labour in the village, rather than migrant work.[5] As stated previously, a sense of pride and accomplishment is attached with migration. For poor upper castes, it is a preferred alternative from local social humiliation.

In rare cases, casual migrant workers are accompanied by family members. It is possible that the migrant's wife works as unpaid attached labour. For example, this was seen in the case of a Giri migrant worker from Dokhgadh, who had worked in Ghaziabad for eighteen years. His work involved washing and packing bottles. Remuneration is piece-rate based. His wife works alongside him, contributing to increased productivity and therefore increased wage. But only the migrant worker – the man – is recognised as an employee and paid.

Male outmigration has added to the work burden of female labour. To quote the female Dhobi contractor from Sapatganj, 'it is difficult to manage household and agricultural work. There is no one to do spade work, to spray fertilizer or drop seeds'.[6] As put by a Baaspur female Dhobi labourer,

> *[M]ale out-migration has increased the responsibility of women vis-à-vis own agriculture . . . . has to do all agricultural work by herself, hire a tractor for ploughing her field etc. Her husband, who operates a rice*

> *mill at home, helps out when he can. When he is not available, not only she has to do spade work in her field, but also harvest sugarcane and help load it. But in badka's fields she does not cut the sugarcane, only cuts the leaves because this is what women do . . . . she will not be physically able to cut sugarcane in badka's fields.*
>
> (Fieldwork Notes, April 2010)

Female labourers bear greater responsibility of household survival on a day-to-day basis: taking care of own cultivation, that is, buying agricultural inputs by incurring debt or through wage earnings, hiring tractors or irrigation facilities, providing exchange labour, etc., in addition to farming the land; livestock responsibilities – milking, grazing, getting fodder; providing for daily family consumption; meeting health and school expenditures and combining care and reproductive economy responsibilities with wage work, etc. Overall, the extent to which male outmigration has led to women's movement from own cultivation to wage labour or intensified wage labour participation is not uniform and depends on factors like the family structure and size, availability of other productive family members in the village and age of women.

But decision-making powers on important social and economic issues related to weddings, land and credit remain firmly in the hands of men. It is claimed by women that decisions pertaining to own cultivation are taken independently by them or jointly taken with male members of the household. In practice, this is hardly the case. Women stated that they independently decided what to cultivate, but when asked if their husbands had any input, they added that they of course 'talked' about it; some reacted with the question that why would they (women) not ask (husbands)? Decisions involving money (hiring labour, tractor, tube well/pipe), are generally taken by men and any 'consultation' with women is merely token. For example, my field assistant would call up her migrant husband and speak to him about tractor hiring, the prevailing rate, if she should borrow money to buy fertiliser, etc. The buying and hiring of inputs involve movement outside the village, so male dependency is not completely eliminated. There are a few cases where women have gone to the market (in the absence of male children or extended male family members in the village) to undertake some essential market work or to sell milk. As far as possible the older women of the house do this or may ask some other male going from the village to do it.

This does not mean that female labour is not aware of how to undertake various agricultural operations or does not take independent decisions at all. It has more to do with the gendering of the social role of female labour as dependents and of men as household heads. In the event of any crisis or urgent expenditure, women do independently approach the wife of the male head of their 'patron' household. A specific example is from Baaspur. A Dhobi woman's husband owns a cycle shop. Its stock has been bought on credit. In the beginning the shop did well but as more such shops came up, income declined. Also, he is an alcoholic and abusive man who does not like his wife undertaking wage labour and presses her to do only housework. She however refuses. She does what she thinks is the best for only then will she be able to save money to pay off the debt. She independently takes decisions regarding the sale of livestock and sold a cow for ₹8,000 and a goat for ₹2,500. Her husband does not help her. One other consequence of male outmigration is that the mobility and actions of the female members of these households have come under closer scrutiny and is consistently monitored by the villagers. This is discussed subsequently.

In Baaspur, an additional consequence of migration (related to the previous point) is the control exerted by comparatively successful male migrant workers on the wage labour participation of their women relatives. They see themselves as proud 'breadwinners', securers of household reproduction. Therefore, from their perspective, their female family members no longer need to undertake degrading agricultural wage labour. Women do not agree with this, given the uncertain and fluctuating remittances and continue to do wage labour, albeit discreetly when the migrant worker is away; or when their economic condition is worsened, and their survival is threatened; and/or they stop undertaking unpaid labour services. This is a case of female labourers being pragmatic without antagonising male authority and position.

To cite one example, a Chamar widow (Baaspur) discontinued with agricultural wage labour and unpaid labour services on her migrant son's insistence. But she does wage labour when he is away. When he is at home, she may try and do wage labour behind his back or organise and send labour for some job. However, she now does wage labour in own village only. Apart from the need factor, this can also be perceived as maintaining old socio-economic relations which serve as a safety net in times of need and a way to avoid an open confrontation.

Finally, regarding the labour markets in the field villages, an important factor vis-à-vis labour relations is the absence of a space (market) where labourers compete to find productive employment. Labour markets operate at different levels and have varying scope. At the most micro-level is the daily labour market in urban areas, that is, usually labourers gather in one location (market in this sense) from where employers take labourers according to their requirements. In the field villages, labourers do not actively search for work, women particularly. Even during peak agricultural season, women wait for work to come by their way through an employer directly or a contractor. Though men do not be actively seek wage employment in the village, their mobility and visibility in public spaces make them more accessible and approachable.

There are three possible reasons for this 'passivity' of female labour. One reason is that in the context of relatively 'closed setting' of the village and a 'fixed' subject operating within the 'village' boundaries, it is more a case of employers knowing who to approach for what work. The second reason has to do with restrictions on female mobility and their social interaction. Related to this is the third reason, that actively searching for wage labour in a village is 'atypical'. As explained by a male Dhobi labourer (Baaspur),[7]

> *[I]n villages, going out in search for work is associated with 'sharm'* (shame). *This is not the case in towns like Kasiya, Gorakhpur or Lucknow.*
>
> (Fieldwork Notes, April 2010)

It is seen as embarrassing and dishonouring the family and particularly the male head.

Specific Aspects of Dalit Rural Female Labour Relations

The specific aspects dealt with here are types of female labour commodification and wage relations, recruitment patterns, forms of labour control, unfree labour relations and intra-labour relations.

Agricultural Labour Commodification and Wage Relations

It is apparent from the mapping of occupational patterns that across field villages female labour is agrarian. There are several reasons for the lack of occupational diversification among female labourers.

One explanation is the threat of public censure for violating socio-cultural traditions and backlash from their families. An added dimension is that these repressive controls are more stringently operative in the absence of migrating male family members. For example, local female labourers do not work in brick kilns even though it is a better waged work. This is because brick kiln work is even more stigmatised than agricultural wage labour. But moreover, their working at kilns would generate gossip among villagers that she wanders in search of work behind her husband.[8] This gossip tantamounts to inviting contempt and reproach on the family. Female labourers' involvement in kilns would be taken as a reflection of inability of their husbands to adequately provide for the family and the loose character of women who cannot make ends meet within their husband's earnings. Such work would require female labourers to be mobile and work in the company of strange men which would be totally unacceptable given the prevailing socio-cultural norms. Drinking and physical harassment are common problems in kilns which scare and further discourage local women.

On further prodding of the issue, women became belligerent. They retorted if, as a woman, I would be able to do such work. They also mocked and belittled incoming migrant female labour (from Ranchi) working at kilns. These migrant women were derided for their peculiar style of draping saris, carrying children on their backs while working, working in the company of unknown men, being loud mouthed and abusive and for manufacturing and selling alcohol to other migrants and locals.[9]

They are the opposite of ideal local females: dependent on male; wear saris in a traditional manner with their heads covered; not engage in verbal fights or are abusive (not entirely true of Dalit women, from what was seen in the field); not challenge the gendered division of labour or established gender roles; work with familiar female companions, employers and operating within a limited geography, etc. According to a female Chamar labourer from Baaspur who had worked as a migrant worker, but since the last fourteen years has been based in the village, local women are not used to any non-agricultural work and therefore they cannot do these. Incoming female labour from Ranchi can do non-agricultural wage labour as in brick kilns or carrying head loads because this is what they have been doing since childhood. Also, they work as a family. From this it is inferred that the presence of 'family' (read husbands or male members) legitimates women working in kilns or for that matter, any non-agricultural occupation. It is also inferred that with a family working together as a unit, the burden of work is shared. This is seen in the third village where women work alongside their husbands in kilns as unpaid attached labour.

The traditional way of village life is itself a limitation. In comparison to a village, caste, religious and gender identities are diluted in cities and towns. Female labourers remarked that in urban locations, women do non-agricultural wage labour.

Sapatganj's Dhobi contractor asserted that she would also have done the same in a town.[10] Several other respondents and villagers in general agreed with this. A few women, from Sapatganj, pointed out that in a nearby town women washed alcohol bottles and made bangles. But such opportunities are not available to female labour in the countryside and even if they went to cities they would not be able to get work because they lack intellect, general awareness and confidence.

The passivity of female labour, limited awareness, the complete absence of women in brick kilns, MGNREGA or non-agricultural work and absence of contractors to recruit and pay female labourers (as is the case in agriculture) are also reasons for lack of female non-agricultural employment. Sapatganj's Dusadh contractor expressed that

> *[S]he has not benefitted from this new source of employment (MGNREGA) because no one calls her for this work. Women come from other areas and do such work. But their pradhan says that women will not be able to do such work. They have never approached any authority above the pradhan, like at the Block level, over this because she cannot go alone and she does not know whom to approach and where. No one would support her. Also, how can she possibly lift head loads of mud and grit if no one takes the contract and responsibility because otherwise if she went, then who would pay her? The men from this*

> *village, who are involved in such work, do not ask women. She would feel shy to work with them and would only go if many of other women go as well.*
>
> (Fieldwork Notes, December 2009)

However, Mosahar women from Dokhgadh worked in MGNREGA projects and this has to be located in a wider context of labour struggles by the Mosahars, as will be elaborated in the following chapter.

The practice of traditional occupations is possibly one form of non-agricultural work in which female labour participation would not be questioned or circumscribed. But there are hardly any examples of this. One example was a Dhobi woman and her husband from Baaspur, who previously engaged in their caste-based occupation (washerman). In Sapatganj, the wife of a Dhobi assisted in ironing clothes (within the village). However, with the changing circumstances, evolving labour market and consumer preferences, this work has fallen into obsolescence. To cite the example of the dhobi couple,

> *[B]oth worked as dhobis till about ten years ago. They were remunerated in kind for this type of work. About nine kilos of rice was given by each customer everysix months or so. Clothes were washed at a dhobi ghaat which was later acquired by the then pradhan. In addition to land dispossession, they now have no access to water as the village pond is dry. People are more fancy and conscious now. Earlier people would bathe when the dhobi returned clean clothes, now they bathe everyday. Surf (detergent) is widely available. People wear synthetic clothes which are easy to wash.*
>
> (Fieldwork Notes, April 2010)

In Dokhgadh, a couple of older Chamar women continued with their caste work of *dais*, assisting in childbirth. Since these are older women and doing their traditional jobs (in other words, not challenging boundaries), socio-cultural restrictions limiting mobility are not seen here. In fact, these women travel great distances for work. They are compensated with clothes, money, grains, livestock or a small piece of jewellery. On special occasions like wedding, some Chamar women are called upon to sing and they may be paid a token amount and/or are served food and sweets. They are not only important sources of income and food but an integrated part of the fabric of village life. Women pointed out that they undertake these activities because of '*vyvhar*' (literally meaning behaviour and implying general social relations here), referring to the common community bond and as wage labourers. This '*vyvhar*', of course also serves to buttress their exploitation as wage labourers. Overall, at the lower end of the labour hierarchy, there has been a sharp disjuncture between caste and traditional occupation which were categorised as polluting. However, as one moves up the caste–class hierarchy, this disjuncture may not be strong. From example, Baniyas still are petty traders, Brahmins and Rajputs are still the major landowners.

Notions of family honour and respect are strongly attached to the economic and social conduct of women. This, together with caste, inhibits diversification of female labour out of agriculture. It is the given duty of men to provide for their families. In this sense, occupational diversification is necessary and preferred to oppressive village-based agrarian relations. But providing for households is not a role traditionally ascribed to women. Moreover, as stressed by the Dhobi female labourer from Sapatganj,

> *[N]o one from this village worked in kilns because they cannot do such intense physical labour. They feel shy. What if a relative saw them moulding bricks while their husbands sit at home? Ranchinis (female labour from Ranchi), don't feel shy because this work is done by their caste group. If she was to wash others clothes, no one would remark on it because her caste does this work. But if a Dusadh was to do it, it would be shameful ('sharm, laaj'). Rather than working in kilns, it is better to incur debt and sit idle at home.*
>
> (Fieldwork Notes, December 2009)

In Sapatganj, an Ahir woman once washed the dirty dishes of my host (Rajput) family but only after she closed the doors of the house so that no outside person could just walk in and see her.

The aforementioned points attest that economic discrimination is closely linked to gendered relations and caste identity. But the language of discrimination does not figure prominently among female labourers' explanations of their exclusion from occupational diversification. It is not a matter of questioning the structural context or challenging the existing power relations. Dalit women have internalised patriarchy; for them, this is how the order of things has always been, what they are used to and identify with. Jassal (2012) has also noted that one reason for the lack of occupational diversification is that the breadwinner is typified as male while women are deemed responsible for care and reproductive activities.

Female labourers' agricultural wage labour participation is influenced and shaped by factors like family structure and size, age and socio-cultural restrictions, site of work and household economic circumstances. As one moves progressively down the labour hierarchy, these factors are not rigidly applied. But even at the bottom, caste and landownership are important determinants of wage labour participation and its nature. In the context of Sapatganj and Baaspur, it was pointed out that upper and medium caste labouring households are either unwilling to take up the wage labour for Dalit employers, did wage labour occasionally or only within a small radius or those with whom they shared close socio-economic relations. In Dokhgadh, in addition to these factors, a Chamar male labour put in that no employer would ask *baba log* (Brahmins) to work in their fields. Other employers also mentioned recruiting labour from *chutkas*. Caste, in this sense, is a ground for discrimination in the village labour market. In other words, upper castes working for upper, medium or lower castes is embarrassing for both employers and labourers.

A landless upper caste household is more likely to undertake agricultural and/or wage labour and more often, in comparison to a landed (even marginal) upper caste household. A Giri woman, from a labouring household in Dokhgadh, pointed out that she was the only woman from her hamlet (predominantly comprising Giris and a few Rajputs and Gonds who are the primary labouring households of this hamlet) to do wage labour. She worked only within the hamlet. According to her, an important distinction between her and Dalit labourers is that she does not haggle with the employer over wages. She merely quotes the going wage rate for that task and the employer pays that rate. She saw wage negotiation as not befitting her caste status. She also mentioned that as a '*Brahmin*' she cannot work for a *chutka*. It is possible that since this is a Brahmin employer–Brahmin labourer employment relation, the employer might be more sympathetic or 'self-embarrassed'. Another reason is that both the employer and the labourer are from the same hamlet and the former serves as a safety net against unforeseen casualties, food insecurity, etc. Once she even went to sing at a *babu's* house, for which she was given ₹100–₹200, food and clothes. So, there exist overlapping socio-economic relations even among upper and middle caste labourers and these possibly circumscribe their bargaining power. Similar cases were observed among several other upper caste female labourers.

Female members of even a Dalit landed labouring household are unlikely to traverse long distances for wage labour. On the other hand are the landless Mosahars in Dokhgadh. Female labourers from these villages even walk to distant blocks for wage labour. Lack of landownership and the minimum food security attached to it is a major reason for this. Mosahars are well known in the field villages as hardy stock, efficient and good agricultural workers, as extremely bold and brazen. This also has to do with their political activism, as we will see later.

As agricultural wage labour, Dalit female labourers have been adversely affected by agricultural transformations like mechanisation, displacement of wages in kind with cash wages, use of chemical inputs and landowners taking to cultivation themselves. I cite one example here, though these points were raised by most respondents from both villages.

A female Dhobi labourer from Baaspur narrated:

> *[S]ince the badkas started using combines for harvesting, not much wage labour is available in katni (harvesting). As cash was not very common, wages were paid in kind. Badkas have large family and they want to save grain for household consumption and now if they have a surplus, they prefer to sell it. When harvesting was manual, she could earn up to ten bhojas. Now men migrate out to earn and they have to*

> *live on that. Chutka employers themselves do katni manually . . . . they are concerned with saving money and therefore, do katni themselves. They would rather spend the saved money on food and not labour wages. Now those who have a little more than ten kathas, may hire labour. These are placed slightly lower than babu log (badkas) . . . It was better when wages were paid in kind.*[11] *Labourers would bring the received grain home, grind it and eat it for two days. Now they get cash wage, go to the market to purchase something and the money is all consumed . . . . In comparison to before, less wage labour is available in sohini (weeding) also. Badkas spray pesticide because of which grass dries. Only in conditions of moisture, will grass grow and there will be need for weeding. Decline in the availability of agricultural employment has led to problems of food and money ('khaane ki pareshani, paise ki pareshani').*
>
> (Fieldwork Notes, April 2010)

The wage structure and relations are very similar across the three villages. It is clear that a gendered division of labour keeps female labour tied to agriculture. Within agriculture, they undertake only certain tasks: sowing (*rupani*), weeding (*sohni*), harvesting and threshing (rice and wheat) and cutting sugarcane leaves on *geda* or paid labour basis.[12] In own cultivation, the sexual division of labour is not rigid – so it is not that women are not capable of doing other agricultural or non-agricultural tasks, but these have to be saved for the men, the heads of the household, the main breadwinners, to preserve the patriarchal power relations. This sexual division of tasks is backed by explanations referring to physical features of the male and female body. Female labour explained that men cannot stoop or sit for long periods of time, in positions, required for sowing or weeding. These tasks are the least paying agricultural operations. One explanation for low wages is that these tasks are mostly done on a daily wage basis which does not pay as much as contract-based work which is common in male tasks. Moreover, regulations on female mobility and their care responsibilities mean that they can undertake only the locally available wage labour and local jobs are likely to be daily waged rather than contract based. Female labour is unlikely to be awarded contract-based work because women cannot do as much labour as men. Another explanation for higher wage rates of male agricultural tasks is that these require greater physical labour.

As the Sapatganj female Dusadh contractor put it,[13]

> *[F]ifteen rupees are paid for weeding because one sits and does it, rupani involves pulling out seedlings and then sowing them, therefore twenty rupees are paid for it. One does spade work for the entire day on just water. By the end of the day, both arms swell and the body aches, so wouldn't one ask for sixty rupees?*
>
> (Fieldwork Notes, December 2009)

An Ansari woman[14] from Baaspur also attested that

> *[M]en undertake spade work and the tasks performed by women involve less hard-work and labour.*
>
> (Fieldwork Notes, April 2010)

Female labour rationalises that their inferior physical strength prevents them from undertaking male agricultural tasks. However, in own cultivation, women may sometimes do these tasks as here they are not subjected to pressures of time or contract. Rather, they can work at their own pace with rest breaks. While true, this should not be read as undermining the role of gendered social relations.

Employers account for the low wage rates of female labour in terms of women not being serious workers and for playing truant from work. Employers explained that they have to call upon female labourers several times before they actually turn up for work. They halt or abandon work in between and 'disappear' to tend to other tasks. This is true to some extent as domestic chores and care and reproductive economy duties are solely the responsibility of women and have to be managed alongside wage labour demands and needs. Local employers rationalise low wages for local labour in terms of labour also accessing their fields for various purposes (grazing livestock, cutting grass for fodder, defecation). The Sapatganj Rajput family defended that Bhumihars do not have the paying capacity to pay the minimum wage.

As stated earlier, female labour is largely employed on a daily wage-rate basis. In Dokhgadh though, women do weeding on contract basis within their village boundaries. Such instances are seen more amongst Mosahar labourers. In paddy transplantation, they are employed on a piece-rate basis. Contractual work is comparatively more profitable, but only male tasks are likely to be given on contract. Regarding contract work, a female Chamar (Baaspur) labourer pointed out that

> *[T]he fewer the men, the better it is.*
>
> (Fieldwork Notes, April 2010)

According to her, if two men are contracted for *kudni* (spade work) of five *kathas* for ₹100 or ₹200, this is split equally between them. This is more than what they would have made working on daily wages, that is, ₹15 per *katha* (and according to one estimate, not more than two to three *kathas* can be done in a day) or a flat rate of ₹40–₹60 per day (wages given by the Baaspur *Pradhan* for *kudni*). Female labourers explained that spade work required more stamina and since, in terms of output, men can achieve more than women, they are recruited on contract basis.

In a few cases female labour may be recruited for contractual work from outside the village. A female Chamar labourer (Baaspur) explained that if there is less *khar* (dry grass, weeds), then four or five women may decide to take up the work on contract basis. If they have been contracted for two days, they finish it in one and a half days, make a profit and then move onto the next job. In this case, wage payment is timely. Generally, the employer gives wages to the contractor who then distributes among labour. But if Khar is more, then it is done on daily wage basis only.

On the whole though, male labour is predominant in contract wage labour. A male Dhobi labourer (Baaspur) pointed out that

> *[I]n contract work wages are paid timely at the completion of the work. In daily wage work, payments are more often than not delayed. Employers say that they do not have cash at home, have to go to the bank etc and they pay several days after the completion of the work.*
>
> (Fieldwork Notes, April 2010)

Therefore, it is not only that as daily wage labourers female labour is paid less but benefits of contract work like timely payment also elude them. It can be inferred that contract work is less humiliating because it does not involve having to ask for due wages time and again. Part wage payment could be a ground for labour's continued dependency on the concerned employer. Contract work does away with this possibility.

In most of the cases, sowing and weeding are tasks that can be done in one day. In a few cases, where it takes two to three days to complete a job, wages are likely to be paid at the completion of work though there is no hard and fast rule and wages are in fact much delayed. However, if any labourer needs money beforehand, she can approach the employer directly. In case of employers from outside it is a common practice to pay the labour at the end of the workday. The employer may come to the field at the end of the workday and give the full amount to the contractor/lead person for distribution among the labourers or the labourers may go to the employer's household at the end of the workday to collect their wages.

During 'season' time, a tight labour market is not uncommon. With respect to female labour one example is in paddy transplantation. Wage negotiations are particularly strong at this time, when it is important that paddy be transplanted at the right time. Also, because wage rates are unlikely to change once fixed at the start of a season. There is no well-structured strategy played out by an organised labour force. Rather, it comes across as a casual and impromptu effort by some labourers. It is usually the case that at the start of the season, labourers talk amongst themselves that their wages should be increased in keeping with the rising living costs and regional or extra-local wage hikes. The more aggressive of these labourers may suggest that wages should be increased by a certain amount and the others tend to agree. The quote is about ₹5–₹10 over the last season's wage rate. As the Baaspur *pradhan* put it, labourers are united in their decision to not work for those who pay less.[15] However, it was evident in interviews with female labourers that there is always the fear that if they haggle too much, someone else from the village will go and do the work or that the employer will recruit labour from another hamlet or village. This was expressed by the Sapatganj Dhobi contractor as such:

> *[T]hey will sit at home for two days and then return to work for the same employer or any where else where they might be employed because what else is there to do in the village?*
>
> (Fieldwork Notes, November 2009)[16]

When an employer calls upon a contractor or the main/lead female labourer, usually at their home, some face-to-face haggling follows. If the employer does not agree to a raise or a mutual agreement is not reached, labourers may refuse. An agreement may be reached between the employer and the contractor, but when the contractor approaches the labourers, the latter may press the contractor into further bargaining with the employer. She would then have to approach the employer again. Negotiations also take place the next day, at the field, as labourers try to wheedle and argue the employer into increasing the wage. Where no agreement is reached, the employer may have to hire labour from outside the village. This is an expensive alternative because these labourers are paid more and have to be served with water and food also. Ultimately, employers have to return to local labour which is cheaper, easily accessible and more regularly available. If arrangements with outside labour do not work out, the employer again approaches local labourers and agrees to a slight increase. Labourers agree to work for this rate, because if they have been unemployed for some time, they cannot afford to let any wage labour opportunity go waste. Labourers may also factor in socio-economic ties of dependency, particularly, if the employer is a *badka*. In this case, labour unity in demanding wage hikes may be fragmented or fragile to begin with.

Nonetheless, all labourers do haggle. As put by the Sapatganj Dhobi contractor,

> *[T]he older generation was scared of badkas, but not now. Now the badkas may get irritated, but then they come around. If one has to live in the village then what of arrogance, badka babu (the eldest son of the Rajput family who takes care of agriculture) sometimes gets angry but then after few days comes to our doorstep.*
>
> (Fieldwork Notes, November 2009)[17]

Another female Dusadh labourer explained that

> *[I]f badka babu was to call her for some work, she would ask for a raise. She may even refuse to go for work, if he did not agree. But then*

> *there is no point in sitting at home. Some other labourers . . . might take on the job. She would be angry with these labourers but after few days' things would be back to normal between them. Some time later, badka babu himself may again have to call her for work when others have refused.*
>
> (Fieldwork Notes, December 2009)

In general, wage hike demands take the shape of negotiations and not open confrontation. The wage rate set by the first petty capitalist to recruit labour becomes the standard rate for the season. This is the case for the region. Employers stick to the rate thus set and in fact, they among themselves also consult and decide rates.[18] It appears that female labour wages increase by about ₹5 every season.

The Sapatganj female Dusadh labourer described the wage negotiation process as such:

> *A contractor attempts to negotiate wage at the time she is approached by the employer or someone on his behalf. Once informed about the task and the land size, she would quote a particular sum and the number of labourers that would be required. The employer would then say that if others pay that much, then he would also pay that. She would then emphasise that everywhere they get that amount and he should also give the same amount. If the employer agrees, she organises a labour group and does the work next day. If the employer does not agree, she may refuse to take on the work and tell the employer to get labour from somewhere else.*[19] *At times, the employer may not agree in the first instance and leave without finalising anything. After giving it some thought, the employer may approach her again. Then she would coax him in a gentle voice that if he were to give them the earlier stated amount, she would do his work as well.*[20] *The employer would then benevolently tell her that he would pay that wage (the quoted wage) and she should get the job done ('Chali, de denge, hamar kaam kar de'). However, if she has gone without wage labour for some time, then she might agree to a lesser amount.*
>
> (Fieldwork Notes, December 2009)

From Baaspur, a female Dhobi labourer explained the process as such:

> *[T]he rate set at the start of the season, remains throughout the season. When the employer calls upon a labourer, some haggling still takes place. Labourers argue with prospective employers or contractors that since everything in the shops have become so expensive, their wages should also increase. Any one labourer who has a sharp mind and can speak up may take the initiative to demand higher wages. Labourers spread, by word of mouth, the wages to be demanded*

and decide among themselves that they will not go for work, unless this is agreed. If the wage offered by the landowner is too less, not enough to provide for food, labourers refuse the job. Employers may hire labour from outside the village, but there is no friction between own village labourers and these. However, after a while, some of the local labour will return to work for lower wages. At times, a low-caste employer may increase the wage and consequently the other employers will have to offer same wages. In demanding wage hikes, labourers may present a unified stand against lower-caste employers. This is not the case vis-à-vis badka employers and anyways they would not increase wages because they provide employment on a more regular basis.

(Fieldwork Notes, April 2010)

Wage rates are more or less fixed but can vary slightly due to several reasons. If the employer is from outside the village, labour has more scope for bargaining the terms and conditions, and in most cases of employment outside the village, wage rates are relatively higher. Female labour takes advantage of the fact that the employer is unable to secure local labour, given the critical timing of the agricultural work like in paddy transplantation and the long distance labourers have to travel. Also, female labourers have to get up very early in the day to tend to domestic chores and other household responsibilities or forsake or delay or pass them onto children for the day. In the case of local employers, the socio-economic dependency restricts scope of bargaining. In Baaspur, a Chamar woman who operated as a contractor mentioned that she might take advance from an outside employer as security against the possibility of delayed wage payment. Because the employer does not live in the village, he will not be easily accessible in case of delayed wage payment. Advance in contract work did not come up in interviews with Sapatganj labourers.

Labour interviews across villages highlighted that OBC and lower caste employers are likely to pay ₹5–₹10 more than the going rate as an incentive to secure labour for timely and efficient work. These employers hire in irrigation sources and can afford limited amounts of fertilisers and pesticides. To make the most of inputs, they need to ensure labour availability in peak season time, particularly in paddy cultivation. They would rather incur higher labour costs than let the crop be affected or bear the expense of hiring in pump sets for longer durations. They pay on time and give labourers cold water and something to eat when they are working in the fields. Several labourers suggested that these employers empathise with them as they understand the problems and needs of labourers. As a Baaspur female Chamar labourer put it,

[O]nly a chutka can understand another chutka's problems.

(Fieldwork Notes, April 2010)[21]

According to her, lower caste employers give wages before labourers ask for it.

According to another labourer from Baaspur, labourers can negotiate with OBC and lower caste employers on a more even basis: they can even fight and verbally abuse lower caste employers, but not the upper caste employers. According to a Sapatganj Ahir female labourer, it is also the case that labourers will not accept low wages from lower caste employers because in times of need, their source of relief is *badlkas*, which privileges his status unlike lower caste employers. According to the Sapatganj Dhobi contractor,

> *[I]n case of any need or emergency, the badkas will help, but of what help can the chutkas be without the resources? In chutkas fields, one does wage labour and comes back home.*
>
> (Fieldwork Notes, November 2009)[22]

She denied any difference between OBC or lower caste employers and upper caste employers on the basis of wage rates, but implicit in her assertion is the differential attitudes labour adopts towards employers on the basis of their castes. This can also be taken as a reflection of the fact that wage rates are not the only consideration on the basis of which labour takes up a particular wage employment opportunity. Also, given that OBCs and lower castes or the petty producers are a very small source of employment in comparison to the *badkas*, employment from petty producers has not mitigated dependency of the classes of labour on petty capitalists.

Wages for women labourers from Dokhgadh are slightly higher and this is attributed to Mosahars. It is usually the biggest landowners who 'open the agrarian season', that is, recruit labourers for, say, paddy transplantation. These employers depend on Mosahar labourers significantly. Mosahars are able to successfully haggle a slightly higher wage rate for the new season. The process of wage negotiation is the same as in the other two villages. The difference between Mosahars and other Dalits is that the former show a high degree of labour unity, no doubt facilitated by the lack of internal economic differentiation. Therefore, they are able to put up a united front against the *badkas*. Unfree labour relations are a characteristic of them also, but as their hamlets are physically isolated and these are single-caste hamlets, the everyday social compulsions and threat of sanctions as seen in the previous two villages are absent. Political pressure is limited since they have successfully accessed block and district administrations for relief. The economic compulsion is omnipresent, but here too unlike other Dalit labourers, Mosahars are not dependent on one or two employers. Above all, by virtue of extremely poor conditions and other reasons, Mosahars are on the 'watchlist' of the local media and government authorities. This, in addition, with the attitude of Mosahars and *badkas'* apprehension of any possible Mosahar action, favours Mosahars in wage negotiations.

On the other hand, Chamar labourers from Dokhgadh pointed out that even if they broadly resolve not to work on last season's wages, one labourer may empathise with a particular employer and work for him on previous rates. Consequently, others will also have to agree to it. The ritual notions of superiority and inferiority, the natural order of things comes across as a much-internalised phenomenon among non-Mosahar Dalits. Their position and status in life are not questioned and there is a feeling that they cannot fight the *badkas*.

Modes of Recruitment

In Sapatganj and Baaspur, whether work is local or undertaken outside the village, women work only in the company of women. One or two familiar men or young boys (relatives of female labourers) may be included, especially when women are working in a different village. This is seldom the case as men are concentrated in different kinds of agricultural tasks, travel much further than women and are more likely to be engaged in contractual and not daily wage work; most of them are also migrants and unavailable. Group work provides a sense of security to women when they are working in a different village. In familiar reliable company there is less threat of social monitoring by other community members. Women also feel less inhibited. They enjoy the company of friends and relatives at work. If one was to go alone, other women would taunt and accuse her of working and earning for herself and not taking others with her. Moreover, paddy transplantation is not a job which can be done by only one person. In own village, women may work individually.

In both villages, with the exception of paddy sowing, agricultural operations undertaken by female labour are remunerated on a daily wage basis. However, if the work is done outside the village, weeding and sowing may be given on contract. In own village, it is easy for employers to individually call upon labour and supervision costs are not high. For outside employers, it is easy to rely on a contractor given the distance and lack of familiarity.[23] In either case, the employer's servant can also approach the labour, but this is not common, particularly in local work.

The starting point in the recruitment process is the employer, whether local or from outside the village. In daily wage works he individually calls upon labourers. In piece-rate-based paddy transplantation or rare local cases where weeding work is contracted out, the employer contacts a female labourer who may have worked for him before or who lives nearby and who is capable of organising a team of labourers. This female labourer in effect becomes the '*thekedar*' (contractor) or is called the main or lead labourer. The employer provides the contractor or the lead labourers with details about the work to be done. The latter then quotes the number of labourers required and the expected wage rate. This takes place at the contractor's house and involves some haggling between the two on wage rates. Later the same day, the contractor or lead labourer approaches other labourers. From the contractor, labourers seek information about the specific task to be done, wage rate, location and whether they be given water and food.

In Sapatganj, two rather well-defined contractors (a Dhobi and a Dusadh widow) exist and each has their work group.[24] Both these contractors reside in the main settlement of the village and their parties draw mostly on classes of labour from this settlement, with a few exceptions. Work parties remain the same throughout a season. However, it is also common that the labourers fall out with their contractor over wages and then go to work with another work group and in the next season return to work for the previous contractor. Depending upon the scale of the work, the two contractors may either recruit only their favourites or if the demand is large, the two contractors and their teams may work together. In this case the contractors first meet for advice and discussion and together take a decision on the job, wages, number of labourers required, who to call upon, etc.

In comparison, Baaspur does not have organised labour parties. The labourers of Baaspur attributed this to the small size of their village. But Baaspur is only slightly larger than Sapatganj. However, the latter does not have contiguous boundaries and the dominant perception is that Sapatganj and its two neighbouring villages constitute one village (socio-economic relations also cut across these villages). This impression is reinforced by the fact that the three villages share one panchayat. The Baaspur labourers extended no clear reason as to what the size of the village has to do with workers being organised or not. However, there are several differences between the two villages which provide a more plausible reason. Sapatganj has fewer labouring households. One way the contractors can secure labour supply in times of seasonal peaks is by organising work groups. They also pay the core members slightly higher wages than the rest. Neighbouring Sapatganj are larger villages with more labouring households and labourers known over the area for their work (for example, the Mosahars of the third village). Labourers from these villages have worked in Sapatganj. In this context, even loosely defined work groups can afford labourers greater bargaining power and voice. In Baaspur, there are relatively more local employers and there is less need of contractors. Here labourers do not show feelings of competition, but then this village has not seen labourers from other villages coming in and 'poaching' their work. In rare cases where they have, intra-labour relations have not been strained.

In Baaspur, a Chamar lead labourer or contractor pointed out that an outside employer may contact her husband in a public place like the market at the village junction and he is given the contract, so to say. But the actual organising of labour, work responsibility and wage allocation is done by her. It is she who haggles with the employer or the person he may send the next day (with tractor-trolley) to collect labour, over wages and advance.

In Baaspur, labourers defined a contractor as someone who is middle aged,[25] has a strong and commanding presence capable of collecting labour, getting the work done and distributing the wages. As put by a Chamar woman whose widowed mother-in-law operated as a contractor:

> *[T]he mother-in-law used to do wage labour from the beginning, she was clever, shrewd, she was always in the front, could organise labour for work and distribute wages among labourer.*
>
> (Fieldwork Notes, April 2010)

The mother-in-law takes on the work of a contractor because in this way she can also earn some money. She recruits labourers from the neighbourhood, her personal social network and mostly from labouring households in own hamlet.

In Sapatganj, labourers defined a contractor or lead labourer as someone with substantial contacts with village women, one whose mobility for some reason is not as restricted as in the case of others and who is strong and commands authority. According to the Dusadh contractor, a contractor is a strong person with a commanding presence capable not only of organising labour into work groups but also getting the work done and of distributing wages.

This Dusadh contractor actually started at a disadvantaged position, but economic needs forced her to take on this role. When she and her husband lost their land in floods, they shifted to her paternal village.[26] Here, the husband became a *sanyasi* (hermit). He later died. She had no brothers to support her, and circumstances pushed her into doing wage labour to provide for her young family. She used to work with an old man who was then the contractor. This contractor's death presented an opportunity for her to make better money. Her one advantage was that she is the 'daughter' of the village, unlike other women who were married into the village. Social norms are more stringently applied to daughters-in-law. The Dusadh contractor benefitted from comparatively uninhibited mobility, visibility and established contacts. This also gave employers ease of access and freedom to engage in direct contact which is not the case with other female labourers.

In both villages, female labourers claimed that there are no fixed criteria in recruiting labour. Nevertheless, as seen, it is common practice to first call upon relatives, neighbours and own street labourers, friends and people with whom the contractor or lead labourer share close social relations. Primarily (though not exclusively), these people would be of the same caste group, though female labourers argue that caste is not a consideration in team selection (only a few respondents outright admitted caste as a selection criteria). However, most of the team members are Dalits and where the demand is for a few labourers, it is the relatives and friends who get the first call. In Sapatganj, they are the core team members, the first 'port of call' and as mentioned previously are also paid a higher sum than other team members. Female labourers mentioned that their huts indicate their labour (class) status to outside employers. In both villages, other factors influencing recruitment that came up included capability, skill, efficiency, who the recruiters get along with, those who are less likely to pick up a fight if wages are low and those more likely to obey the recruiters.

How caste, class and local politics underscore who works for whom is very clear in Sapatganj. Here, the two most landed and important sources of employment are Rajput and *pradhan* (Ahir) households. The two are economic rivals. Their political rivalry has to do with gaining political position and power directly or through their proxy candidates to be exploited later for economic benefits and social prominence.

Villagers commented on how both households, in order to create their spheres of influence, tried to incite villagers to register false complaints against one another. Both households have their own lobbies among the villagers based on caste, locality and debt. There are several Ahir households that, because they belong to the *pradhan*'s caste and live near him, are under direct pressure and control. This is the case even for those outside debt-based labour relations who still cannot take up employment outside the *pradhan*'s sphere of influence. This is true of several other Ahir households living in other parts of the village. But these households try to seek a balance rather than distinctly aligning with either side. Men from these households may not do wage labour for a Rajput family, but instead send their wives and children (uncommon). In this way, female labour plays an important role in maintaining male patron–client relations.

In Sapatganj and Baaspur, labour interviews reveal debt-based recruitment is found in the case of male labourers working at brick kilns. They take advance of up to ₹4,000 from kiln managers or owners in the off-season. On the one hand, this credit is crucial to labour reproduction in the lean season and on the other hand, the credit secures chimneywallas' (brick kiln owners or managers) labour for brick kiln season. The advance is adjusted against labour wages in the season. In Sapatganj, a male labour contractor, advanced money for travel expenses to those he recruited for migrant work. This was later adjusted against their wages. This contractor's wife was a source of credit in the village for small amounts. In case of large amounts, she could mediate between labourers and prospective creditors (fallouts between her husband and migrant workers from the village also led to 'tension' between her and the concerned migrant worker's wife).

In Sapatganj, debt 'tied' female labourers to creditor households. This is best exemplified with reference to the Rajput family and a Dusadh household located just behind their house. This Dusadh household's history of borrowing from the Rajput family can be traced back to the previous generation. Over the years, they borrowed to meet wedding expenses, purchase food and fertilisers, for roof repairs, etc. Recently, the current male head of the household had, with the help of the eldest son of the Rajput family, taken a loan from a bank. Though taken on the pretext of livestock rearing, it was used to repay a previous debt which had been incurred against part of their land. The entire loan amount was not sufficient for this, and some additional money was borrowed from the Rajput family. The Dusadh family pays interest on this amount.

Both the male head of the Dusadh household and his wife provide priority labour to this household and the rate paid is less than the market wage rate. Wage payments are much delayed. In instances when the wife had worked as an agricultural wage labour with a bigger group in Rajput's fields, she was paid less, if at all, or paid much later than the others. She cannot work elsewhere without first checking with the creditor family. She is expected to first finish their work. She is also expected to check with the wife of the male head of the Rajput household, if she can go and work elsewhere and if there is no work to be done for them. She cannot work for households in conflict with this household. Tied labour relations have debilitating consequences for labourers, given the extremely limited work opportunities for female labour. The Dusadh couple also provided unpaid labour services to the Rajput family. The husband has to tend to the livestock and sweep the front courtyard every day. His wife may also do this (eventually she was 'hired' for this) in addition to doing scooping or drying the grain within the household.

Nonetheless, for this Dusadh household, the 'patronage' of the Rajput household is crucial: the Rajput family serves as a mediator and safety net in times of crises and otherwise as well. For example, a Rajput family member may plough their field. In Sapatganj, there are other households indebted to the Rajput family, but members of these households are not as attached to the Rajput family as this Dusadh household. Physical proximity of the latter to the Rajput household is a major factor in reinforcing the tied and unfree labour relations. The Dusadh family has often considered shifting to their field, but this has been actively discouraged by the Rajput family who pacify the Dusadh family with various promises. This aside the fact remains that the Dusadh family itself does not have the resources that such relocation would entail.

Dokhgadh is mostly similar to the other two villages where recruitment of labourers is concerned. Like Baaspur, the village does not have well-defined labour parties or female contractors. The only difference with other two villages is that Mosahars underplayed the role of caste, capability and personal preferences in the selection of team members. Given the absence of other *chutkas* in their hamlets, caste obviously does not figure in their recruitment strategies. However, Mosahars are known not to forge alliances with other labourers in their struggles and no other Dalit group also stated working with them. Recruitment is hamlet based. Mosahars of one hamlet do not call on Mosahars of another hamlet for work purposes. The two hamlets are also at opposite ends of the village. Within hamlets also, the immediate neighbourhood (and by implication, relatives and people with whom they are likely to share greater social and economic rapport) appears as a preferred area for recruiting labourers.

Another difference between Sapatganj, Baaspur and Dokhgadh's non-Mosahar labouring households on the one hand and Mosahars on the other hand is that the latter deliberately denied limiting the number of workers for a contract job and forged a community spirit, that is, lead labourers think that as many as possible should work in a contract job because then they will all earn.

Like Sapatganj and Baaspur, overlapping socio-economic and political allegiances are important determinants of labour arrangements, as is debt-based recruitment in brick kilns. These may manifest within patron–client relations. These factors are also grounds for unfree labour relations.

Labourers who openly aligned themselves with either of the two dominant Brahmin households or another petty capitalist resident in or nearer to their hamlet did not work for the other or seek redress from them. For example, female labourers from the first hamlet said they did not approach the de facto *pradhan* for their problems with MGNREGA or pensions because they did not vote for him and so do not expect him to help. They get no benefits from the de facto *pradhan*. They supported a resident petty capitalist Brahmin. Several women elaborated that they voted for him because he is the largest employer of wage labour in their hamlet, their lands are adjoining, labourers take their goats to his fields for grazing, and he is the first person they would approach in times of crisis. This petty capitalist has in the past mediated with government authorities on behalf of labourers, as has the Brahmin household other than the de facto *pradhan*'s. Efforts of the former led to developments like electricity, paved roads and drainage facilities in the hamlet. Women were confident that he would help them in the future as well. Importantly, this petty capitalist also harboured political aspirations, so his actions were not really benign. In a similar way, labourers also rationalise and base their decisions on a cost–benefit analysis.

According to female Mosahar labourers, some employers allow only those labourers to harvest grain who undertook weeding and paddy transplantation work in their fields. In this way employers ensure the availability of labour at peak season and also limit their bargaining scope. Since harvesting is remunerated in kind, it is an important element of households' food security. Mosahars spoke of this arrangement with reference to upper caste employers from another neighbouring village.

It was indicated in the mapping exercise that brick kiln recruitment is based on an advance system. This is similar to Sapatganj and Baaspur. Unlike in these two villages, male labourers, particularly the Mosahars, take out loans from brick kiln owners/managers to survive in the off-season. Though this work is onerous, and exploitative, brick kiln work is crucial to their survival. Some did not consider it as socially degrading, unlike the labourers of the other two villages. Rather, for them it is better to take credit from kilns rather than repeatedly appealing to the *badkas*' benevolence. Also, at kilns, labourers claimed that wage rates are not only higher but also timely paid. In general, debt appears as a means of survival in

Dokhgadh but limits labourers' bargaining power vis-à-vis employers, as in Sapatganj and Baaspur. These survival relations are evident in unfree labour relations as well.

Unfree Labour Relations

So far in this chapter, we have seen that scarcity of employment, access to fields, credit for various purposes, access to public resources, mediation with local government structures, etc. underscore labourers' dependency on *badkas*. Also, we saw that these are the bases of unfree labour relations: debt based, priority, unpaid or tied labour arrangements enforced by a combination of caste, class and political factors. Such labour relations permeate village life in Sapatganj and Baaspur and are even willingly submitted to or upheld. I will cite a few examples explaining the shift from traditional labour bondage to unfree labour relations; how labour rationalises unfree labour relations and very briefly, again look into the role of patron–client relations.

In neither of the two villages, old-style labour bondage – based on feudal exploitation, backed by physical violence, a generalised terror of *badkas* and reinforcment with discriminatory caste ideology – existed. Traditional labour bondage has been replaced with 'free' labour relations characterised by unfreedom to varying extents. There is certainly no more physical violence. However, the discourse of superiority–inferiority styled on the basis of caste and class divisions is still deeply engrained in villagers. The spread of education and administrative changes are associated with the decline of bonded labour. Examples of land of bonded labourers being appropriated by their employers also serve as a caution. Monetisation of the economy has necessarily meant that labourers need to earn a cash wage and cannot work in exchange for food only. There is now greater yield from own cultivation and the opening up of the rural economy has meant that men can migrate out to earn and support the family.

In Sapatganj, an Ahir woman explained that many years ago her in-laws did unpaid agricultural labour for a Bhumihar. In exchange, the Bhumihar gave them a plot (about three to four *kathas*) for own cultivation. However, when the Bhumihar's sons grew up, they took back the land and now they cultivate it themselves. According to her, now there was no benefit for labourers in doing such work. Another Dusadh female labourer from Sapatganj, accounted for the shift from bonded labour to unfree labour in the following way:

> *The Rajput household of the village used to have a bandhak. He was from another village. This naukar (servant) had to do all the work and he would be beaten up if he did not do it. The present era is different from earlier, there is fear of police in all. Rice and wheat are produced in every household, poverty has decreased from before.*
>
> (Fieldwork Notes, November 2009)

According to a woman from a labouring Dhobi household (Sapatganj), whose male ancestor was a bonded labourer of the Rajput family, now people refuse to work without wages. Making cow dung cakes and washing dirty utensils in houses of others is a matter of humiliation, impropriety and is disapproved by the society.[27] Earlier, labour could not say no to their employers and would get very less wages . . . Now labourers can state that they will go to work only if they are paid and paid a certain wage. But her (the respondent) household is in a different position. Her father-in-law was a bonded labourer of *badka babu's* (the eldest son of the Rajput family) grandfather. It is a matter of social ties and association.[28] When she is called upon by them for work, she does not negotiate or answer back and does whatever is asked of her. In the past, *badka babu* has helped her in times of need. For her daughter's delivery, he took them to a hospital in Faazilnagar block in his car and did not ask for any money. . . (Fieldwork Notes, December 2009).

In Baaspur, a Chamar woman narrated the example of her husband who worked for ten years for a *babu* in a neighbouring block, several decades ago. For tending their livestock, he was given food and about ten kilograms of grain every six months. He lived in their house and would come home once a week or so. If he asked for wages, he would be threatened with physical violence, so out of fear he continued working for them. But later he ran away. The employing family reported it at a police station and accused him of stealing cash and jewellery. He was taken by the police for interrogation and his family had to pay some money to secure his release. After that, he never went back.

A Dhobi couple, from Baaspur, explained:

> *There are no 'bandhaks' (bonded labourers) in the village. Instances of these could be found three to four decades ago, but not now. Now people are clever and no one will submit to such a relationship or work only for food. Taking advantage of a personalised and dependent relationship, badkas (who owned bandhaks) appropriated the land of their bandhak's.*[29] *This is why badkas own so much land today. There is begari however. They (respondents) did begari in the pradhan's household, but since the pradhan claimed a part of the Gram Sabha land as his own, there is 'tension' between them . . . . Earlier, they tended to his livestock, made cow dung cakes, swept the areas outside their house, scooped rice and wheat etc. Now they do not even go to his place on weddings and such occasions. Many others do begari because of fear . . . Earlier people would be scared and hide in their huts on seeing the police. The administration was different then. But now as people gain education, they become intelligent. They are not scared of the police now and tell whatever they know.*
>
> (Fieldwork Notes, May 2010)

In Sapatganj, a non-indebted Dusadh female labourer attributed her non-involvement in unpaid labour within *badka* households to her being a daughter-in-law of the village. This held even in relations with the Bhumihar from whom her family had leased in land. This is not really the case. There are other daughters-in-law of the village who are involved in unpaid labour for *badkas*. However, these are also women who are 'pure' wage labourers and are not young. The same respondent asserted that nonetheless, if the Rajput family was to call her for work, she would abandon any other wage work she may be doing at the time and do the Rajput family's work first. According to her, *badka babu* lets her cut grass from his fields for fodder and take livestock to his fields for grazing. Her kids defecate in his fields and play there. It is beneficial to work for *badka babu* whose field neighbours her house in comparison to working for the *pradhan* whose field is at some distance, so not of much use or benefit (Fieldwork Notes, December 2009). A female Dhobi labourer, from Baaspur, said that she would first work for a *badka* (pointing towards the *pradhan*'s house) employer because she lives near his house, his fields surround the village, and she has to go through them for anything. Money is not the most important criterion. A *chutka* employer can be patient, but *badka* is easily annoyed and angered (Fieldwork Notes, May 2010).

Unfree labour relations often appear as a part of patron–client relations. As indicated in this chapter, patron–client relations operate as mechanisms through which public and private resources are accessed and distributed. The *badkas* are more aware of government schemes, possess the crucial networking with bank officials, help with the paperwork, act as guarantor, etc.[30] Through acts of 'patronage', *badkas* cultivate vote and labour lobbies. Other than debt, patronage can be of other types, often of everyday variety, which are nonetheless very important. These are not credit based, but function to oblige labour and cement patron–client relations. For instance, allowing a migrant member from a labouring household to call on the patron's phone to speak with their family, providing their vehicle free of cost to transport people to hospital in emergency cases, in rare cases ploughing their labourers' fields, allowing villagers to charge their cell phones (especially during elections), providing a needy family with milk/curd/tea, etc.

In Sapatganj, fieldwork showed that these informal networks operated also as 'conduits of information'. For instance, an elderly Ahir woman who lived near the Rajput family visited the wife (Amma) of the male head of this family almost everyday in the evening. She was served tea. Her interactions with Amma pertained to everyday issues of village life. Almost everyday, in the morning and evening, the male head of the household would be joined by a few other local males (from own and neighbouring villages and all mostly upper caste) in the front courtyard, where they would hold a panchayat over tea. However, in this case, the networking is patterned along the lines of a socio-economic 'lobby' rather than a patron–client relation between capital and labour.

In Dokhgadh also no bonded labourers were seen, but labour relations and wider social relations show features of unfree labour relations.

How credit or overlapping socio-economic and political ties circumscribe labour relations has been dealt with. As in Sapatganj and Baaspur, here as well, women from classes of labour category provided unpaid, paid-in-kind labour or labour remunerated with a token amount by *badkas* within their homes. These women were mostly Dalits, but unlike, in the other two villages, a few upper caste women from labouring households also delivered unpaid labour services. For example, a landless Baniya woman – deserted by her husband – did agricultural wage labour to support herself and her son. She even did *begari* for which she was remunerated in kind with ration. However, she does these within the hamlet only. She felt shy and self-conscious to go to other hamlets. This woman stressed that whenever she went to a Rajput household near her house, she was never returned empty-handed.

Providing *begar* services depended on the caste configuration of hamlets. Mosahar hamlets or those dominated by OBCs either did not reflect *begar* or did so to a very limited extent. But these labouring households do *begar* for petty capitalist households in nearby hamlets. Generally, these services are remunerated with a token amount of ₹5 or ₹10 or labourers are given grains. On ceremonies, some labourers may go for singing or playing the *dholak* (musical instrument) at a *badka's* place for which they are paid more and often also given food and/or clothes. A few Chamar women mentioned that when they were called for cleaning and such work at weddings, the *badkas* gave them only some food.

It is common for women (but not in case of young ones) whose husbands are involved in brick kiln work to work with them as unpaid attached labour, but not if the wife is young. Men leave for kilns at about four in the morning. At around ten or eleven in the morning, women take lunch to kilns for their husbands. While they eat and take a short rest, women continue with the work. They are not actually involved in moulding the bricks but rather spread out and water the bricks, make the mixture, etc. Brick kiln work is remunerated on a piece-rate base. So women's participation is important as they enhance productivity and therefore wages.

Tied and priority services are common as well and take place along the same lines as in Sapatganj and Baaspur. In addition, in Dokhgadh, these may be tied to leasing arrangements. In one leasing arrangement, going back ten years, the lessee household provided tied and priority labour services to the landowners which were remunerated at a much lower rate than the going wage rates. There is an implicit understanding that if they stop working for the owner, the leased land will be taken back. The leased land is important for this landless household for reasons of food security and also because they cultivate sugarcane on half the land and therefore, it is a crucial source of money. In another case as well, land had been leased out to a wage labourer who worked for the landowning household. In Sapatganj, we had seen a similar arrangement wherein the Rajput family had leased out a plot of land to a labourer who looked after their crops since the field was far away from their house.

Mechanisms of Labour Control

At a broad level, debt, locality and otherwise attached labour relations are a means of control over classes of labour. These have previously been discussed in the description on general social relations.

Methods of labour control exercised vary according to the nature of work. In daily wage work, the employer or someone from his family is present to supervise the labourers. This acts as a check on the labour which otherwise attempts to draw out the work for an extra day.[31]

As put by the Sapatganj Dusadh female contractor:

> *[I]n cases of daily wage work, labour works slowly and tries to draw out work. Labourers work leisurely, chat amongst themselves about working slowly so that they can come tomorrow to finish the work.*
>
> (Fieldwork Notes, December 2009)[32]

The landowner tries to cajole the labourers into working efficiently and finishing the work on the same day. He constantly monitors the labourers because otherwise labourers chat and do not work properly. In his presence, the female contractor scolds labourers that either they work properly or leave.

According to a female Dhobi labourer from Baaspur, when a *badka* employer is not present at the field for supervision, labourers work slowly and take rests. They try to draw out the work. But if the employer is present, then foot-dragging is not possible. If labourers are working properly but still the employer keeps hollering at them, they deliberately continue weeding at the same spot and laugh it off saying that labour is in any case infamous (Fieldwork Notes, April 2010).

According to a Chamar female lead labourer from Baaspur, *badkas* pay lesser wages than *chutka* and this is why their work is not done properly. Local employers are present on field for supervision in daily wage work. They keep egging on labour to hurry. If a labourer even tried standing up, the employer shouts at him to not stand and keep working. If the employers are not present on site, then labourers work slowly and procrastinate. In contrast, when labourers are working outside the village, they are given water, sweets and paid in the evening. No one stays at the field hollering at labour. Here labourers work properly (Fieldwork Notes, April 2010). This also reflects how labourers' attitude towards employers differ. This was the case in Sapatganj as well.

In cases of contractual work undertaken in own or different villages, the contract acts as a sort of in-built control as labour attempts to finish a task as soon as possible and move on to the next one in an attempt to maximise the profit. In contract work, the onus of labour control is on the contractor. If it is done within the village, the employer may come to the field a few times to check on labour. The employer may pay the contractor ₹10–₹20 more to ensure that labourers do not run away or take too many breaks and that the work finishes on time and is done properly.

In Sapatganj, labourers mentioned that the contractor worked alongside her team. She keeps inciting them to work faster and threatens of wage cut if work is shoddy and not finished on time. However, labourers also claimed that the contractor leaves for long periods of time on some pretext and hardly puts in any actual work. If the work is completed before time, the contractor pockets the extra money. Well aware of this, even in contract work labour tries to prolong the work and haggles with the contractor (and this after some of the work has been done because then the employer cannot afford to simply turn them down without trying for a compromise) who in turn bargains with the employer that work would take time and therefore the initial amount should be increased. According to the Dusadh contractor, at times when the employer has not agreed to such additional payment, or he paid less than what was agreed upon, she has had to pay from own pocket.

Where the employer is from the labourers' village and particularly if he is an upper caste-class, payments are almost always delayed. Delayed wage payment and/or withholding a part of the due wages is also a common form of labour control directed at ensuring continued availability of labour, greater labour efficiency and productivity.

Mechanisms of labour control in Dokhgadh are similar: employer supervision in the case of daily wage work and contractor supervision, in addition, to the in-built incentive of the contract in contract-based work. Petty producer employers may work alongside labourers in daily wage work to avoid deliberate procrastination of work and ensure timely completion of good quality work. Regarding the profit motivation in contractual work, the de facto *pradhan* commented:

> *[I]f male labour is given spade work on katha basis, they do up to five kathas per day, but on daily wages they do only two katha even if per day wage is hundred rupees.*
>
> (n.d.)

Similarly, as in Sapatganj and Baaspur, where *badkas* pay less than the going wage rate (as is likely to be the case), it is common for labour to deliberately do shoddy work, whether in contract or daily wage rate. The contractors work alongside labourers and keep up a fast pace of work. But, according to a few employers, though lead labourers and labourers get the same wage, the former do not do as much work or supervise properly. Delayed wage payment and/or withholding a part of the due wages is also common and a way to ensure labour supply in peak season particularly. In case of local upper caste employers, payments are almost always delayed because of socio-economic ties of dependency.

Intra-Labour Relations

In both villages, everyday female intra-labour relations are fraught with altercations on varied and even trivial issues.

As put by a Sapatganj Ahir labourer, in today's world, there is no mutual understanding and harmony.[33] If one wears good clothes and eats well, then others get jealous. This is true not only in case of Chamars and Bhumihars but the case of the village, the whole region and the world. According to Sapatganj's Dhobi female contractor,

> *[T]here is no consensus and unity among the Dhobi caste or even among the poor. People think that if they do not benefit then others should also not benefit.*[34] *There are fights and tension between households on petty issues and if people get angry on small issues then how will there be consensus?*[35] *Sometimes people live in harmony and agreement and sometimes they fight.*
>
> (Fieldwork Notes, December 2010)

Similar feelings were expressed by Baaspur labourers. Ansari women stressed that people are concerned with their own success, and they do not like to see others do well.[36]

Intra-labour relations are beset with everyday clashes. A Dusadh labourer from Sapatganj elaborated,

> *[T]here is a lot of fighting among labouring households, among her caste people, over issues like animals straying in others' fields and causing some damage, between their children when parents are at work, within families over some member not working or doing domestic chores, if the field boundary is crossed by mistake during ploughing. In this people are known to have even filed complaints with the police and so on. It is difficult for labourers to be united. Some would work for some badkas even if they were told not to because they would be threatened by badkas that their livestock would be harmed if it entered their fields, some labour would agree to work for lower wages etc.*
>
> (Fieldwork Notes, November 2009)

Such sentiments are widely shared amongst women labourers from both villages. Not only are labourers divided by caste, neighbourhood and personal networks, these are also played upon and possibly manipulated by the dominant classes as pointed out elsewhere in this chapter. Feelings of jealousy, animosity and competition are common among labourers and more so outside economic relations. According to a woman Dhobi labourer from Baaspur,

> *[E]ven though labour or lower-castes are numerically dominant, they do not present a unified stand on common problems relating to ration or job cards. People do what they think is correct. It is common for people to lie and embroil others in some petty dispute, in showing off their importance. The pradhan or members of his house do not mix extensively with the villagers socially, nonetheless, they are fed all types of information by villagers who have their own agendas. They are served tea when they go to his house. This is how the pradhan comes to know of everything. As the pradhan's fields borders those of many villagers, there is always the fear of repercussions such as the pradhan cutting off their access to his fields for grazing livestock, for defecation or create other problems for labour in accessing their own fields.*
>
> (Fieldwork Notes, May 2010)

Altercations on issues of slacking and foot-dragging are common in case of piece-rate work like sowing. According to a female Dusadh labourer (Sapatganj), clashes among members are common on petty issues of who has sown more than others, another member not working fast enough or just sitting out. She adds that

> *'[N]etagiri' (petty politics) is common among labourers . . . . Recalling a fight between her husband and another Dusadh male member (of the petty producer household which could not be accessed), she says that the latter lodged complaints at two police stations and paid twenty thousand rupees each to bring in her husband and beat him up. However, though the police took the money, they did not take any action and said that it was a false case. It is common in villages for people to create trouble for others, on incitement from other people.*[37]
>
> (Fieldwork Notes, November 2009)

It is claimed by employers and accepted by labourers that where they are paid less or late, they deliberately do shoddy and incomplete work. As one female Dusadh labourer from Sapatganj stated, if there is too much grass to be weeded then they will not pull it out, but just press it down with their feet and hurry back to their houses when it is time.[38] It is more common for labourer to resort to these tactics in other villages. There they simply take the money and run back to the refuge of their homes. But in own village, where will one run to? Employers from own village may even report them to the panchayat (Fieldwork Notes, December 2009).

Wages are another most common ground for tensions among labour while factors like kinship, caste and locality also cut across. In contract work, on the surface it is claimed that all are paid equal wages, but this is not the case in practice. As pointed out elsewhere, the female Dusadh contracter (Sapatganj) accepted that in reality, the main party members (relatives, same caste, neighbours) are paid more, and this is justifiable because they work more than the others. These are also people who are contacted first if the work to be done is of small scale and requires only a few labourers.

According to labourers, the contractors are paid a little extra for '*chai-paani*'.[39] Some labourers suggested that this is because contractors put in more hard work than others in organising labour, taking them for work and ensuring that it gets done well and on time.

However, on top of this, contractors or lead labourers also cheat labour. This is so in both the villages. For example, at the beginning of the work the contractor bargains with the employer that labourers will not work for less than₹20 per day. It may be that the employer agrees to this rate, but the contractor tells the labourers that the employer has said that he will think it over. At the end of work, the employer gives money on the basis of ₹20 per day per labourer to the contractor to distribute. But the contractor distributes wages on the basis of ₹15 only and tells the labourers that this is what she was given by the employer. There is some heated verbal exchange, and the contractor takes the moral stand that if the labourers don't trust her they should ask the employer themselves. Labourers may then go to the employer to confirm but are actually helpless because the work has already been done so they might as well take the money offered. Contract work is generally undertaken outside own village and as such it is rare that female labourers would actually confront the employer and various taboos restrict female mobility and interaction with outsiders.

As pointed out by the Sapatganj Dusadh female contractor, labourers fight and then cool down. Labourers enter into heated verbal exchanges but do not lodge formal reports against each other. They fight and then unite. In the village, people need each other (Fieldwork Notes, December 2009). Labourers are aware that an open confrontation would be debilitating in the long term as these contractors are an important source of work. Labourers may rebel by joining the party of another group. However, in view of economic vulnerability and food insecurity, they may go back to working for the same contractor and employer. The Sapatganj Dhobi female contractor agreed with the Dusadh contractor that labourers get angry with her when she does not recruit them. She tries to rationalise with them that she can recruit only as many as are required by the job. If she were to take them all, then would they not have to return empty-handed? If one contractor bags more jobs than others or does not consult the others at times, the latter are jealous and get angry with that contractor (Fieldwork Notes, November 2009).

Regarding wages, there are two further sources of strained relations between labourers in both villages. That there is always a section of labourers willing to work for low wages when another section of labourers may be insisting on increased wages is a cause of friction and fragmentation among female labour. Delayed wage payment is another cause of intra-labour tension, particularly where there is a contractor or 'point-woman' involved. It has happened that if the employer has not paid till after a few days of work completion or has paid less than what was agreed upon, the labourers confronted the contractor. A heated verbal exchange follows, abuses are traded, and the contractor is forced to pay from her pocket or in turn confront the employer.

Exchange labour relations (referred to as *adla badli* or *janvahi*) is another area of conflict (or cooperation) among women belonging to the classes of labour. Exchange relations are organised along the lines of caste-class, neighbourhood and social relations. Exchange relations exist only in female tasks of sowing, weeding or *katni* and takes place among Dalits owning some land with available family labour. It is often the case that fights break out over whose work should be done first, one not turning up in return, sending children instead of capable and efficient adults or procrastinating. In retaliation, if the labourer on the receiving end is asked to recruit labour in future, she will not recruit that labourer.

In Sapatganj, local Dalit labour against Dalit labour from outside adds another dimension to intra-labour relations. Different terms and conditions of work and difference in the treatment meted out to them lead to fractious relations between them and foreclose any grounds of cooperation. Local employers resort to calling labourers from neighbouring villages when the local labourer insists on a wage hike. They are more likely to be given the work on contract basis and even if given on daily wages, it will be higher than the local rate and they will be offered food and old clothes. In Sapatganj, there have been instances when the Rajput family has hired Mosahar labour from a neighbouring village. Mosahars are known in the region for their hard labour, activism and are generally able to command and get a better wage rate and contract-based work. Sapatganj labourers acknowledged that it is generally with them that the season's wage rates open. Nonetheless, when Mosahars come to Sapatganj, confrontational exchanges between the two are common.[40]

Lack of a common ground among regional labour is an important factor why local labour cannot afford a consistent confrontational stand against the local *badkas*. Cheap labour is always accessible from neighbouring areas in the case of female labour as it does not migrate. Terms and conditions of work are always more favourable to incoming labour who would face similar problems in their village. Working outside their village is a very good source of income and therefore the possibility of outside labourers ever aligning with local labourers is very low. As such, a non-confrontational approach is the only recourse to local labour to wrest benefits from local *badkas* without losing out on 'privileges' associated with such patronage.

According to a male member of the Sapatganj Rajput family, a big drawback of local labourers is that they are unorganised. Because labourers are satisfied with their material conditions, they will never progress, be mired in petty issues and want instant results. As was put by him:

> *Villagers want instant results. They do not work hard. He once tried to organise villagers on the issue of MGNREGA, particularly women. But women would ask him if they would also have to go to work on roads and if they worked for so many days, would they get this much money? Lack of organisation is the most negative point. There are four to five self-help organisations in the village, but these are again completely ineffective. People have taken loans from banks to start SHGs, but mostly they have appropriated the funds. Benefits have not percolated to the public. Loans are given for livestock rearing also, but there is no willingness to take initiative.*
>
> (Fieldwork Notes, November 2009)

Even if SHGs or some other source extended loans to people, it is doubtful if it would be used for intended purposes. For instance, in Indira Awaas Yojna, beneficiaries get ₹25,000. Out of this, ₹7,000–₹8,000 would be the *pradhan*'s share. Then the beneficiary would probably buy a goat or some animal. In the leftover money, the beneficiary will buy some bricks for house construction. In this village, a few have got Indira Awaas Yojna. Obviously, it has not been utilised for house construction as can be observed from the huts. People say that

> *'hum to aise rahe hi rahe hai, humko kya? Jisko rahna hoga voh banvaye ga' i.e. people think that they are anyway living like this, so why should they bother? Those desirous can build concrete houses. Officials have ideas about what can be done, but they do not want to make an effort. He himself wants to start a SHG of women that teaches them stitching and embroidery.*
>
> (Fieldwork Notes, November 2009)

Despite the aforementioned issues, intra-labour relations are an important social and support network. In times of personal crises or against a common enemy (*badkas*), female labourers show solidarity, albeit a temporary one. One instance is that of labour coming together for wage negotiations. In another case, the young son of a Dusadh (Sapatganj) was seriously injured by a pig and villagers collected *chanda*, that is donations to help the family meet medical expenses. Where a labouring household is unable to meet expenses such as those related to weddings, their relatives and friends help out in any small way they can, for example, putting them in touch with possible sources of credit or even borrowing on their behalf. Successful organisation of these occasions in a manner befitting their status and fulfilling the societal expectations is a matter of the community's respect. Similarly, another example is where several women get together to hold religious ceremonies.

Dokhgadh findings are same as for Sapatganj and Baaspur on various issues: everyday issues; work-related issues such as who has done how much work and unequal wage distribution between lead labourers and other labourers of the team; on the fragmentation of labourers along lines of caste, locality, kinship and wider socio-economic relations; and exchange labour issues. There are two areas of differences between Dokhgadh and the other two villages on this theme. The first is to do with the labour solidarity among the Mosahars which is facilitated by a high degree of socio-economic homogeneity among them and the second pertains to the relation between them and other labourers.

The first aspect is evident in the occupational profile of Mosahars. It has been mentioned earlier in the chapter how this uniformity within the village favours Mosahars' bargaining position. It was observed in other villages and hamlets in this village that labouring households face different socio-economic circumstances, varying land position and are beset with petty issues along neighbourhood and caste lines. Relative labour solidarity on issues like wage negotiation is temporary and undercut by independent economic circumstances of labouring households and personal ties. The total absence of *badkas* and other socio-economic grounds of differentiation bind Mosahar households together and give it a stronger leverage vis-à-vis employers.

On the other hand, the success of Mosahars in accessing public resources and setting higher wage rates have been a cause of jealousy and friction with other labourers who have not managed to secure these. Even the Mosahars of the last hamlet claimed to have been sidelined by the Mosahars of the bigger hamlet in their struggles, though the latter denied this. My field findings and observations show that though the latter are the main protagonists, the former have not been as marginalised as they claim and have also benefitted from these struggles. Chamar labourers (mainly women) berate the Mosahars for having no sense of shame and modesty, no 'vichar' (consideration, judgement). They are different from Chamar labourers. Even if Chamars go to panchayat, they sit separately and are scared to speak up for fear of being scolded. They have a sense of modesty, a consciousness of their *chutka* status and their behaviour towards *badkas* is appropriately circumspect. The Mosahar angle will become clearer in the next chapter.

Notes

1 To quote her, '*ghoos ka jamana hai*'.

2 NREGA provides for unemployment benefit where it is unable to provide employment on demand. Men do approach the *pradhan* for job cards and work. However, it is unlikely that villagers are aware that NREGA is a demand-driven

programme. They approach the *pradhan* more in the hope that he will provide them with work when any such project is introduced. There have been NREGA projects around the villages. A very limited number of people were aware of the unemployment allowance clause called *baithaki* (from the word sitting) locally and in fact, a criticism of NREGA has been its non-payment. As such, it is doubtful whether, the reference here is to wages received for work done or unemployment benefit received, particularly since this was not systematically investigated because NREGA was not the focus of study here. Rather, what was stated was taken at face value. Discrepancy between number of workdays and wages received was clearly borne out by fieldwork: for one to receive ₹6,000, one would have worked for sixty days, however, no villager in Sapatganj said they had worked for more than ten to fifteen days under the scheme. In Baaspur, the discrepancy was evident in the few job cards which were with the labourers and could be accessed. These cards had been returned to them after the wages had been collected (see Dreze and Khera, 2009; Dreze in Mahaprashasta, 2009).

3 To quote her, '*usko daud-dhoop karni padti hai, tel-paani kharch hota hai, paisa do to awaas dilayenge*'.

4 Several respondents mentioned how the growing trend of consumerism puts an added pressure to provide better and more things – motorbikes instead of cycles, mobile phones, television and CD players and more than anything else the burden of providing dowry for daughters and making elaborate ceremonial arrangements. To finance this, often the relatives and friends of the concerned individual also borrow on their behalf as it is a matter of honour and pride of the community/hamlet/village.

5 To quote her, '*aisa deh le kar yeh kaam karte. . . . bahar jaakar nahi kamate*' (Fieldwork Notes, April 2010).

6 As put by her, '*apna ghar ka kaam mein, kheti ke kaam mein pareshani hoti hain, Koi kodne ko, khaddar cheetne ko, beej cheetne ko nahi*' (Fieldwork Notes, November 2009).

7 '*Dehaat, dehaat hai aur shahar, shahar hain*', said the labourer.

8 This is seen in female labourers' common refrain: '*shikayat laagi ki aadmi ke peeche ghoom-ghoom kar kaam kari*'.

9 Alcohol drinking is particularly perceived as an economic and social menace by local women. Men spend a significant portion of their earnings on alcohol and are also known to get abusive when drunk.

10 To quote her, '*Town hota to na*' (Fieldwork Notes, November 2009).

11 Jassal's (2012) work mentions the custom of *lehana* under which a labourer could claim as much harvested grain as he could carry with both hands. Such a custom was not noted in my field villages. What is important to note here is that gender wage gap is seen across cash and in-kind wages, and this is justified with similar explanations. For example, under the *lehana* custom, able-bodied male labourers could carry more grain than women labourers. This alludes to the difference in physical strength which is taken as natural.

12 Sugarcane harvesting is mostly done on *geda* basis. Labourers are hired when the quality of sugarcane is poor (basically if leaves have dried; labourers have no use of these and therefore do not cut such sugarcane on *geda* basis) or where sugarcane cultivation is extensive, as in the case of petty capitalists. In the latter case also, a significant portion is harvested on *geda* basis.

13 To quote her,

> sohni pandrah rupaye hain kyunki baith kar karte hain; rupani mein pehle beej ukhadte hain, phir raupte hain, is liye bees rupiye hain; kudari paani peekar din bhar chalate hain, dono haat phool jaate hain, dahi dard karat hain, to saat rupiye nahi maange ge?

14 As put by her, '*hum mard hai, kudari chalate hai, aurat kam mehnat ka kaam karti hai*'.

15 '*Unity bana li hai ki kam denge to uska kaam nahi karenge*'.

16 '*Do din ghar par bethenge, phir uske paas kaam par chale jaayenge, kahi aur kaam milega to vha chale jaayenge. Aur dehat, gaon mein kya karenge?*'

17 '*Jab yaha rehna hai, to kya ghamand, badka babu khisyaat jaat hai, phir dwar par aate hain thode din baad*'.

18 This is so according to the interviewed female labourers, but it seems unlikely where the main employers in the same village are often at loggerheads.

19 To quote her, '*Khethaar* (landowner) *se kehta hain itna paisa mili to hamar jana jaayega, varna jaakar kahi aur se dhood le*'.

20 '*A babu, humko de na utna, to tumhar kamo kar di*'.

21 '*Chutka hi jaanta hai dusre chutka ke pareshani*'.

22 '*Badka se kabhi koi kaam fasa, koi jarorat padi, emergency hui, to badka madad karega, chhut kya karega? Koi sadhan ho to na, uske khet mein to majoori karo aur bas apne ghar chali aayi*'.

23 An elderly Ahir woman distinguished this from recruitment a few decades earlier. Then Bhumihars would seldom come to labourers' door, rather recruitment was routed through their servants who were also responsible for supervision.

24 It was claimed by some labourers and the Dusadh contractor that there is a third contractor, a Gupta woman as well. However, this was denied by the said woman. During my stay in the village, I did not see her in operation as in the case of the other two contractors. Also, the Dusadh and Dhobi contractors figured most prominently in labour interviews. The Dhobi contractor's daughter also worked as a contractor at times (she and her mother operated as one unit).

25 The lead labourers in Baaspur and the two contractors in Sapatganj are middle aged.

26 Since she and her sister did not have any brothers, they had inherited land from their parents.

27 To quote her, '*dusre ke ghar mein gobar pothne mein, chauka bartan karne mein shikayat hogi, laaj aat*'.

28 '*Unka vyavhar hai*'.

29 '*Bandhako ko khilaate-khilaate kitno ka khet apne naam kar liya*'.

30 However, it should be noted that in informal sources of credit primarily *badkas* are preferred. Credit is a means of survival primarily, mostly directed towards meeting living expenses, school fees, marriages, agricultural investment, etc. Formal sources like banks are not approached because of lack of any asset which can be offered as collateral. Given the lack of a secure source of income, there is a real possibility of defaulting on monthly instalments leading to an accrual of interest and a real threat of losing the only possible form of collateral, that is, land. In informal borrowing, land may or may not be mortgaged since collateral is not necessary for access to credit. Where it has been mortgaged, the debtor is not charged interest. Instead, he loses the right to cultivate the land till such time that the debt is repaid. So there is a possibility of temporary dispossession rather than one losing land to bank permanently. Also, unlike in banks, there is a notion of the debt being transferred on to the next generation so there is at least a far-fetched possibility that ultimately the land will revert back to the indebted family. There is no limit on the repayment period and no pressure for monthly instalments where the existence is already hand-to-mouth. In most cases, overhead costs (which includes bribe and misappropriation of relief money given by government under various schemes) and the hassle of paperwork are avoided through informal borrowing.

31 Of relevance here is an example from Jassal (2012). Though she has used this example to emphasise on the clout of a particular landlord's house, I use this

story as exemplifying labour control and one way of deciding wages. This landlord would sit under an umbrella at one end of his field for the entire day while labourers worked. His presence can be construed as direct supervision of labourers. At the end of the workday, he would measure with a wooden stick the distance covered by each labourer while weeding, sowing, etc. On this measurement, wage would be decided. So, while women could sing and talk occasionally while working but can do nothing that interrupts their work and would adversely affect their wages.

32 '*Jana dheere-dheere karte hain, baatein karat hain, kahte hain ki dheere-dheere karo, bihane aayi kaam kare*'.

33 '*aajkal ke zamane mein kaun sahmati?*'

34 '*Hamara bhala nahi hoga, to tumhara bhala bhi nahi hoga*'.

35 '*Chotti-chotti baat par tension, ladai, muh phula lete hain, to kha se sahanmati hogi?*'

36 To quote one Ansari woman, '*voh apne ghar ka, hum apne ghar ka, sab bigadne pe hi tule rahte hain*'.

37 '*Gaon mein yeh netagiri hoti hain ki kisi ke kehne pe koi bhi kisi ko fasa deta hain paise ke liye*'.

38 '*theek se nahi nuchenge, laat se daba denge, nauchenge nahi, kaam chod kar ghar bhaag jaayenge time par*'.

39 This literally refers to some tea and snacks, but what is implied by this is that this little extra given as advance to the contractor is to get her on the good side of the employer so that she keeps a tight control on labour, that the work is done well and finished on time.

40 Though this is denied by the Mosahars.

5 Negotiating for Every Penny

Labour Resistance and Struggle

This chapter deals with the various ways in which labourers attempt to improve their positions vis-a-vis their employers or capitalists. I argue that labour struggles mostly take the form of 'weapons of the weak' (Scott, 1985, 1986) and 'negotiations' (Jeffery and Jeffery, 1996) within existing power structures. They can occur within unfree labour relations and patron–client relations. The outcomes of these labour struggles are important to the extent that female labourers have managed to extract limited economic gains and that these struggles symbolise their politicisation and assertion. However, it is also possible that such attempts may either not have the desired outcomes or may lead to a backlash, the most common example being that of withdrawal of patronage or denying employment to a particular Dalit labouring household.

This chapter begins by providing readers with a brief on how the regional political context has changed in UP since the 1990s and how these shifts impact the conditions of Dalits. I then move on to describe evidence from my field. This part of the discussion is limited since there is not as much empirical evidence to present as in the previous chapters. One reason is that women are still largely restricted to the realm of the private; their movement into the public domain as labourers does not translate into 'political' as owners and decision-makers in matters of property or marriage or as participants in political affairs such as *panchayats*. This, however, does not mean that they are not politically aware or do not mobilise on 'political' issues. As I show later, female labourers from the Dalit classes of labour category have on occasions challenged their oppressors and exploiters, the *badkas*. This is evident in their understanding of general village politics and struggles to influence their position as labourers.

Regional Political Context

Identity politics is a defining feature of electoral competition in India and the state of UP is the prime playing field. Since, the 1990s, the state has been ruled by different political parties and alliances. Nonetheless, the material position of Dalits remains largely unchanged. The years of

DOI: 10.4324/9780429321894-5

Mayawati-led BSP's rule were an attempt to unite the Dalits, sections of backward castes and Muslims into a cohesive vote bank. One should note however that Dalits are not a homogenous category. Rather, the many *jatis* have their own politics and grievances. To capture state power, Mayawati, at one point of time (Pai, 2007) entered into alliance with BJP – the party of upper caste Hindus or the oppressors of Dalit labourers. As one of my respondents explained, to rule *chutkas* need to work with *badkas*. At the level of the village, the BSP periods of rule did provide Dalits with a sense of security and dignity. But ultimately, the endemic corruption, development failures, the shift from *bahujan* to *sarvjan*[1] and the refusal to disturb the status quo, which made the agitational style of Dalit politics as seen in Bhim Army[2] more attractive, spelled the doom for BSP. In fact, according to an early 2020 newspaper report, thousand BSP workers from just one eastern UP district joined SP (Vij, 2020). This was attributed to the image of SP's main campaign face Akhilesh Yadav[3] as young, clean, focussed on development issues. Why then did SP face such a dismal failure in the state elections in 2017 and then again in the 2019 national elections which it fought as an alliance partner of the multi-caste BSP–SP–RLD *Mahagathbandhan*?[4] According to Sudha Pai (2019), SP failed over the years to bring all OBCs together and continued to be seen as a party of Yadavs. This at a time when education and urbanisation created greater class differences within caste groups. According to Pai (2019), in UP caste still matters, but it is the failure of parties like BSP and SP to tap into precisely this 'upwardly mobile aspirational class' that played into the hands of Narendra Modi-led BJP. The BJP has built on the weaknesses of BSP and SP and this was reflected in its resounding success in the 2019 national elections – it has promised economic development (sops such as toilets, LPG cylinders, insurance schemes, higher MSPs, etc.), built a formidable caste alliance as its vote base by using its leader's caste identity to rope in the disgruntled non-Chamar, non-Yadav sections, the vicious communalisation of the political discourse by the BJP which trumped even the Mahagathbandhan and of course, the portrayal of BJP as the only force capable of protecting the country's borders.

These shifts in the political terrain are actually illustrative of a few important ground realities that were visible even during the course of my research in eastern UP. First, *jati* rather than caste is the primary medium through which people identify each other. Second, class is very relevant to politics. Class itself has to be understood as not just an economic category but how it is also shaped by identities such as gender and caste. Third, both caste and class are politically salient. At a general level, Dalits expressed support for Mayawati, but just below this surface an awareness of differences and tensions at the level of *jatis* simmered – an awareness that Chamars were favoured by Mayawati and her loyalists in distributing scholarships, MGNREGA jobs, etc. or that Mosahars were the most polluted. Even while forging production relations, *jati* is an important organising principle. At the top, whether rich or poor, the upper castes opt for the BJP which is seen as the saviour of their caste and religion. Amongst the OBCs, there is clearly a sense amongst the labourers that the better-off Ahirs corner most of the benefits, not only because *sapa* (SP) favours them when it is in power but also because the village-level power might be in the hands of Ahirs. Despite this, when I did my fieldwork, non-Ahirs also expressed support for the SP. Village-level politics even then could not be understood in terms of only caste or class. It is these simmering fissures, the *jatis* and classes within OBCs that felt neglected which were exploited by the BJP (on this see, Jaffrelot, 2014). Fourth, to understand the politics of labouring women, their gender identity and position are also important. Only then can one understand why politics of Dalit women labourers takes the form that it does or why women are hesitant to speak about certain issues even though they are politically conscious about them. Finally, all of these trends are indicative of the larger reality of growing inequalities.

How Women Labourers Relate to Politics

Caste is the most popular form of identification. A *pradhan* is identified by his caste and not party affiliation or policies. Political support is more often than not expressed along caste lines. In Sapatganj and Baaspur, Dalits, without any exception, spoke out in favour of Mayawati. In Baaspur, a male Dhobi labourer, explained voting as a caste–class exercise:

> *[H]arijans vote for the elephant (BSP), Muslims vote for the cycle (SP), Brahmins and Rajputs vote for either lotus or palm (BJP or Congress respectively).*
>
> (Field notes, September 2009)

He attributed the phenomenon of caste-based voting to the decline of the grand old umbrella party of Congress and post-Indira Gandhi phase when identity politics came to dominate the Indian political stage.[5]

However, as was the case in labour relations (and wider social relations), caste as a medium of identification also encompasses a class consciousness. In the field villages, the upper caste-classes are the dominant political powers: they either occupy positions of authority such as that of *pradhan* or they are the actual power behind proxy figures. Female labourers believe that even if one of their own caste was to be in a position of power and authority, it would bring no relief to them because this person would act under the influence of upper caste-class. The caste-class overlap is evident in how labourers refer to themselves. Labourers see that it is them, the Dalits, who are agricultural labourers, who live in huts, who are poor and who are not *pradhans*. A common refrain among women is that no one is for the poor and that once in power, these positions are used to further self-interest and benefit their '*khaas aadmi*'[6] (favourites, loyalists).

Women in general do not participate in *panchayat* meetings (though some admitted to eavesdropping) and male labourers also go only when called upon specifically. Lack of confidence and knowledge underline female labour's exclusion from or low participation in formal political institutions and operations. Many expressed problems in articulating and expressing themselves in an acceptable manner. Presence of women in a predominantly male congregation where issues seen as coming under purview of the male domain/family head are discussed as a transgression of established roles and the boundaries of which women also don't question. However, in the absence of the male head of the household, it is acceptable for the woman to attend the *panchayat* but only if the matter to be taken up that day directly involves that household and only if she has been asked to attend the day's proceedings. Also, these meetings more often than not turn volatile, with abuses and accusations liberally thrown around and as such classes of labour generally tend to avoid them.

There was one example of a woman being a mainstream participant in the *panchayat* proceedings. This was the Dusadh female labour contractor from Sapatganj. Her involvement was 'natural' as she represented the SC woman quota in the *panchayat*. She explained her role as follows: she attends all *panchayat* meetings. Though she does not benefit from being a *panchayat* member because the *pradhan* does not pay her anything, her purpose in attending these meetings is to support the *pradhan*. Discussions over budget take place there, various decisions are made such as whether a gate should be built here or a house, to act as a witness along with four or five other people, etc. She puts her thumb impression on paper and sometimes her son signs for her. She was chosen as a member because she can articulate and speak up, she can answer back and does not hide. She does not get any money from the *pradhan*. She does this job because the *pradhan* is from own village and she feels that she should support and help him whenever he needs it because so would he in times of need (Fieldwork Notes, December 2009).

Female labourers' understanding and critique of politics is based not on any systematic study of party policies or ideology but is expressed in pragmatic and practical terms, drawing on their everyday experiences. Women are not familiar with the BSP, but they recognise its leader, Mayawati, from various posters and propaganda in the villages. Their understanding of the government machinery is restricted to the village, block and zilla or district. Beyond this, they do not distinguish between the levels of government. Schemes like mid-day meals in schools, scholarships to Dalit students and MGNREGA are attributed to Mayawati's government. In Baaspur, an Ansari woman pointed out that at election time, a man from another block comes to the village for propaganda purposes. He is from Mayawati's party and is paid ₹100 per day. The *pradhan* is supplied with alcohol for distribution among his main people as a way of vote lobbying. The lack of MGNREGA's benefits actually reaching the villagers is attributed to corrupt middlemen like their *pradhan*. A common refrain among labourers is '*sarkar mein kami nahi, beech ke aadmi, pradhan ki kami*', meaning the problem is not with the government but with middlemen like *pradhan*.

The overlapping caste and class consciousness is reinforced from what labourers observe in village-level political proceedings. In Baaspur, a Chamar was the *pradhan* in the recent past. The villagers mocked him for his inability to discharge office functions and duties without the prior knowledge and consent of village *badka*s. This *chutka pradhan* had promised allocation of *abaadi* land, but after a behind-the-doors discussion with the *badka*s of the village and several middle-level officials, a primary school came up on the proposed land. Several female labourers, from both villages, astutely remarked that even Mayawati is forced by political compulsions and calculations of running a government to accommodate the *badka* combine.[7] Female labourers come across as very well informed of the political themes of the moment, for instance, on the statues installed by Mayawati in Lucknow or the speculations surrounding the relationship between Mayawati and the BSP founder Kanshi Ram. Many female labourers criticised Mayawati for inflation and increasing the procurement price of sugarcane. They explained that benefits of the latter accrue to the *badka*s who cultivate sugarcane substantially since they have more land and eventually this increase in the procurement price would consequently raise the price of sugar.

One of the biggest achievements of Mayawati's rule for *chutkas*/labourers, according to women, has been the direct and easy access to police in recent years. Female labourers pointed out that their reports are duly noted and immediate action taken. They don't know the details of the SC/ST Act[8](referred to as *harijan* locally) but are aware of its potential or practical implications. This extends to them a feeling of security, a protective measure deployed against upper caste atrocities and abuse. A female Dhobi labourer (Baaspur) explained that the politics of *badka*s centre on keeping the *chutkas* subjected. They do not like the *chutkas* to get food, clothes, be educated or get better employment, so that *chutkas* do the work of *badka*s. The *chutkas* live in fear of *badka*s because their children may cut sugarcane from *badka*s' fields, or their livestock may wander into their fields. But the Mayawati government has put *badka*s on the back foot. If they say anything, they can be blamed under the SC/ST Atrocities Act (Fieldwork Notes, May 2010). The control of police and crime data have since long been important political tools in UP. For example, whether BSP or SP, the ruling party recruits 'their' personnel to staff police stations and crimes against Dalits' rise during periods of BSP rule (Sethi, 2016).

An Ansari woman emphasised that the Mayawati government had not benefitted her community. She gave the following example: the Mayawati government has benefitted the *harijans* a lot. At one time, from the Chamar hamlet, two carloads of people went to Deoria, where they stayed in a hotel free of cost, they were given blankets and saris. Both, men and women had gone. Dhobis and Kamkars also do not fear the *badka*s and they even abuse *badka*s just as the latter abuse them (Fieldwork Notes, April 2010). There are two assertions implicit here. One is that only Dalits have benefitted under Mayawati and not other castes. This sentiment was reverberated by *badka*s as well. The second is manifest in terms of the differences between different caste (or religion) labourers. Suffice it to say here that only certain sections of labourers have managed to access corridors of power in their successful struggles for resources and benefits. Antagonisms and jealousy between these labourers and the rest of the labourers are common and prevent intra- and supra-village labour solidarity.

Since my work focussed on Dalit women labourers, their narratives here reflect more on the 'public' aspects of politics. However, politics is everywhere. For example, Jassal's (2012) research on folk songs of women in Jaunpur is quite revealing on the politics in the domain of family. For example, one of the folk songs reveal the relief of the father *aka,* the patriarch at his daughter's wedding, presumably because after her marriage the daughter will not stake claim in the patrilineal property. Another folk song throws light on how women, by embarrassing young men and thereby forcing them to vacate the room, seek to carve out a comfort zone for themselves in the house away from the male gaze. In line with my findings, these examples also show how women deal with patriarchy and unequal relations without subverting the established structures. Jassal (2019) has documented other such folk songs that reflect on power relations within the home and family. An interesting point made by her is how these songs may actually end up reinforcing prescribed caste and gender roles by cautioning women about the consequences for breaking acceptable code of behaviour. Jassal rightly points out that through songs women find it easier to express themselves on issues they would otherwise hesitate to speak on. My own fieldwork shows how certain subjects like property and politics are seen as male domains and women felt that they cannot speak on these topics because of their lack of knowledge and, confidence – this discourse was internalised even though this might not be the case in reality.

Labour Struggles

Overall, the structural position of labourers remains unchanged. Dalits clearly identified themselves as *harijans* and not with their specific caste. They share a deep sense of being poor, isolated and alone, of being unworthy and inferior which has been internalised and only symbolically shunned. For instance, girls did not like to be photographed while cutting grass, tending to livestock and particularly when touching cow dung. So they would cover their faces with scarves. Educated young men, when asked if they took animals for grazing, expressed offence. Some insisted on their names being appropriately prefixed with 'Shri' (Mr) or 'Shrimati' (Mrs). Education has certainly given the younger generation a sense of respect but has not necessarily led to significant improvement in their economic situation. But the labourers are aware of the ground reality and their prospects for improvement. Respondents often remarked that without land or education, they are unlikely to make any progress.[9] As put by a Koeiri male labourer,

> *[I]f a labourer earns fifty rupees a day, then would he buy food or send his children to school? What will we do if not wage labour, how will we survive?*[10]

Labourers hesitate to assert any demand for fear of being denied. The fact that they are lower castes is itself something to be ashamed of. In addition, a refusal is seen as an insult to their self-respect and an embarrassment. There is also an apprehension that *badka*s may do something untoward. Labourers do not like to ask employers for wages repeatedly. A Kharwar woman from Baaspur cited apprehension of what the *badka* may say on being asked for wages, as a reason for not asking wages. This was widely agreed upon amongst female labourers.[11] A female Dhobi labourer, also from Baaspur, retorted that Bhumihars should think that labourers have worked hard and should be paid. But he does not give of his own will, then to ask is to demean oneself.[12]

Another reason for the lack of labour action is overlapping socio-economic ties of dependency, as explained previously. In Baaspur, two Ansari women stressed that the number of labourers does not make any difference. The whole area is under the influence and fear of the *pradhan*. If labourers' ancestors were afraid of *badka*s, then why should they not be afraid now? It would have been a different story if only from the beginning labourers had not adopted a submissive attitude.[13] A generalised fear of *badka*s is a major limitation. A woman's sense of self-respect, modesty and a certain expected way of behaving are also cited as limitations on labour action. In Baaspur, a female labourer said that when the *pradhan* campaigned for votes, he touched everyone's feet, but now one would not even spit on his hand. When her husband approached the *pradhan* for a job card, he was refused as he had not voted for the *pradhan*. But 'ladies have respect' ('*ladies ki izzat hoti hai*'). Another said that they (labourers) are genial and loving individuals but can also be opportunistic and serving when need be.[14]

However, as was flagged in the discussion on unfree labour relations, it is not that there are no labour struggles or that labourers have not successfully acted to improve their position.

It was mentioned earlier that unfree labour relations do not preclude the possibility of defiance and insolence on the part of labour towards their oppressors. Here, I cite examples from Sapatganj and Baaspur to support this.

In Sapatganj, a Dhobi female labour narrated:

> *Today also Badka Babu has a bandhak. An old man (over sixty years old) works for him . . . He earns about five hundred rupees a month. He is also given his meals by them. When he goes home, he is given some*

token amount or even grains . . . . the old man had once got very angry that he was not given flour or new shoes and he left work and went home for about six months. Then badka babu's younger brother went to his place to placate and cajole him into coming back to work. He was given new shoes and was asked to have his meals at their house.

(Fieldwork Notes, November 2009)

A Dusadh female labourer stated that

[I]f she has fought with an employer, she does not work for him as long as she is angry. But since she lives in the village, she is helpess and obligated to work for them (gaon mein rahi to laachar hoi to jaayeke padi).

(Fieldwork Notes, November 2009)

In Baaspur, some Ansari families exemplify how stable and successful migration can decrease dependency of female members of these households on wage labour. In these cases, everyday humiliating experiences of being inferior may be limited, but a wider sense of duress and threat exists. But these do not preclude the possibility of defiance on the part of labour. This is usually expressed in subtle forms like withdrawal from such work or procrastination. One Ansari woman, living in close proximity of the *pradhan*'s house and whose husband migrated to Saudi Arabia about six years ago, explained the situation as follows:

He (husband) is involved in various types of casual work including construction, painting, flooring etc. Presently he owns a small tailoring shop which he operates at night and during the day he works in a cloth store. He is able to send home between ten thousand and fifteen thousand rupees once every two to three months . . . . Till about two years ago, she undertook agricultural wage labour . . . for the Pradhan only. He is the major employer in the village and owns so much land that labourers from other villages come to work on his fields . . . The other Bhumihars live in other parts of the village and hire labour from there . . . the pradhan thinks that they (the respondent and her family) have so much money, but do not think of the expenses involved. If she goes to his house to ask for few chillies, she is told to purchase it from the market . . . So now she purchases everything from the market, even if it has to be on credit.

(Fieldwork Notes, April 2010)

Previously, she did unpaid labour within the pradhan's house, but not any longer. Because of her caste (read religion), she did not undertake work such as washing utensils or cooking . . . She was called for tasks like scooping. On religious functions like Ramnavmi, she would be asked to make a mud stove and on these rare occasions, she is allowed

> *to touch few utensils. . . 'Pradhan tang karte hain' i.e. the pradhan harasses. He controls everything. The pradhan's fields border hers and he does not allow the latter to take her goats there for grazing. A dirt road leads to the fields but this has been taken over by the pradhan who cultivates sugarcane on it. The pradhan is known to have threatened them with cutting off their access to their fields. She asserts that one cannot be silent* (passive) *all the time. She now takes her goats alongside the road for grazing where neither chutkas nor badkas can complain, though those whose field borders the road may do so. She says that she hesitates and even feels shy to sit alongside them because they are badkas. If she is called upon for some work by the pradhan's house, she does not outright decline but forwards excuses such as her keeping unwell. They have to 'respect' the pradhan because they have to cross his fields to reach theirs.*
>
> (Fieldwork Notes, April 2010)

This story indicates that extra-economic coercion and a fear of the consequences of threats and sanctions are a major root cause that perpetuates dependency on petty capitalists, even in situation of relative economic prosperity. Even outside of immediate labour relations, their movement and actions are not free but designed to evade *badka*s' domination rather than challenging it. This also limits their bargaining scope in terms of wage relations vis-à-vis local *badka*s. So, for Ansaris, it has been more a case of coexistence fraught with occasional petty conflicts and exchange of taunts.

The scope of bargaining and resistance is greater in the case of households not located in close proximity of dominant *badka*s. This was seen earlier in the case of Sapatganj Rajput family and the Dusadh family. In Baaspur, labouring households from other hamlets who are not dependent on the *pradhan* for access to their fields reflect greater autonomy and agency in staking their rights in all domains. This does not mean open hostility or confrontation, rather it is a constant attempt to have their say and win some leeway on issues such as wages. The crucial difference is that unlike in the earlier case, there is no constant and real threat to the very means of their livelihood and subsistence. There are a greater number of wage labourers in other hamlets. They also undertake wage labour in surrounding villages which means that they are not solely dependent on availability of local opportunities. When they get called upon for domestic labour (like scooping, tending to the livestock, sweeping, etc.) by the *badka*s, they get some grain or ₹15–₹20 for a day's work, unlike in the earlier case where such work was not remunerated.

Forms of labour resistance are largely modelled as 'weapons of the weak'. Scattered and isolated incidents/actions expressing resistance do not challenge notions of deference or the system but nevertheless give labour some limited leverage which they use to wrest important concessions. Through persistent negotiations, demands and haggling, female labour is able to win certain concessions in terms of work as explained previously.

One specific example is from Sapatganj. The Kharwar woman who washed dishes in the Rajput household did not come to work for several weeks, despite a member of the family personally calling on her at her house. This was her way of resistance or expressing discontent with low and delayed wages, treatment meted out to her, that is not been given clothes, tea, being served dinner late or given leftovers. Some villagers speculated that it was because her son was back in the village, and he did not like his mother working in their house. There could be some truth in this.

Generally, the refusal to work if the wage offered is much below the going rate or if wage hike demands are not agreed to is also a type of resistance. Whether or not labourers take this route depends upon their specific economic position at that point of time. Doing shoddy work, abandoning work in the middle, not turning up for work until the employers have asked them twice or thrice are other examples. In the absence of *badka*s, they are very assertive, vociferously critical and even abusive and threatening. But in actual practice this is very rare. Nonetheless, *chutkas* see the power to raise their heads, look in the eye and speak up to *badka*s, to negotiate and argue with them as important tools of their assertion and improvement in their position.

A Dusadh labourer (Sapatganj) attributed these changes to Mayawati's *raj* and contrasted this 'empowerment' with previous decades when labourers lived in fear of Bhumihars:

> *Labourers would hide in their huts whenever they saw a Bhumihar coming towards them. They could not go up to the doors of Bhumihars houses, could not sit in front of them, labourers would lower their head in shame and listen to Bhumihars. They could not refuse doing work and could even be physically threatened. Even rich chutkas were scared of badka zamindars. Previously, labourers did not have any money or possess any sense. Today, even if Mayawati was no longer in power, a labourer would not revert back to old ways. Even if one does not have any money, one has intellect now. The ability to assert their rights provides an impression of some control and maintains labour's sense of dignity. Labourers now produce enough to eat.*
>
> (Fieldwork Notes, December 2009)

One way of bypassing the structures of oppression in the village like the *pradhan* is to directly approach the block administration for relief. However, here the role of middlemen is not eliminated. For example, in Baaspur, one respondent had approached the district administration for accessing old age pension with the help of the previous *pradhan*. This can be attributed to the fact that people like *pradhan* are aware of whom to approach, can access them and they write applications or argue on behalf of villagers, etc.

Increased and easier access to the police and immediate and effective police action on their complaints is a powerful tool in the hands of labouring classes. It serves as a deterrent to *badka* brutalities. Labourers have been known to file police complaints (even false ones) or use the threat of doing so to counter *badka* oppression. Though as pointed out elsewhere, the action may be backed by a Bhumihar for personal reasons, and it may even be that the labourer is coerced into it due to unfree labour relations.

While labourers claim that *badka*s are now scared to get into fights with *chutkas*, this is denied by upper castes who argue that in reality labourers are still scared to approach the police by themselves and labourers ask them to mediate. This may or may not be the case depending upon the parties involved and the nature of the case. But for most part it is true that labourers feel more secure now. In several cases, labourers have even filed false reports against other villagers (upper and lower castes). There may be two reasons behind this: one, petty fights with neighbours and other villagers where reports are filed out of spite and second, Dalit labourers may be incited by the *badka*s to file cases against rival *badka*s using the pretext of wrong allocation of BPL cards, refusal to make job cards, not giving the stipulated amount under IAY, etc.

A female Ahir labourer from Sapatganj added that now even children do not hesitate in picking up fights with Bhumihars. Labourers are supported by their relatives. Labourers can fight Bhumihars in their homes.[15] In previous decades, labourers lived in terror of Bhumihars because they could not provide sufficient food for their households through farming. This labourer and another Ahir labourer elaborated that the yield would be very low in those times. There was no fertiliser other than cow dung and no irrigation source other than one canal. Now fertilisers are available in the village and there is tube well irrigation. Now, people can produce much more.

In a village close to Sapatganj, an incident of physical violence against an untouchable had resulted in all low castes uniting against the perpetrator who was a dominant landlord. Both sides verbally abused the other and threatened. Ultimately, after a few days the landlord had to apologise to the victim under collective pressure and boycott (and actually also under the very real threat of being jailed under the Prevention of SC/ST Atrocities Act). In Sapatganj, could the absence of any such violent and immediate threat be taken as a cause for the absence of collective labour action? When a woman from the village where the aforementioned incident had taken place and a female labourer from Sapatganj were asked to explain the difference, I was told that in the former, the Bhumihars are Brahmins while in Sapatganj they are Rajputs who are feared more. According to the woman from the village where the incident had taken place, an important reason for labourers' united stand was fear that if a stand was not taken now, in future the violent oppression would only increase.

In Baaspur, one Chamar household traced their family's legal struggle with the *pradhan*'s family, over some land, back to more than two decades.

Ultimately, the *pradhan* lost the case in court. However, sometime later, on the contested land, the married women of Bhumihar households constructed '*chhatts*' (tiny hut-like mud constructions which are worshipped on a religious function). This had put the Dalit household under pressure, and they were unable to farm the land. When the male head of the Dalit household had argued against it, he was beaten up. Many *harijans* had even acted as witnesses and provided evidence against the *pradhan*. However, later, the *harijans* did not pursue the matter, the statement was changed and the *pradhan* let off the hook. These *chhatt* structures have religious importance and cannot be destructed. The male head of the Dalit household was also thinking of extending the area under '*chhatt*' because this will bring him blessings. Nonetheless, according to him tensions between the two households will continue for lifetime.

Again, in Baaspur, a Dhobi female labourer, wrongly accused of cutting crop from the *pradhan*'s field, reported him to the police under the SC/ST Act. Though nothing happened to the *pradhan*, this act itself is in stark contrast to previous decades when the very name of police was equated with terror and physical violence and even the sight of men in uniform was enough to send *chutkas* into hiding. But whenever BSP is in power, their reports are lodged and action taken immediately. As such, BSP's rise to prominence has contributed to labour's empowerment. The difference is also explained with reference to the greater spread of education among the classes of labour.

A resident, of a village neighbouring Baaspur, filed a complaint against the acquisition of *banjar* (barren) land by the current *pradhan* in his wife's name (this village and Baaspur together constitute one *panchayat*). According to one respondent, the matter was quietly closed when the *pradhan* gave the Superintendent District Magistrate some money. In another instance, a team of inspectors had come to Baaspur for a surprise inspection of the MGNREGA work being undertaken. A labourer when asked how much wage he was paid said ₹80. Again, the *pradhan* had to bribe some officials. The respondents took pride in narrating such instances and though the culprit evades the law because of his financial and political clout, it does reflect the increasing propensity of labour to challenge the dominance of and discrimination by *badka*s. At the same time, such actions do have repercussions for labouring classes: the labour who had mentioned a lower wage rate (previous example) was thereafter not called for work by the *pradhan* under the MGNREGA project or in his personal capacity. However, the labourer was not aware that the query had come from an inspector and therefore, it was possible that he would not have given the actual rate if he had known so and there have been precedents to this fact as well. On the positive side, the *pradhan* henceforth started giving the stipulated wage but at the same time continued making money on the side by making false entries in the job cards.

These modes of resistance are shaped and conditioned by the specific socio-cultural and economic positioning of female labourers. Whether or not they lead to desired results, female labour is not a muted subject. But unlike, male labour it cannot afford overt methods of labour struggles or even sit out for longer periods of time as ultimately it has to reconcile given the limited work options it has as compared to male labour. Nonetheless, their importance cannot be discounted. Being aware of their dependency on capital, female labourers avoid a confrontational approach and does not seek structural change or equality. Rather, they seek to work around it and win concessions.

On political expression, there are no different findings from Dokhgadh. Labouring households' understanding and practice of politics are framed by caste, locality and everyday events and often follow lines of patron–client relations. This is not different from what was seen in Sapatganj and Baaspur. For example, like Baaspur, female labourers in Dokhgadh drew a parallel between the Mayawati–Brahmin coalition and the Chamar–de facto *pradhan* relationship. Or for example, the parallel between how Mayawati's government came to power on the platform of Dalit votes, but benefits have accrued to *badka*s more and how *badka*s have cornered government measures like loan write-offs or extension of subsidised credit. Yet another example is their belief that though government is astute because it reserves the *pradhan*'s seat for *chutkas*, at times for women, in reality, the poor cannot become *pradhan* because they do not have the money to contest elections. There are other such similarities across villages, for instance, in some cases, women admitted attending (sitting apart from the main group) or eavesdropping *panchayat* meetings, but they do not participate because of the way the role of women is conceived and for fear of repercussions and public humiliation. Some female labourers noted that when government officials participate in the *panchayat*, labourers are not allowed to participate.

Female labour struggles, modelled on the basis of weapons of the weak, also do not show any variation from what was described in the case of Sapatganj and Baaspur. Like in Baaspur, there are scattered, isolated incidents of labourers taking complaints to block or district administration. For instance, a group of Chamar labourers had approached the district magistrate to complain about their ration provisions and since then these households get a regular supply of ration. However, the initiative was taken by someone from outside the hamlet.

Here, I will focus on labour struggles of the Mosahars, men and women. It should be noted that where labour relations are concerned, Mosahar women show similar attempts (weapons of the weak and negotiations) at improving their position. Nonetheless, their struggles outside of immediate labour relations do have consequences for their employment relations, as indicated elsewhere in this book.

The extreme poverty and abject living conditions of Mosahars have been mentioned earlier. Their plight came to light with the death of a Mosahar man (from the larger Mosahar hamlet, the last hamlet in the list) in front of a police station. He was begging there, in a desperate attempt to save his family from starvation. Shortly before the death of this Mosahar, a local political activist had visited the hamlet and promised help to the Mosahars. But the incident happened before he could address the issue.

The death of the Mosahar immediately focussed media and political spotlight on this hamlet. His wife was given compensation. All Mosahar households (including the ones in the smaller hamlet) now possess red BPL cards. They even have their job cards with them and though there are a few entries, they are correct, and correct dues have been paid. The administration has constructed public toilets in the hamlet. Other labourers cribbed that whenever any public authority visited, they are taken to the Mosahar hamlet to show 'development efforts'. The administration held more checks, new schemes are advertised in the Mosahar hamlet first, and good quality ration is timely distributed in stipulated quantity. A disabled man has been given a loan for the purchase of a sewing machine. A *panchayat bhawan* came up in the hamlet. The widow became a popular symbol of struggle and frequently attends block- and district-level meetings over Mosahar issues. This is unlike in Sapatganj, Baaspur and possibly atypical of other villages in the region as well. But then, so is the struggle for their rights.

The political activist is well known in the region for his work among the Mosahars. He has organised them across villages over issues of job and BPL cards, payment of dues, provision of more work under MGNREGA, against corruption, etc. He has stood by the Mosahars through various crises, provides them with food, clothing, blankets, etc. whenever they have to travel to the district or capital city for holding or participating in a protest or rally. He has organised Mosahars (both men and women) to participate in rallies, hunger strikes, *dharnas*, *gheraos* at the block- and district-level administration and state level.

With the fear of starvation death, a sense of collective has emerged. While earlier, Mosahars worked on daily wages, they can now get contract work. The stipulated amount is paid to them and if payments are not made on the same day, labourers stop working for those employers. A very strong sense of dignity and capability has emerged. Other factors that appear to have enabled Mosahars' labour struggles have been previously stated.

Such activism has its limitations. The leading political activist is not from the village and visits only occasionally or contacts his 'point-man' who then spreads the passed information among the labourers. There is no person who has been trained as an indigenous leader from the Mosahar hamlet. Though I was informed by the villagers that the widow of the man whose death sparked off Mosahar resistance was an active political participant – an isolated case. She and the widowed Dusadh labour contractor from Sapatganj referred to previously in the book show that their disadvantaged position actually worked to their benefit. In other words, there was no male relative to control their movements and actions. Their respective position as a widow and daughter of the village meant that similar socio-cultural values and norms did not apply to them as in the case of daughters-in-law.

Ciotti (2009)'s work on BSP and women's political agency makes a similar point. Despite repeatedly asking, the Mosahars did not extend details of how they can afford such actions when other Dalit labouring households claim that they cannot afford to take time out for such activities. Neither did they explain how from their meagre wages they are able to afford and pool money for transport to Lucknow (as the Mosahars claimed to fund their transport to different locations), etc.

Such activism does not incorporate other Dalits and no explanation was furthered by the Mosahars on this other than remarking that those labourers want to benefit without struggling for the 'spoils'.

The other Dalit groups remarked that they are never included by the Mosahars and that they cannot argue and fight like the Mosahars who have no shame and self-respect. Other Dalit groups also allege that Mosahars go for rallies and strikes because they get free lodging, food, blankets and not because they are motivated by a political or economic cause. But the fact remains that the Mosahars are definitely more aware of their rights. The fact that the *panchayat* is wary of them means that even under the limited availability of work under MGNREGA, the Mosahars are put to work first. The differential treatment meted out to Mosahars by the local administration and the fact that they have benefitted much more than other Dalit labourers is a major source of envy among the non-Mosahar Dalit classes of labour.

Why have the labour struggles of the Mosahars gone beyond the weapons of the weak? Singh's (2013) analysis explains why Mosahar labour relations and struggles have recently become so different from those of other Dalits in the area. According to Singh (2013), the critical harbinger of change was an NGO which had worked with Mosahar women and men in two districts of eastern UP, Kushinagar and Maharajganj, for about five years. At the start, the NGO engaged extensively with Mosahar communities in the two regions and made them aware that they were losing out badly, because of their absolute exclusion by local elites, from government development programmes. With time, the self-perception of Mosahars changed quite remarkably, from seeing themelves as a despised, helpless community that was resigned to its fate, to seeing themselves as the equals of others in development projects. The NGO organised 'interface camps' between the Mosahar communities and the local bureaucracies. The exposure of the latter to the Mosahars' pitiable living conditions and media advocacy by the NGO resulted in concrete action – Mosahars were given IAY, Antyodaya cards, etc. My own research corroborates this. The NGO facilitated rallies on various issues – food for work, self-respect, etc. These efforts raised the profile of Mosahars in the public consciousness and therefore forced the local administration to prioritise Mosahars in its developmental assistance. One indicator of the Mosahar's growing confidence and political consciousness has been their gradual shift from their earlier *modus operandi* of meek cooperation with the authorities to rallies and *dharnas* to demand their rights. However, Singh (2013) acknowledges that this tactic of public assertiveness has to coexist with local structures of *badka* dominance and *chutka* subjugation. Also, she explicitly states that the NGO has never questioned local structural inequalities. The Mosahar story cannot be generalised, though this NGO's intervention indicates why today, very unexpectedly, it is the 'poorest of the poor', the Mosahars, who are more united, conscious and aggressive than any other Dalit sub-caste.

Whether Mosahars' labour struggles are an anomaly or an aberration in the region is a matter of further investigation. Can non-state actors facilitate Dalit empowerment? Given the paucity of village-level descriptive work in eastern UP, it is difficult to establish a general trend. Jassal (2012) also mentioned in her work that the work of an NGO in her field area had led to greater consciousness amongst Dalits about their rights and the same had supported Dalit workers of a village in their struggle against an upper caste landlord who had attempted to sexually violate a Dalit woman labourer. The struggle of Dalit women in this case began as a fight for their honour and dignity and it became more broad based and eventually women labourers were able to achieve higher wages and in fact, Jassal notes that for some tasks wages for men and women were the same. The social and economic conditions of Dalits generally remain pitiful and there is similar evidence from other villages in the regions (for example, see Dhuru, 2008).

It is clearly the case that Dalit women labourers do have political awareness and agency. They are conscious of their rights and aware of the bases of their exploitation. But Dalit women are, above all, pragmatic and canny – and they appear to have, realistically, concluded that more can be gained by their 'working the system', through 'negotiations' and 'the weapons of the weak' than by openly opposing it. In these circumstances, they can pose only a very limited challenge to capitalist agrarian structures and thus their work continues to benefit Dalit men and male capitalist accumulation more generally. Even though such struggles by Dalit labourers, especially women, have not led to substantive material improvements in their conditions or posed any systemic challenge, they cannot be discounted and are reflective of their active attempts to improve their position. Success has been intermittent and limited, but benefits have been wrested. One need only take the example of Usha, a Dalit, from Savitribhai Phule Dalit Mahila Sangarsh Morcha in Jaunpur, who leveraged her personal experiences to mobilise and organise on issues of caste, labour and land (Dalit Camera, 2017). Unfortunately, till date there has hardly been any research on labour relations or political consciousness of Dalit labouring women in eastern UP.

Notes

1 *Bahujan* means majority. The BSP in its initial years sought to capture state power on the basis of a voting block of SCs, STs, OBCs and religious minorities which together are a numerical majority in the state of UP. In the 2000s, the party adopted a stance of *sarvjan hitay*, that is welfare of all, as it fielded

candidates from across caste groups and not just Dalits and not just Chamars within Dalits which were the core base of the BSP at its founding.

2 Founded in 2015 in UP, the Bhim Army is an organisation that seeks to empower Dalits and other minorities. It believes in confrontational style of politics such as *dharnas* and *gheraoes*.

3 The son of the founder of SP, Mulayam Singh Yadav.

4 BSP–SP–RLD *Mahagathbandhan* refers to an electoral alliance between the BSP, SP and the Rashtriya Lok Dal for the 2019 national elections. The purpose of this *Mahagathbandhan* was to present a formidable challenge to the BJP by bringing together the votes of Jatavs, Yadavs and Jats – the core constituency of BSP, SP and RLD respectively.

5 On the decline of the Congress System, see Rai and Kumar (2017).

6 '*Garib ka kauno saath nahi deb, aur khud ko kaha se kaha bana liya*'.

7 At different times, the BSP has formed governments in alliance with the BJP, a party traditionally associated with an upper caste base. Mayawati has also made deliberate attempts to woo other castes. Though still drawing on the populism attached with a Dalit identity, her political strategy is marked by a shift from *bahujan* (majority i.e., Dalits) to *sarvjan* (everyone).

8 A GOI initiative to prevent caste-based atrocities.

9 '*Garib aadmi kauno aadmi hai, din bhar kaam kari, kin kar lai, to shaam ka khai*' (Fieldwork Notes, May 2010).

10 '*Majdoori nahi karenge to karenge kya, jiyenge kaise*' (Fieldwork Notes, May 2010).

11 '*Maangne mein sharm, laaj lage ki badka kuch kha na de. Hum chutka hai to yeh sharm ka baat hain nahi?*' (Fieldwork Notes, April 2010).

12 Karya karke chali aaye, paisa maangne mein sharm aai. Voh bhumihar ko nahi sochak chahi ki itni mehnat se kaam karat to paisa nahi dek chahi? . . . voh apne man se nahi kahange ya denge aur maangne mein aithi laage. (Fieldwork Notes, April 2010)

13 '*Yeh sara elaka pradhan ka hai. Do hai to kya? Jab baap, dada dare, to beta nahi darega?. Shuru se seena taan ke rahte to alag baat thi*' (Fieldwork Notes, April 2010).

14 '*Hum prem bhaav ke hain, ka puchi? Jarorrat padi to siyaar bani*' (Fieldwork Notes, May 2010).

15 '*Ghar mein ghus kar lad lete hain*' (Fieldwork Notes, November 2009).

6 Conclusion

In this concluding chapter, I bring together the major findings and arguments made in each chapter.

I began this book by bringing out the vacuum in research on village-based Dalit women labourers from eastern UP. Class, women, labour, caste, livelihoods, village – these are central to my work. Unfortunately, in most works these themes get bound by disciplinary boundaries – management studies on labour; economists' focus on measuring inequality, poverty, land patterns, labour participation, etc. using statistical tools; sociological works on caste, village, mobility; cultural studies on folklores and women studies on issues of gender, sexuality and power. Rooting my work in agrarian political economy and using Bernstein as the theoretical frame have hopefully allowed me to move beyond these disciplinary boundaries to some extent. For example, nature of agrarian transition; how capitalism has evolved; how different classes have been impacted and what are the features of different types of capital and labour today; understanding structural sources of exploitation in capitalism with reference to class relations but also hierarchies of gender, caste, religion, etc.; debate on the relevance of peasantry; the fluid boundaries between rural–urban, etc.

This book is also an exercise in making a case for the benefits of using a political economy analyses wherein class relations and power dynamics are central. A political economy framework such as Bernstein's has strong explanatory and analytical power. What is the overarching structural context of neoliberal capitalist globalisation? How is domination maintained? What are the sources of surplus and accumulation? What are the different types of small farmers and the variety of their experiences in relation to capitalism in agriculture and outside of it? How are classes formed? The strength of class analyses lies in providing answers to such questions. The following summary reflects on these questions and further builds on them in describing the prevailing labour relations of Dalit women belonging to the category of classes of labour.

Occupational Mapping

To start with, a case was made for Henry Bernstein's framework as the best way to understand neoliberal agrarian transformations and labour. Bernstein's

DOI: 10.4324/9780429321894-6

notion of 'classes of labour' is taken as the point of departure for this work. Classes of labour refer to those petty commodity producers who struggle to reproduce themselves as labour. Members of households belonging to classes of labour category are simultaneously engaged in various types of irregular and exploitative wage labour, self-employment activities and other value-adding labour activities. These are combined with small-scale farming. Logically then, labour is highly mobile, fragmented and straddling different production locations and spaces in the divisions of labour. Though the concept of classes of labour has been previously used in the Indian context to understand the informal labour more generally (for example, Mezzadri, 2009; Lerche, 2010; Pattenden, 2011), Bernstein's framework of petty commodity production differentiation has not been applied. This book is probably the first instance of understanding socio-economic differentiation in small-scale production in rural India, which does not use the traditional class categories of landlord, farmer and peasantry. Are pre-modern concepts of landlord and peasantry still relevant today? What is to be gained by using them? Peasant, for example, refers to a pre-industrial, pre-capitalist class location based on landownership or access to land through feudal lords and characterised by some sort of an idyllic and subsistence-oriented socio-economic lifestyle outside the market. There were also the serfs who were landless and bonded. The ground reality today is far from this. I elaborate on this in the following, but one should also note that capitalism penetrates spaces and relations in different ways and in varying extents (for example, see Harriss-White et al., 2009).

In terms of knowledge creation, this book makes an important contribution in general to the literature on eastern UP, one of the least studied regions in India. When I began reading on rural labour in eastern UP, there was no definite knowledge on labour relations of Dalit women. A few works exist on male rural labour relations and these provided some pointers about women labourers. The gender- and caste-based occupational mapping undertaken in this research provides definite first-hand information about the rural labour market in eastern UP. Also, it sheds light on aspects such as the lived experience of caste, non-waged labour and how the village itself is seen. What are the important conclusions which can be extracted from this mapping?

In many ways, the traditional village has changed but caste still defines everyday lives to a huge extent – where one lives, in what utensils one is served food, who one eats with, formation of work groups, etc. My fieldwork showed that the *jati* identity is the prevalent mode of caste identification. Not only is recognition with socio-political derivations or the official three-fold caste categorisation limited, but there is disjuncture between *jati* and government categories as well. Caste and class coincide to a large extent. This overlap is reinforced through a strategic confluence of political and economic power and social status. Caste, class and gender intersect to varying degrees across the rural social structure and mediate women's position, socio-economic choices and conduct within the household and outside.

At a general level, these observations find mention in other works cited in the earlier chapters of this book – Srinivas (1966, 1989) on the *jati* understanding of caste; Srinivas (1966), Deliege (1997) and Kapadia (1990) on local variations in caste perception. Studies on rural labour from Gujarat (Breman, 1985b), Tamil Nadu (Kapadia, 1995; Heyer, 2001) and Andhra Pradesh (da Corta and Venkateshwarlu, 1999) show a correspondence between labourers and low caste status. The interconnectedness among caste, class and gender is also well established, for example, Srinivas (1989), Ilaiah (2005) and Dube (1996).

In eastern UP, Lerche (1998) and Srivastava (1999) point out a caste–class overlap and Sharma (1985) has shown how caste, class and gender relations interact. In this area, this research makes an important contribution. The detailed mapping of socio-economic relations builds substantially on these areas. Regarding the first aspect, the detailed mapping of socio-economic relations undertaken in this research show that there is a caste–class overlap. At a broad level, the petty capitalists continue to accumulate and consolidate their dominance. Agriculture is an important but not the only source of surplus as petty capitalists have diversified into lucrative businesses such as transport, construction, agri-trades like milling. Their domination is based on their owning most land in the village, being upper caste, from being in politics or indirectly accessing state and using its resources to bestow 'patronage' and operating as a source of social protection. At the other extreme, the classes of labour are caught in a poverty and debt trap, constantly struggling to secure their survival. Economic polarisation is a fact. At a disaggregated level, within class economic differentiation has also occurred as seen in the case of some OBCs and a few Dalits who have managed to access public employment and/or stable non-agricultural employment or migrant work. It is notable that there was no instance of a Dalit petty capitalist.

Regarding the second aspect, Sharma's is the only existing work that draws linkages on caste, class and gender in eastern UP. She does this in the context of capitalist developments in agriculture. This research does more than this. In line with Sharma, the findings of this research also show polarisation between men and women. This is observed in the labour market, production process, own cultivation and unfree labour. Mediated by class position, social status and backed by a patriarchal ideology, it is interpreted as a natural division, is internalised and maintained by female labourers themselves. After all, if women can do physically arduous spade work in own cultivation, then why not in wage labour? The socio-cultural repression might not be so rigidly observed in the case of Dalit women, but it is true even in their case that female subjugation and exploitation have enabled and sustained male 'freedom' as seen in men cornering better waged, better status work or resorting to migration due to economic and social reasons. While women are concentrated in jobs typified as female (paddy transplantation, for example) or jobs that are no longer considered worthy of being done by men as they may be seen as dirty and low waged such as agricultural labour.

The empirical application of Bernstein validated its theoretical relevance and applicability in an Indian setting. This occupational mapping is a rich description of the classes in the villages and their features. Also it provides information on the processes of class differentiation. It definitively countered the notion of a subsistence-oriented homogenous peasantry and reiterated the complex variation within small farmers whose subsistence is commodified. It helped us to understand their class locations and how gender and caste do indeed mediate with class positions and shape the experience of exploitation and oppression. That identification of class locations required reference to conditions outside of immediate farming relations and agriculture is borne out by strategies of capitalist accumulation on the one end and occupational multiplicity as encompassed in labour mobility and fragmentation in mechanisms of labour reproduction on the other end. Class analysis cannot be premised on a reductionist method of categorising classes on the basis of ownership of means of production. A household can simultaneously be exploiter and exploited, as with some petty commodity producers. Class locations are not static, but a dynamic process and social relation, combining elements of capital and labour.

In village labour markets, job distribution is shaped by gender and caste. A further aspect to the gendering of labour market is the sexual division of labour in agricultural wage labour. Gendered wage gap is a common phenomenon. This finding finds support in Harriss-White (2003, 2004, 2005), Rigg (2006), Kapadia (1995) and Heyer (2011) in Tamil Nadu and da Corta and Venkateshwarlu (1999) and Garikipati (2009) in the context of Andhra Pradesh. However, until now, we did not have this information for eastern UP. At best, male movement out of agriculture could be inferred from Lerche (1999), Srivastava (1999) and Diwakar (2004), who indicated increasing availability of alternative employment with reference to male labour.

Another conclusion is that the occupational structure reflects a gendered caste–class hierarchy, as described by Chen (2008), Harriss-White (2003, 2004, 2005) and Lerche (2010). At the bottom of the village labour market are the agricultural and casual wage labour and brick kiln work. These are the most stigmatised, tedious, and exploitative forms of wage labour and often linked with debt and other forms of unfree labour. Non-agricultural forms of self-employment activities are far in between and appear as survival activities. Women are into agricultural wage labour only and they bear a disproportionate burden of unfree labour. The worst-off Dalits work at brick kilns. Based on his field study in eastern UP, Srivastava (1999) had noted in relation to male labourers that occupational diversification coincides with socio-economic status and labourers may resort to it as a way out of demeaning agrarian relations. This is borne out in this work as well – occupational diversification by men has not necessarily led to prosperity, but still local non-agricultural work or migrant work is better than dirty agricultural work which pays less and is not available round the year and importantly signifies freedom from village-based exploitation on the basis of caste and religion. In eastern UP, a comprehensive and systematic caste- and gender-based mapping such as undertaken here is not available. How intersecting caste, class and gender identities shape the role of women in the market and private sphere is either not taken into account or clearly established in works on rural female labour relations. There are stand-alone references such as Garikipati (2009) and Kapadia (1995) or Paris et al. (2005) in eastern UP. As such, this book substantially adds to existing knowledge on this front at the general level and also specifically in eastern UP.

The gendering of occupational diversification leads to a very pertinent question. Untouchability is a ground reality. Inside the village, it is a fact of life as explained previously. The market too continues to socially and economically discriminate against the Dalits especially Dalit women. In this scenario then, could it be possible that the state is the only logical hope of them procuring better waged and dignified employment, as teachers, para-health workers and in MGNREGA? This is despite the MGNREGA's limited benefits and it reifying existing power relations. Even though women are unwilling to disturb the established gendered division of labour – a source of unequal gender relations and power – state-sponsored work programmes can potentially challenge establish gendered roles by providing work to men and women under similar terms and conditions of work (provided women are educated about their rights). Such 'non-traditional' female wage labour participation is likely to find wide societal acceptance as well. Also, to be noted here is that even within formal jobs, there is a hierarchy. On the one hand there are jobs in the defence, paramilitary, bureaucracy which are considered very prestigious, are salaried with the provision of pension and come with other perks. These are the preserve of men – likely upper castes and some sections of OBCs like Yadavs and some sections of Dalits, notably Chamars. On the other hand are jobs like para-health workers and teachers which are done by women. These are also jobs that are not salaried or paid on the basis of work done, pay much less in either case and are not seen as prestigious work.

Decentralisation of agriculture in the reproduction of capital and labour is an important theme in literature (for example, Bryceson et al., 2000; NCEUS, 2007). My findings show that the dependency on agriculture in the reproduction of capital and labour needs to be studied at a disaggregated level and has to be qualified on the basis of caste and gender. On this, there is no uniform picture. For example, my findings suggest that there are certain petty capitalist and petty producer households completely reliant on agriculture only. They are either surplus-producing farmers as is the case with petty capitalist or their caste is a limitation on their local wage labour participation as is the case with small surplus-producing petty producer Brahmins for whom credit against their land and limited practice of their traditional occupation are the major sources of sustenance. At the other extreme are Dalit classes of labour. In this case, own cultivation is a minimum buffer against hunger and abject poverty. Agricultural wage labour is crucial for female labourers wherein they are the day-to-day providers of their households in the face of male outmigration. Here, the importance of agriculture cannot be denied and to this extent, female labourers are dependent on agricultural wage employment and on landowners for various socio-economic reasons.

That migration takes place along gender and age lines was borne out by the fieldwork. This is supported by Lerche (1999), Srivastava (1999) and Paris et al. (2005) in eastern UP. Even though migration was not systematically investigated in the field, the findings presented in this book on this aspect are important interventions. The mapping exercise also showed that at a broad level, migration is a significant trend for social and/or economic reasons, but at a disaggregate level, the link between classes of labour and migration as a mechanism to cope and spread risk is not straightforward.

Declining participation of male migrants in own cultivation has added to the burden of women who anyway faced increasing responsibility for ensuring daily household reproduction in the absence of men. Yes, migration is undertaken for social and economic reasons, but not only does the repressive patriarchal gendering of social roles deny women this opportunity, but it may even lead to their maginalisation/withdrawal from production processes and thereby concentrate accumulation only in the hands of men. On top of it, male outmigration has pushed women into performing unfree labour, as a part of debt or patron–client relations. Finally, the weak link between migration and the landless position is contrary to those of Paris et al. (2005). However, as pointed out by de Haan (1997, 1999), in certain situations, the poorest and landless are less likely to migrate because they cannot afford even the minimum expense involved in migration and because they are likely to lack contacts in source or destination areas that could facilitate migration. In my field villages, both factors hold true in addition to others identified in the text.

Rural Labour Relations of Dalit Women Belonging to Classes of Labour

On this topic, the book makes an original contribution in the area. At best, the existing literature on eastern UP either indirectly hints at or refers to isolated specific aspects of female rural labour relations as a consequence of changes in male labour relations. Where such evidence exists, I will relate it to my field findings.

Rural labour relations are a part of the wider framework of unequal power structure and overlapping socio-economic relations in the villages. There are various aspects to this, all reinforcing labour dependency on the dominant caste-class for food, credit, access to fields for grazing livestock, fodder collection, defecation, *badkas*' mediation to access to loans and other government provisions and protection from structures of authority and power. The extent of dependency is influenced by factors like proximity, history between the 'patron' and the 'client' households and geographical layout of the village.

We saw that caste and cultural ideology are important determinants of wage labour participation and practices, as are other factors like the caste equation between employers and labourers, the prospective cost–benefit analysis by labourers, 'rurality' wage labour and passivity of female labour (Dreze and Khera, 2009). These factors are not accorded central importance in most literature. In the case of eastern UP, only Sharma (1985) has made limited references to one or two aspects.

On wage structure and relations and modes of employment, my findings conform to those of Kapadia (1995), Heyer (2001), Ramachandran (1990) and Athreya et al. (1990). Based on my findings, I agree with Harriss et al. (2010) that wage structure is influenced by government policies and level of politicisation of labourers. On the issue of wage negotiations, my findings differ from the aforementioned. The major point of departure is that contrary to Kapadia (1995) or Lerche (1994, 1995) and Srivastava (1999) in eastern UP, my findings establish that rather than an organised and confrontational approach, wage hike demands take the form of informal, unstructured persistent negotiations and haggling. However, there are similarities as well between my findings and the general and eastern UP literature, for example, regarding timing of such demands or how these may be limited by individual socio-economic circumstances and patron–client relations that serve to keep labour divided. My findings differ from other works in highlighting the role of limited economic polarisation (in addition to other factors) and in the creation of a strong labour lobby in wage negotiations. In eastern UP, though Lerche (1995, 1999), Srivastava (1989) and Ruthven and Kumar (2002) argued that general dependency of male labour on capital underscored wage relations, we did not have details of these aspects vis-à-vis female labourers till now.

The labour recruitment and discipline patterns in the field villages are as found in existing general literature highlighting how the mode of employment determined recruitment type, the role of local identities, individual tied or patron–client relations and general grounds of labour dependency in securing and controlling labour. This is seen in Kapadia (1995), Pattenden (2011) and Athreya (1990). I did not find tied harvest and labour arrangements as described by Garikipati (2009) and da Corta and Venkateshwarlu's (1999) fieldwork in Andhra Pradesh. In Dokhgadh, harvest wage labour was linked to transplantation wage labour. This secured timely labour in peak season and also limited their bargaining leverage when the labour market is tight and there is a higher possibility of successfully getting a wage raise. Nonetheless, this was not common. In eastern UP, no information was available till now on recruitment style and labour control mechanisms of female labourers other than Lerche (1999) and Srivastava (1999) highlighting employers accessing unpaid family labour in tied labour and leasing arrangements as a means of securing cheaper and on-demand labour.

On labour bondage, my findings support the generalisation that old-style labour bondage is displaced with the development of various unfree labour arrangements as a part of capitalist social relations (Ramachandran, 1990; Garikipati, 2009; Da Corta and Venkateshwarlu, 1999; Kapadia, 1995; Heyer, 2001). Shankar (1996), Ruthven and Kumar (2002), Lerche (1995, 1999, 2003) observe the same in eastern UP.

Conspicuous by its absence in the field chapters is the concept of neo-bondage. Elements of unfree labour relations observed in the field cannot be subsumed under Breman's (1985b) definition of neo-bondage. These unfree relations are not just economic, contractual or impersonal. Other than credit, they are based on labourers' social and economic expectations from their patrons and very much draw on a personal familiarity and shared history. In eastern UP, Bardhan and Rudra (1978) and Ruthven and Kumar (2002) pointed out that unfree labour relations are associated with advantages like access to food, employment, etc. Neither can these unfree labour relations be associated with the dissolution of inherited notions of purity–pollution-based superiority–inferiority between *badkas* and *chutkas*. Contrary to Breman (1985b) and da Corta and Venkateshwarlu (1999), women still reflect a strongly engrained sense of superiority/inferiority and the embarrassment cum humiliation of being a Dalit, the only exception being the highly politicised Mosahars of Dokhgadh. This is not seen in the case of men though.

As shown in the book, it may often be the case that these unfree labour relations are willingly undertaken by women. This has to do with a general fear of *badkas*, general grounds of labour dependency on their employers, wider patron–client relations that serve as an insurance and safety net and increasing responsibility of women to provide for the household on a daily basis in the absence of migrant male members. de Neve (1999, 2005) showed that labourers sought advance from their employers, for economic reasons, but their attempts to maximise advance and changing employers are symbolic of their struggles against these employers. Heyer (2001) made a similar point, arguing that this reinforced their dependency. Pattenden (2011) has also linked patron–client relations to unfree labour relations. In the context of eastern UP, Bardhan and Rudra (1978) and Ruthven and Kumar (2002) pointed out certain labourers, the worst-off especially, may even seek to maintain these. But again, this is done with reference to male labour.

From eastern UP, the evidence on unfree labour relations shows that it generally takes the form of interlocked tied labour-credit relations (Bardhan and Rudra, 1978; Srivastava, 1989; Lerche, 1999; Rajni, 2007). Though debt as an important basis of securing cheap and priority labour was borne out in my fieldwork as well, this was not linked to land via leasing or tenancy arrangements. Rather, unfree labour relations appear as tied and priority labour services, unpaid attached family labour, *begar* provided by women within *badkas* households and a very few land–labour–credit tied relations.

Until this research, the element of unfreedom in labour relations of Dalit women from the classes of labour households had not been investigated in eastern UP, other than referring to them as attached family labour in tied credit, labour and land relations (Lerche, 1999; Srivastava, 1989). In documenting unfree labour relations of women as independent labourers or as part of a household, this book makes an original contribution to the theme in eastern UP. The most important finding is that there appears to be feminisation of unfreedom – women bear a disproportionate burden of unfree labour relations.

Intra-labour relations have not been an important subject of study within works on rural labour relations. One exception is Kapadia (1995), which lends support to my findings. In this case, the findings presented in the field chapters add to the limited available literature generally and specifically in eastern UP, where data on this is also scanty. For example, Ruthven and Kumar (2002) highlighted strained relations between local and incoming migrant labour and Lerche (1999) highlighted the different socio-economic power matrices confronting male labourers of different hamlets. The former point was not explored in this research. On the latter point, my findings are the same. This is the sum of available evidence, apart from the general remarks about labour fragmentation along social and economic lines. As such, this research can be seen as making a valuable contribution on this front.

Political Expression and Labour Struggles

Here, the purpose was to gain an understanding of the ways in which female labourers challenged their domination and sought to improve their position as labourers. On this theme, no work exists in eastern UP.

My findings show that, commonly, labour struggles take place along the lines of Scott's (1985, 1986) *weapons of the weak* thesis and Jeffery and Jeffery's (1996) analysis of how women negotiate with, rather than confront, structures of oppression. In the second chapter, it was suggested that labour struggles are likely to take these forms in view of the nature of classes of labour-fragmented, embedded in local and particularistic identities and lacking a common class interest. On the politicisation of labourers and their struggles, Lerche (1994, 1995, 2003) and Srivastava's (1999) works provide detailed evidence on male labourers in eastern UP. My findings on female labour struggles conform to their assertions and add new insights regarding female labourers.

I agree that an overlapping caste–class consciousness is the principle organising fulcrum of labour struggles, despite economic differentiation among caste groups. While the demands of wage hike or BPL cards can be perceived as class issues, this is not separated from an overlapping caste consciousness. Struggles of Dalit labourers from one hamlet do not include Dalit labourers from another hamlet, much less from other non-Dalit labouring households. Even within the same hamlet, the worst-off are likely to stay away from participating in these struggles, an observation made by Lerche also.

My field findings show that in the case of women, caste is the most basic medium of associating oneself with a particular political party. Women's understanding and critique of politics are based on their everyday observations and experiences. These reflect that for them caste is not delinked from class. Women are able to relate village politics to regional-level political phenomenon, albeit on a limited basis. This is despite their marginalisation from village political processes due to gendered roles.

As observed by Lerche and Srivastava, labour struggles are restricted to the hamlet level and circumscribed by specific social, economic and political contexts in which households operate, including individual economic circumstances and patron–client relations. Nonetheless, as Lerche has argued labour struggles can occur even within the framework of unfree labour relations or patron–client relations. At a more general level, Alavi's (1973) conclusion that labourers' political response is limited by their dependency on oppositional landlords is found to be true in the field villages.

Both Lerche and Srivastava stress on the role of occupational diversification in enhanced labour assertion. My findings show that this could indeed be the case, but the examples are few and far in between. Occupational diversification might have greater social consequences in terms of male withdrawal from demeaning work, but for women this occupation diversification may create new grounds for economic dependency and which in any case, does not eliminate the general rounds of labour dependency on *badkas*. In fact, male occupational diversity might end up reifying existing gendered relations. For example, we saw that some migrant workers pressure the women of their households to withdraw from wage labour and by extension, further limit their scope in the public domain. But we also saw that in the absence of migrant family members, women are likely to continue with wage labour. This is reflective of their economic vulnerability and general dependency on the *badkas*. In this sense, da Corta and Venkateshwarlu (1999) have rightly pointed out that women's exploitation subsidises male labour struggles. This is also evident in declining participation of returning male migrants in agriculture.

Overall, the BSP regime had imparted Dalit labourers a sense of security and empowerment. However, the BSP's 'politics of dignity' does not appear to have successfully countered the shame and embarrassment of being a *chutka* that female labourers expressed. This has to be read in conjunction with women's lack of confidence and their compartmentalisation as male dependents.

Such labour struggles constitute more of a symbolic rather than a systemic challenge to generalised *badka* dominance. They have not led to substantive material improvement in the work and living conditions of Dalit labourers. These struggles are erratic and issue based and often reflect personal vendetta. Female labourers' awareness of their exploitation and even a comparatively high level of politicisation, as seen in Mosahars, does not translate into a class for itself action. This is because classes of labour are internally divided along social and economic lines. This limits the evolution of a purely class-based collective conflict and at the same time reinforces capitalist dominance. This is similar to what Lerche observed in relation to male labourers. But whatever said and done, the fact remains that these *weapons of the weak* and negotiations with oppressors are important means through which women assert themselves and wrest concessions. Importantly, they show that female labourers are not ignorant and passive victims of capitalist exploitation. They are fully aware of the limitations of their struggles and the structural context of employment scarcity which perpetuates their subjection to *badkas*. I did not come across any open confrontation between employers and female labourers. The latter are not engaged in a struggle between classes in a Marxian sense. Depending upon individual circumstances, female labourers seek benefits by working with the tide so to say, rather than against it. The element of physical aggression by capitalists that Lerche and Srivastava write of is not found vis-à-vis female labourers. Here, the gender factor could be a positive.

The Dokhgadh Mosahars present a different picture. At one level, female labourers resort to similar weapons of the weak and negotiations. But beyond the village (the outcomes are village based though), they have taken on a more aggressive and directly confrontational stance, have successfully managed to access political power and have gained economically from this. This is facilitated by a few other factors indicated in the previous chapter. It is notable though that at this level, female labourers have not achieved this independently of male labourers. Here, labour struggles draw on a strong gender and caste labour solidarity. But this solidarity, as well as that seen in labour struggles for wage hikes in other villages, should not be interpreted as a conventional Marxian class struggle, despite being driven by extreme economic deprivation. The capital–labour contradiction is diluted by fragmentation among labourers on various non-class identities which preclude the formation of a strong unifying class identity and along the lines of patron–client realtions. In Dokhgadh, the labour solidarity is limited to the Mosahars in the hamlet. There is no attempt to integrate the Mosahars from another hamlet or Dalit labourers from other hamlets. It is indeed true that Mosahars are the worst off among Dalits and the 'advertisement' of their plight has taken on a strong caste hue. Even in this hamlet, the organisational initiative has come from an external source. So, their dependency on middle people has not been eliminated even though village-level politics are bypassed. The Mosahars show the strongest connections between the local-, meso- and regional-level politics and reflect a stronger sense of confidence and self-worth. But their struggles continue to be sporadic, issue based and take place within the existing unequal power structures.

Overall, this research is an important contribution on understanding and analysing labour relations of female labourers from the classes of labour category in a much under researched area. On the one hand, its microscopic focus is advantageous: it affords a detailed analytical research on a subject which has been marginalised and muted in the mainstream literature. This countered established dominant perceptions and provided interesting insights. As such, this research could be an important input in relevant policy formulation processes, to understand the myriad and complex web of identities and relations in which women operate, how they are inhibited by these and how women bend or work around these. On the other hand, the microscopic nature of this fieldwork is disadvantageous because it leaves unanswered the question of to what extent can the findings of this book be generalised. This book did not focus on agriculture, but it definitely highlighted its continued importance for female labourers essentially and therefore the need to bring back agriculture again to the centre of Indian policy discourse. Similarly, this research highlights that in an Indian context how tightly are class, caste and gender identities (and possibly others, depending upon the motives and work of individual scholars) woven together. An obsession with either one of these without considering the others is at best a partial investigation.

This knowledge of rural labour markets and agrarian relations in eastern UP is important because only the basis of this data can appropriate policies be formulated to benefit classes of labour and especially women. For instance, feminisation of agriculture also calls for feminisation of policies, in a manner of speaking. Women need to be placed at the centre of infrastructural provision by the state – credit, irrigation, marketing, storage, etc. Two, the government has to play a major role in generating employment for women through labour-intensive rural industrialisation – arts and crafts, packaging and processing, etc. My fieldwork shows that women are likely to participate in government programmes as these are better paying and not demeaning. Women are likely to also participate if such opportunities are near their homes and come with childcare facilities. Third, considering that health, education and food expenditures are major reasons for indebtedness of classes of labour, delivery of public services at the level of villages needs to be made more robust and corruption needs to be tackled. Apart from considerations of efficiency, quality is also an issue. For example, Dalit families send their children to public schools, but they are well aware of the poor quality of infrastructure, teacher absenteeism, poor standards of teaching, etc. Those who can afford, send their children to private schools even though these are not of quality standard. As such, there is definitely a need to strengthen public education.

References

Agarwal, Bina. (1994). *A field of one's own: Gender and land rights in South Asia*. Cambridge: Cambridge University Press.

Akram-Lodhi, A. Haroon. (1993). Agrarian classes in Pakistan: An empirical test of Patnaik's labour-exploitation criterion. *Journal of Peasant Studies*. 20(4). 557–589.

Akram-Lodhi, A. Haroon and Cristobal Kay. (2010a). Surveying the agrarian question (part 1): Unearthing foundations, exploring diversity. *Journal of Peasant Studies*. 37(1). 177–202.

Akram-Lodhi, A. Haroon and Cristobal Kay. (2010b). Surveying the agrarian question (part 2): Current debates and beyond. *Journal of Peasant Studies*. 37(2). 255–284.

Akram-Lodhi, A. Haroon, Cristobal Kay and Saturnino Borras. (eds.). (2009a). *Peasants and globalization: Political economy, rural transformation and the agrarian question*. London: Routledge.

Akram-Lodhi, A. Haroon, Cristobal Kay and Saturnino Borras. (2009b). The political economy of land and the agrarian question in an era of neoliberal globalization. In A. Haroon Akram-Lodhi and Cristobal Kay (eds.). *Peasants and globalization: Political economy, rural transformation and the agrarian question*. London: Routledge.

Alavi, Hamza. (1973). Peasant classes and primordial loyalties. *Journal of Peasant Studies*. 1(1). 23–62.

Athreya, Venkatesh B., Goran Djurfeldt and Staffan Lindberg. (1990). *Barriers broken: Production relations and agrarian change in Tamil Nadu*. New Delhi: Sage Publications.

Bardhan, Pranab. (1984). *The political economy of development in India*. Oxford: Basil Blackwell.

Bardhan, Pranab and Ashok Rudra. (1978). Interlinkage of land, labour and credit relations: An analysis of village survey data in east India. *Economic and Political Weekly*. 13(6–7). 367–384.

Bardhan, Pranab and Ashok Rudra. (1980). Types of labour attachment in agriculture: Results of a survey in West Bengal, 1979. *Economic and Political Weekly*. 15(35). 1477–1484.

Beneria, Lourdes and Gita Sen. (1997). Accumulation, reproduction and women's role in economic development: Boserup revisited. In Nalini Visvanathan, Lynn Duddan and Nan Wiegersma (eds.). *The women, gender & development reader* (Ch. 3). New Delhi: Zubaan.

Bernstein, Henry. (1996). Agrarian questions then and now. *Journal of Peasant Studies*. 24(1–2). 22–59.

Bernstein, Henry. (2001). 'The peasantry' in global capitalism: Who, where and why? *Socialist Register*. 25–51.

Bernstein, Henry. (2002). Land reforms: Taking a long(er) view. *Journal of Agrarian Change*. 2(4). 433–463.

Bernstein, Henry. (2003). Farewells to the peasantry. *Transformation*. 52. 1–19.

Bernstein, Henry. (2004). 'Changing before our very eyes': Agrarian questions and the politics of land in capitalism today. *Journal of Agrarian Change*. 4(1–2). 190–225.

Bernstein, Henry. (2006a). Is there an agrarian question in the 21st century? *Canadian Journal of Development Studies*. 27(4). 449–460.

Bernstein, Henry. (2006b). Once were/still are peasants? farming in a globalising South. *New Political Economy*. 11(3). 399–406.

Bernstein, Henry. (2008). Agrarian change in globalising world: (Final) farewells to the peasantry? *Journal of Agrarian Change* workshop on 'Agrarian Questions: Lineages and Prospects'. London: School of Oriental and African Studies, University of London. 1–2 May.

Bernstein, Henry. (2010). *Class dynamics of agrarian change*. Halifax: Fernwood Publishing; Sterling, VA: Kumarian Press.

Bernstein, Henry and Terence J. Byres. (2001). From peasant studies to agrarian change. *Journal of Agrarian Change*. 1(1). 1–56.

Beteille, Andre. (1965 [1996]). *Caste, class and power: Changing patterns of stratification in a Tanjore village* (2nd ed.). New Delhi: Oxford University Press.

Beteille, Andre. (1997). Caste in contemporary India. In C.J. Fuller (ed.). *Caste today* (Ch. 6). New Delhi: Oxford University Press.

Beteille, Andre. (2007). *Marxism and class analysis*. New Delhi: Oxford University Press.

Bhalla, Sheila. (1999). Liberalisation, rural labour markets and the mobilisation of farm workers: The Haryana story in an all-India context. In T.J. Byres, Karin Kapadia and Jens Lerche (eds.). *Rural labour relations in India* (Ch. 2). London: Frank Cass.

Borras, Saturnino M. (2003). Questioning market-led agrarian reform: Experiences from Brazil, Colombia and South Africa. *Journal of Agrarian Change*. 3(3). 367–394.

Borras, Saturnino M., Marc Edelman and Cristobal Kay. (eds.). (2008). Transnational agrarian movements: Origins and politics, campaigns and impact. *Journal of Agrarian Change*. 8(2–3). 169–204.

Bourgois, Philippe. (1988). Conjugated oppression: Class and ethnicity among Guaymi and Kuna banana workers. *American Ethnologist*. 15(2). 328–348.

Brass, Paul. (1980). The politicization of the peasantry in a North Indian state: I. *Journal of Peasant Studies*. 7(4). 395–426.

Brass, Tom. (ed.). (1994). New farmers' movements in India. *Journal of Peasant Studies*. 21(3–4).

Breman, Jan. (1985a). Between accumulation and immiseration: The partiality of fieldwork in rural India. *Journal of Peasant Studies*. 13(1). 5–36.

Breman, Jan. (1985b). *Of peasants, migrants and paupers: Rural labour circulation and capitalist production in West India*. New Delhi: Oxford University Press.

Breman, Jan. (1990). 'Even dogs are better off': The ongoing battle between capital and labour in the cane-fields of Gujarat. *Journal of Peasant Studies*. 17(4). 546–608.

Breman, Jan. (1994). *Wage hunters and gatherers: Search for work in the urban and rural economy of South Gujarat*. New Delhi: Oxford University Press.

Breman, Jan. (2003). *The labouring poor in India: Patterns of exploitation, subordination, and exclusion*. New Delhi: Oxford University Press.

Breman, Jan. (2007). *The Poverty regime in village India: Half a century of work and life at the bottom of the rural economy in South Gujarat*. New Delhi: Oxford University Press.

Breman, Jan, P. Kloos, and A. Saith. (eds.). (1997). *The village in Asia revisited*. New Delhi: Oxford University Press.

Bryceson, Deborah F. (2000). Peasant theories and smallholder policies: Past and present. In D. Bryceson, C. Kay and J. Mooij (eds.). *Disappearing peasantries?: Rural labour in Asia, Africa and Latin America* (Ch. 1). London: ITDG Publishing.

Byres, Terence J. (1977). Agrarian transition and the agrarian question. *Journal of Peasant Studies*. 4(3). 258–274.

Byres, Terence J. (1986). The agrarian question, forms of capitalist agrarian transition and the state: An essay with reference to Asia. *Social Scientist*. 14(11–12). 3–67.

Byres, Terence J. (1996). *Capitalism from above and capitalism from below: An essay in comparative political economy*. London: Macmillan Press.

Byres, T.J. (2003). Structural change, the agrarian question and the possible impact of globalization. In J. Ghosh and C.P. Chandrasekhar (eds.). *Work and well-being in the age of finance* (pp. 171–211). New Delhi: Tulika Books.

Chakravarty, Uma. (2012–2013). In her own write: Writing from a Dalit feminist standpoint. *India International Centre Quarterly*. 39(3–4). 134–145.

Chandrasekhar, C.P. (2017). The roots of the agrarian disress in India. *BloombergQuint*, 27 June 2017. Retrieved from https://www.bloombergquint.com/opinion/2017/06/27/farm-loan-waivers-and-the-roots-of-agrariandistress-in-india#gs.76WQ5aQc [Accessed 22 November 2018].

Chandrasekhar, C.P. and J. Ghosh. (2002 [2004]). *The market that failed: Neoliberal economic reforms in India* (2nd ed.). New Delhi: LeftWord Books.

Chandrasekhar, C.P. and J. Ghosh. (2018). India's services sector boom has failed on the jobs front. *Business Line*, 19 November. Retrieved from https://www.thehindubusinessline.com/opinion/columns/c-p-chandrasekhar/indias-servicessector-boom-has-failed-on-the-jobs-front/article25540761.ece [Accessed 25 January 2019].

Chen, Martha. (2008). Informality and social protection: Theories and realities. *IDS Bulletin*. 39(2). 18–27.

Ciotti, Manuella. (2002). *Social mobility in a Chamar community in Eastern Uttar Pradesh, Northern India*. PhD Thesis. London: School of Economics and Political Science, University of London.

Ciotti, Manuella. (2009). The conditions of politics: Low caste womens political agency in contemporary North Indian society. *Feminist Review: South Asian Feminisms: Negotiating New Terrains*. 91. 113–134.

Cleaver, Harry M. (1972). Some contradictions of capitalism: The contradictions of the green revolution. *American Economic Review*. 62(2). 177–186.

Cohn, B.S. (1987). The pasts of an Indian village. In Vandana Madan (ed.). *The village in India*. New Delhi: Oxford University Press.

da Corta, Lucia and Davuluri Venkateshwarlu. (1999). Unfree relations and the feminisation of agricultural labour in Andhra Pradesh, 1970–95. In T.J. Byres, Karin Kapadia and Jens Lerche (eds.). *Rural labour relations in India* (Ch. 4). London: Frank Cass.

Dalit Camera. (2017). *"Before I go out, I'll create as many Dalit women leaders as I can" – Usha* [Online]. Retrieved from www.dalitcamera.com/go-ill-create-many-dalit-women-leaders-can-usha/ [Accessed 22 July 2020].

Das Gupta, S. (2019). *Class, politics, and agrarian policies in post-liberalisation India*. New Delhi: Cambridge University Press.

Deere, Carmen Diana and Alain de Janvry. (1981). Demographic and social differentiation among Northern Peruvian peasants. *Journal of Peasant Studies*. 8(3). 335–366.

de Haan, Arjan. (1997). Rural-urban migration and poverty: The case of India. *IDS Bulletin*. 28(2). 35–47.

de Haan, Arjan. (1999). Livelihoods and poverty: The role of migration-a critical review of the migration literature. *The Journal of Development Studies*. 36(2). 1–47.

Deliege, Robert. (1997). At the threshold of untouchability: Pallars and Valaiyars in a Tamil Village. In C.J. Fuller (ed.). *Caste today* (Ch. 3). New Delhi: Oxford University Press.

De Neve, Geert. (1999). Asking for and giving *baki*: Neo-bondage, or the interplay of bondage and resistance in the Tamilnadu power-loom industry. *Contributions to Indian Sociology*. 33(1–2). 379–406.

De Neve, Geert. (2002). *Weaving rugs for IKEA: The dynamics of subcontracting work for the global market in rural Tamilnadu*. Occasional Paper No. 4. Centre of South Asian Studies. Cambridge: Cambridge University Press.

De Neve, Geert. (2005). *The everyday politics of labour: Working lives in india's informal economy*. New Delhi: Social Science Press.

Dhuru, Arundhati. (2008). *Musahars: Bonded to poverty* [Online]. Retrieved from www.thesouthasian.org/archives/2008/musahars_bonded_to_poverty_1.html [Accessed 16 November 2009].

Dirks, Nicholas B. (2002). *Castes of mind: Colonialism and the making of modern India*. New Delhi: Permanent Black.

Diwakar, D.M. (2004). Living condition and survival strategies of agricultural labour in Uttar Pradesh. In U. Kalpagam, Nisha Srivastava and D.M. Diwakar (eds.). *Labour and poverty (studies on Uttar Pradesh)* (Ch. 10). New Delhi: Segment Books.

Djurfeldt, Goran, Venkatesh Athreya, N. Jayakumar, Staffan Lindberg, A. Rajagopal and R. Vidyasagar. (2008). Agrarian change and social mobility in Tamil Nadu. *Economic & Political Weekly*. 43(45). 50–61.

Dreze, Jean. (1997). Palanpur, 1957–93: Occupational change, land ownership, and social inequality. In Vandana Madan (ed.). *The village in India 2002*. New Delhi: Oxford University Press.

Dreze, Jean and Reetika Khera. (2009). The battle for employment guarantee. *Frontline*. 26(1) [Online]. Retrieved from www.frontlineonnet.com/fl2601/stories/20090116260100400.htm [Accessed 29 August 2012].

Dube, Leela. (1996 [1997]). Caste and women. In M.N. Srinivas (ed.). *Caste: Its twentieth century avatar* (Ch. 1). New Delhi: Penguin Books.

Duncan, Ian. (1999). Dalits and politics in rural North India: The Bahujan Samaj party in Uttar Pradesh. *Journal of Peasant Studies*. 27(1). 35–60.

Ebrahim, Alnoor. (2000). Agricultural cooperatives in Gujarat, India: Agents of equity or differentiation. *Development in Practice*. 10(2). 178–188.

Forest Rights Act. (2006). *Act, rules and guidelines*. Retrieved from https://tribal.nic.in/FRA/data/FRARulesBook.pdf [Accessed 21 November 2021].

Foundation of Agrarian Studies. (2015). *Nature of Income diversification in village India with a special focus on Dalit households*. New Delhi: Indian Council of Social Science Research.

Fraser, Nancy. (2012). *Feminism, capitalism and the cunning of history: An introduction*. HAL Working Paper Series. Paris: FMSH.

Fuchs, Stephen. (1981). *At the bottom of Indian society: The Harijan and other low castes*. New Delhi: Munshiram Manoharlal.

Garikipati, S. (2009). Landless but not assetless: Female agricultural labour on the road to better status, evidence from India. *Journal of Peasant Studies*. 36(3). 517–545.

Geertz, Clifford. (n.d.) *Thick description: Toward an interpretive theory of culture 1973* [Online]. Retrieved from http://people.ucsc.edu/~ktellez/geertz1973.pdf [Accessed 17 August 2012].

Geetha, V. (2009). *Patriarchy*. Kolkata: Stree.

Ghosh, Jayati. (2005). *Trade liberalization in agriculture: An examination of impact and policy strategies with special reference to India*. Occasional Paper, Human Development Report Office [Online]. Retrieved from http://hdr.undp.org/en/reports/global/hdr2005/papers/HDR2005_Ghosh_Jayati_12.pdf [Accessed 11 June 2012].

Ghosh, Jayati. (2007). A policy for unfreedom. *Frontline*. 24(16) [Online]. Retrieved from www.frontlineonnet.com/fl2416/stories/20070824501910100.htm [Accessed 8 August 2012].

Ghosh, Jayati. (2015). India's rural employment programme is dying a death of funding cuts. *The Guardian*. Retrieved from https://www.theguardian.com/global-development/2015/feb/05/india-rural-employmentfunding-cuts-mgnrega [Accessed 14 January 2019].

Gidwani, Vinay. (2001). The cultural logic of work: Explaining labour deployment and piece-rate contracts in Matar taluka, Gujarat. Part II. *The Journal of Development Studies*. 38(2). 75–108.

GoUP. (2006). *Uttar Pradesh human development report*. Lucknow: Department of Planning, Government of Uttar Pradesh.

GoUP. (2008a). *Statistical abstract: Uttar Pradesh*. Lucknow: Economic and Statistics Division, State Planning Institute, Uttar Pradesh [Online]. Retrieved from http://planning.up.nic.in/apd/hdr-2006/HDR.html [Accessed 27 February 2011].

GoUP. (2008b). *District-wise development indicators: Uttar Pradesh*. Lucknow: Economic and Statistics Division, State Planning Institute, Uttar Pradesh.

GoUP. (2008c). *Sankhiyakiya patrika 2008: Janpath Kushinagar*. Lucknow: District Economics and Statistics Officer, Kushinagar.

Government of India. (2007). *Uttar Pradesh development report*. New Delhi: Planning Commission, Government of India [Online]. Retrieved from http://

planningcommission.nic.in/plans/stateplan/index.php?state=sdr_up.html [Accessed 27 February 2011].
Government of India. (2019). *All India report on number and area of operational holdings*. Agriculture Census Division, Department of Agriculture, Co-operation and Farmers Welfare, Ministry of Agriculture and Farmers Welfare. Government of India.
Government of India. (2020). *Economic survey 2020*. New Delhi: Government of India.
Govinda, Radhika. (2014). On whose behalf? Women's activism and identity politics in contemporary Uttar Pradesh. In R. Jeffery, C. Jeffrey and J. Lerche (eds.). *Development failure and identity politics in Uttar Pradesh*. New Delhi: Sage Publications.
Govinda, Radhika. (2017). Different Dalit women speak differently: Unravelling, through an intersectional lens, narratives of agency and activism from everyday life in rural Uttar Pradesh. In S. Anandhi and K. Kapadia (eds.). *Dalit women: Vanguard of an alternative politics in India*. Abingdon: Routledge.
Guerin, Isabelle P. (2013). Bonded labour, agrarian changes and capitalism: Emerging patterns in South India. *Journal of Agrarian Change*. 13(3). July.
Guerin, Isabelle, P. Subramanian, G. Vankatasubramanian and S. Michiels. (2012). Ambiguities and paradoxes of the decent work deficit: Bonded migrants in Tamil Nadu. *Global Labour Journal*. 3(1). 118–142.
Gupta, Jyoti. (2002). Women second in the land agenda. *Economic & Political Weekly*. 37(18). 1746–1754.
Guru, Gopal. (1995). Dalit women talk differently. *Economical and Political Weekly*. 30(41–42). 2548–2550. 14–21 October.
Harriss, John. (1999). Comparing political regimes across Indian states: A preliminary essay. *Economic & Political Weekly*. 34(48). 3367–3377.
Harriss, John, J. Jeyaranjan and K. Nagaraj. (2010). Land, labour and caste politics in rural TamilNadu in the 20th century: Iruvelpattu (1916–2008). *Economic & Political Weekly*. 45(31). 47–61.
Harriss-White, Barbara. (2003). Inequality at work in the informal economy: Key issues and illustrations. *International Labour Review*. 142(4). 459–469.
Harriss-White, Barbara. (2004). *India working: Essays on society and economy*. Cambridge: Cambridge University Press.
Harriss-White, Barbara. (2005). *India's socially regulated economy*. Queen Elizabeth House Working Paper Series-QEHWS133 [Online]. Retrieved from http://www3.qeh.ox.ac.uk/pdf/qehwp/qehwps133.pdf [Accessed 11 June 2012].
Harriss-White, Barbara. (2008). *Rural commercial capital: Agricultural markets in West Bengal*. New Delhi: Oxford University Press.
Harriss-White, Barbara and Nandini Gooptu. (2001). Mapping India's world of unorganized labour. *Socialist Register*. 89–118.
Harriss-White, Barbara and John Harriss. (2007). *Green revolution and after: The 'North Arcot papers' and long-term studies of the political economy of rural development in south India*. QEH Working Paper Series-QEHWPS146, Working Paper Number 146. Oxford: University of Oxford Press.
Harriss-White, Barbara and Matthew McCartney. (2000). *The 'intermediate regime' and 'intermediate classes' revisited: A critical political economy of Indian economic development from 1980 to Hindutva*. Queen Elizabeth House Working Paper Series- QUEHPS34 [Online]. Retrieved from http://www3.qeh.ox.ac.uk/pdf/qehwp/qehwps34.pdf [Accessed 11 June 2012].

Harris-White, Barbara, Deepak K. Mishra and V. Upadhyay. (2009). Institutional diversity and capitalist transition: The political economy of agrarian change in Arunachal Pradesh, India. *Journal of Agrarian Change*. 9(4). 512–547.

Hart, Gillian. (1991). Engendering everyday resistance: Gender, patronage and production politics in rural Malaysia. *Journal of Peasant Studies*. 19(1). 93–121.

Hasan, Zoya. (1998 [1999]). *Quest for power: Oppositional movements and post-congress politics in Uttar Pradesh*. New Delhi: Oxford University Press.

Heyer, Judith. (2001). *The changing position of agricultural labourers in villages in rural Coimbatore, Tamil Nadu, between 1981/2 and 1996*. Working Paper No. 57, QEH Working Paper Series, QEHWPS57 [Online]. Retrieved from http://www3.qeh.ox.ac.uk/pdf/qehwp/qehwps57.pdf [Accessed 8 July 2012].

Hobsbawm, E.J. (1973). Peasants and politics. *Journal of Peasant Studies*. 1(1). 3–22.

Ilaiah, Kancha. (2005). *Why I am not a Hindu: A sudra critique of Hindutva philosophy, culture and political economy* (2nd ed.). Kolkata: Samya.

Institute for Human Development. (2014). *India labour and employment report 2014: Workers in the era of globalisation*. New Delhi: Academic Foundation.

Jaffrelot, Christophe. (2014). The class element in the 2014 Indian election and the BJP's success with special reference to the Hindi belt. *Studies in Indian Politics*. 3(1). 19–38.

Janakarajan, S. (1997). Village resurveys: Issues and results. In J. Breman, P. Kloos and A. Saith (eds.). *The village in Asia revisited* (pp. 397–428). New Delhi: Oxford University Press.

Jaoul, Nicolas. (2007). Political and 'non-political' means in the Dalit movement. In Sudha Pai (ed.). *Political process in uttar pradesh: Identity, economic reforms and governance*. New Delhi: Pearson Longman.

Jassal, Smita Tewari. (2012). *Unearthing gender: Folksongs of North India*. Durham and London: Duke University Press.

Jassal, Smita Tewari. (2019). Agrarian production and the archiving of folksong. *Review of Agrarian Studies*. 9(1).

Jeffery, Craig and Jens Lerche. (2000). Stating the difference: State, discourse and class reproduction in Uttar Pradesh, India. *Development and Change*. 31. 857–878.

Jeffery, Patricia and Roger Jeffery. (1996). *Don't marry me to a plowman! Women's everyday lives in rural North India*. Boulder: Westview Press.

Jetley, Surinder. (1977). *Modernizing Indian peasants: A study of six villages in Eastern Uttar Pradesh*. New Delhi: Asian Educational Services.

Kannan, K.P. (2018). Macro-economic aspects of inequality and poverty in India. In Alpa Shah, Jens Lerche, Richard Axelby, Dalel Benbabaali, Brendan Donegan, Jayaseelan Raj and Vikramaditya Thakur (eds.). *Ground down by growth: Tribe, caste, class and inequality in Twenty-first century India* (pp. 32–48). New Delhi: Oxford University Press.

Kapadia, Karin. (1990). *Gender, caste & class in rural South India*. PhD Thesis. London: The London School of Economics and Political Science, University of London.

Kapadia, Karin. (1995). *Siva and her sisters: Gender, caste, and class in rural south India*. Boulder: Westview Press.

Kapur, Devesh, Chandra Bhan Prasad, Lant Pritchett and Shyam D. Babu. (2010). Rethinking inequality: Dalits in Uttar Pradesh in the market reform era. *Economic & Political Weekly*. 45(35). 39–49.

Kay, Cristóbal. (1981). Political economy, class alliances and Agrarian change in Chile. *Journal of Peasant Studies*. 8(4). 485–513.
Kerkvliet, Benedict and J. Tria. (2009). Everyday politics in peasant societies (and ours). *Journal of Peasant Studies*. 36(1). 227–243.
Khan, M. (2007). *Governance, economic growth and development since the 1960s* [Online].Retrieved from www.un.org/esa/desa/papers/2007/wp54_2007.pdf [Accessed 30 June 2012].
Kumar, Deepak. (2017). Landholdings and irrigation in the study villages. In M. Swaminathan and Arindam Das (eds.). *Socio-economic surveys of three villages in Karnataka*. New Delhi: Tulika Books.
Lanjouw, Peter and Nicholas Stern. (eds.). (1998). *Economic development in Palanpur over five decades*. Oxford: Clarendon Press.
Lerche, Jens. (1994). *New wine in old bottles: Caste, local action, social movements and general elections: Scheduled caste agricultural workers in Uttar Pradesh, India*. CDR Working Paper 94.12. Copenhagen: Centre for Development Research.
Lerche, Jens. (1995). Is bonded labour a bound category? Reconceptualising agrarian conflict in India. *Journal of Peasant Studies*. 22(3). 484–515.
Lerche, Jens. (1998). Agricultural labourers, the state and agrarian transition in Uttar Pradesh. *Economic & Political Weekly*. 33(13). A29–A35.
Lerche, Jens. (1999). Politics of the poor: Agricultural labourers and political transformations in Uttar Pradesh. In T.J. Byres, Karin Kapadia and Jens Lerche (eds.). *Rural labour relations in India* (Ch. 6). London: Frank Cass.
Lerche, Jens. (2003). Hamlet, village and region: Caste and class differences between low-caste mobilization in East and West UP. In Roger Jeffery and Jens Lerche (eds.). *Social and political change in Uttar Pradesh: European perspectives* (Ch. 7). New Delhi: Manohar.
Lerche, Jens. (2008). *Class, agrarian questions, and neo-liberal growth in India* (mimeo). London: Sage Publications.
Lerche, Jens. (2010). From 'rural labour' to 'classes of labour': Class fragmentation, caste and class struggle at the bottom of the Indian labour hierarchy. In Barbara Harriss-White and Judith Heyer (eds.). *The comparative political economy of development: Africa and South Asia* (Ch. 4). London: Routledge.
Lerche, Jens. (2011). Agrarian crisis and agrarian questions in India. *Journal of Agrarian Change*. 11(1). 104–118.
Lerche, Jens and Roger Jeffery. (2003). Uttar Pradesh: Into the twenty-first century. In Roger Jeffery and Jens Lerche (eds.). *Social and political change in Uttar Pradesh: European perspectives* (Ch. 1). New Delhi: Manohar.
Lerche, J. and Alpa Shah. (2017). Tribe, caste and class – New mechanisms of exploitation and oppression. In Shah, Alpa, J. Lerche, R. Axelby, D. Benbabaali, B. Donegan, J. Raj and Vikramaditya Thakur (eds.). *Ground down by growth: Tribe, caste, class and inequality in twenty-first century India* (pp. 1–31). New Delhi: Oxford University Press.
Lerche, Jens, A. Shah and B. Harris-White. (2013). Introduction: Agrarian questions and left politics in India. *Journal of Agrarian Change*. 13(3). 337–350.
Levien, Michael. (2012). The land question: Special economic zones and the political economy of dispossession in India. *The Journal of Peasant Studies*. 39(3–4). 933–969.
Lieten, G.K. and Ravi Srivastava. (1999). *Unequal partners: Power relations, devolution and development in Uttar Pradesh*. New Delhi: Sage Publications.

Mahaprashasta, Ajoy Ashirwad. (2009). 'Entitlements under NREGA violated': Interview with Jean Dreze, development economist. *Frontline*. 26(16) [Online]. Retrieved from www.frontlineonnet.com/fl2616/stories/20090814261604000.htm [Accessed 29 August 2012].

Mahaprashasta. Ajoy Ashirwad and Venkitesh Ramakrishnan. (2011). Producers' plight. *Frontline*. 28(26) [Online]. Retrieved from www.frontlineonnet.com/fl2826/stories/20111230282602100.htm [Accessed 8 August 2012].

Mandelbaum, David G. (1972). *Society in India: Continuity and change* (Vol. 1); *Change and continuity* (Vol. II). Mumbai: Popular Prakashan.

Mazumdar, Vina, Kumud Sharma, and Lotika Sarkar. (1992). Agricultural development with women: Policy and legislative approaches. In R.K. Punia (ed.). *Women in agriculture*. (pp. 133–153). New Delhi: Northern Book Centre.

Mehrotra, Ishita. (2017). Subsidising capitalism and male labour: The scandal of unfree Dalit female labour relations. In S. Anandi and K. Kapadia (eds.). *Dalit women: Vanguard of an alternative politics in India*. London: Routledge.

Mehrotra, Ishita. (2019). Inequality and rural employment: Agrarian distress and Dalit women. In *Mind the gap: The state of employment in India*. New Delhi: Oxfam.

Mendelsohn, Oliver and Marika Vicziany. (1996). The untouchables. In Oliver Mendelsohn and Upendra Baxi (eds.). *The rights of subordinated peoples*. New Delhi: Oxford University Press.

Mezzadri, Alessandra. (2009). *The architecture of production and labour control in the Indian garment industry: Informalisation and upgrading in the global economy*. London: School of Oriental and African Studies, University of London.

Mezzadri, Alessandra. (2017). *The sweatshop regime: Labouring bodies, exploitation, and garments made in India*. Cambridge: Cambridge University Press.

Mies, Maria. (1976). The Shahada movement: A peasant movement in Maharashtra (India)-its development and its perspectives. *Journal of Peasant Studies*. 3(4). 472–482.

Mondal, Bidisha, Jayati Ghosh, Shiney Chakraborty and Sona Mitra. (2018). *Women workers in India. CSE Working Paper 2018-3*. Bengaluru: Centre for Sustainable Employment, Azim Premji University.

National Commission for Enterprises in the Unorganised Sector. (2007). *Report on conditions of work and promotion of livelihoods in the unorganised sector* [Online]. Retrieved from www.nceus.gov.in/Condition_of_workers_sep_2007.pdf [Accessed 30 September 2008].

National Commission for Enterprises in the Unorganised Sector, Government of India. (2008). *A special programme for marginal and small farmers* [Online]. Retrieved from www.nceus.gov.in [Accessed 3 December 2008].

National Sample Survey Office. (2013a). *Key indicators of land and livestock holdings in India* (70th Round, January-December, 2013). Retrieved from http://mospi.nic.in/sites/default/files/publication_reports/KI_70_18.1_19dec14.pdf [Accessed 15th September 2020].

National Sample Survey Office. (2013b). *Household ownership and operational holdings in India* (Report No. 571(70/18.1/1). Retrieved from http://mospi.nic.in/sites/default/files/publication_reports/Report_571_15dec15_2.pdf [Accessed 15th September 2020].

Nayyar, Dhiraj. (2011). Expressway to growth: UP Polls 2012: Uttar Pradesh's economic performance now matches the national average. *India Today* [Online].

Retrieved from http://indiatoday.intoday.in/story/india-today-opinion-up-polls-2012-bihar-gujarat/1/163683.html [Accessed 11 August 2012].
Neale, Walter C. (1962). *Economic change in rural India: Land tenure and reform in Uttar Pradesh, 1800–1955*. New Haven: Yale University Press.
Omvedt, Gail. (1978). Women and rural revolt in India. *Journal of Peasant Studies*. 5(3). 370–403.
Oxfam International. (2016). *An Economy for the 1%*. Retrieved from https://d1tn3vj7xz9fdh.cloudfront.net/s3fs-public/file_attachments/bp210-economy-onepercent-tax-havens-180116-summ-en_0.pdf [Accessed 2 February 2019].
Oxfam International. (2017). *An Economy for the 99%*. Retrieved from https://d1tn3vj7xz9fdh.cloudfront.net/s3fs-public/file_attachments/bp-economy-for-99-percent160117-summ-en.pdf [Accessed 2 February 2019].
Oxfam International. (2018). *Move over 'Sons of the soil': Why you need to know the female farmers that are revolutionizing agriculture in India*. Retrieved from https://www.oxfamindia.org/women-empowerment-india-farmers [Accessed 7 February 2019].
Oya, C. (2007). Agricultural maladjustment in Africa: What have we learned after two decades of liberalisation? *Journal of Contemporary African Studies*. 25(2). 275–297.
Pai, Sudha. (2007). From Dalit to *Savarna:* The search for a new social constituency by the Bahujan Samaj party in Uttar Pradesh. In Sudha Pai (ed.). *Political process in Uttar Pradesh: Identity, economic reforms and governance*. New Delhi: Pearson Longman.
Pai, Sudha. (2019). *Indian politics has undergone a tremendous change: Uttar Pradesh results the proof* [Online]. Retrieved from https://economictimes.indiatimes.com/news/elections/lok-sabha/uttar-pradesh/indian-politics-has-undergone-a-tremendous-change-uttar-pradesh-results-the-proof/articleshow/69498432.cms [Accessed 22 July 2020].
Paris, Thelma, Abha Singh, Joyce Luis and Mahabub Hossain. (2005). Labour out-migration, livelihood of rice farming households and women left behind: A case study in Eastern Uttar Pradesh. *Economic & Political Weekly*. 40(25). 2522–2529.
Patnaik, Utsa. (1976). Class differentiation within the peasantry: An approach to analysis of indian agriculture. *Economic & Political Weekly*. 11(39). 82–101.
Patnaik, Utsa. (1986). The agrarian question and the development of capitalism in India. *Economic & Political Weekly*. 21(18). 781–793.
Patnaik, Utsa. (1987). *Peasant class differentiation: A study in method with reference to Haryana*. New Delhi: Oxford University Press.
Patnaik, Utsa. (1988). Ascertaining the economic characteristics of peasant classes-in- themselves in rural India: A methodological and empirical exercise. *Journal of Peasant Studies*. 15(3). 301–333.
Patnaik, Utsa. (2003). Agrarian crisis and distress in rural India. *Macroscan* [Online]. Retrieved from www.macroscan.org/fet/jun03/fet100603Agrarian%20Crisis_1.htm [Accessed 18 February 2011].
Patnaik, Utsa. (2006). The agrarian crisis and importance of peasant resistance. *People's Democracy*. 30(5) [Online]. Retrieved from www.cpim.org/pd/2006/0129/01292006_utsa.htm [Accessed 11 June 2012].
Patnaik, Utsa. (2010). *The new primitive accumulation and the poverty*. Abstract of P. Sundarayya Memorial Lecture, Hyderabad. 19 May [Online]. Retrieved

from http://indiacurrentaffairs.org/the-new-primitive-accumulation-and-the-peasantry-utsa-patnaik/ [Accessed 11 June 2012].

Pattenden, Jonathan. (2011). Gatekeeping as accumulation and domination: Decentralization and class relations in rural South India. *Journal of Agrarian Change*. 11(2). 164–194.

Racine, J. and Racine, J. (1997). *Viramma*. New York: Verso.

Rai, Praveen and Kumar, Sanjay. (2017). The decline of the Congress party in Indian politics. *EPW*, 52(12). Retrieved from https://www.epw.in/journal/2017/12/web-exclusives/decline-congress-party-indian-politics.html [Accessed: 31 August 2021].

Raikes, Philip. (1978). Rural differentiation and class-formation in Tanzania. *Journal of Peasant Studies*. 5(3). 285–325.

Rajni, Vijaya. (2007). Casual labour contracts of agricultural labourers in East and West Uttar Pradesh. *Economic & Political Weekly*. 42(2). 154–160.

Ramachandran, V.K. (1990). *Wage labour and unfreedom in agriculture: An Indian case study*. Oxford: Clarendon Press.

Ramachandran, V.K. and Vikas Rawal. (2010). The impact of liberalization and globalization on India's agrarian economy. *Global Labour Journal*. 1(1). 56–91.

Ramachandran, V.K., Vikas Rawal, and M. Swaminathan. (eds.). (2010). *Socio-economic surveys of three villages in andhra pradesh: A study of agrarian relations*. New Delhi: Tulika Books in Association with Foundation for Agrarian Studies.

Ramakrishnan, Venkitesh. (2012). Lopsided growth. *Frontline*. 28(25) [Online]. Retrieved from www.frontline.in/fl2825/stories/20111216282501300.htm [Accessed 11 August 2012].

Ramamurthy, Priti. (1994). Patriarchy and the process of agricultural intensification in South India. In Alice Clark (ed.). *Gender and political economy: Explorations of south Asian systems* (pp. 179–214). New Delhi: Oxford University Press.

Reddy, Narasimha D. and Srijit Mishra. (eds.). (2009). *Agrarian crisis in India*. New Delhi: Oxford University Press.

Rege, Sharmila. (1998). Dalit women talk differently: A critique of 'difference' and 'towards a Dalit feminist standpoint position'. *Economical and Political Weekly*. 33(4). WS39–WS46. 31 October–6 November.

Right to Fair Compensation and Transparency in Land Acquisition, Rehabilitation and Resettlement Act. (2013). *Arrangement of sections*. Retrieved from https://legislative.gov.in/sites/default/files/A2013-30.pdf [Accessed 21 November 2021].

Rigg, Jonathan. (2006). Land, farming, livelihoods, and poverty: Rethinking the links in the rural South. *World Development*. 34(1). 180–202.

Rodrik, D. (2004). *Growth strategies* [Online]. Retrieved from www.hks.harvard.edu/fs/drodrik/Research%20papers/GrowthStrategies.pdf [Accessed 30 June 2012].

Rudra, Ashok. (1978a). Class relations in Indian agriculture: I. *Economic & Political Weekly*. 13(22). 916–923.

Rudra, Ashok. (1978b). Class relations in Indian agriculture: II. *Economic & Political Weekly*. 13(23). 963–968.

Rudra, Ashok. (1978c). Class relations in Indian agriculture: III. *Economic & Political Weekly*. 13(24). 998–1004.

Rustagi, Preet. (2015). *Employment and inequalities. Round table on addressing economic inequality in India, Bengaluru*. Retrieved from https://vdocument.in/employment-and-inequalities-undp-in-india-employment-and-inequalities-preet-rustagi.html [Accessed 8 January 2015].

Ruthven, Orlanda and Sushil Kumar. (2002). *Moving mud, shifting soil: Change and development in wage labour livelihoods in Uttar Pradesh, India*. Working Paper 176. London: Overseas Development Institute [Online]. Retrieved from www.odi.org.uk/resources/docs/2698.pdf [Accessed 3 March 2012].
Saad-Filho, A. (2005). From Washington to post-Washington consensus: Neoliberal agendas for economic development. In A. Saad-Filho and D. Johnston (eds.). *Neoliberalism: A critical reader* (Ch. 12). London: Pluto Press.
Saha, Partha and Sher Verick. (May 2016). *State of rural labour markets in India*. ILO Asia-Pacific Working Paper Series. Retrieved from https://www.ilo.org/wcmsp5/groups/public/---asia/---ro-bangkok/---sro-new_delhi/documents/publication/wcms_501310.pdf [Accessed 29 August 2018].
Saith, Ashwani. (1990). Development strategies and the rural poor. *Journal of Peasant Studies*. 17(2). 171–244.
Saith, Ashwani and Ajay Tankha. (1972). Agrarian transition and the differentiation of the peasantry: A study of a West UP village. *Economic & Political Weekly*. 7(14). 707–723.
Sampat, Preeti. (2016). Dholera: The emperor's new city. *Economic & Political Weekly*. L1(17). 59–67.
Scott, James. (1985). *Weapons of the weak: Everyday forms of peasant resistance*. New Haven: Yale University Press.
Scott, Jim. (1986). Everyday forms of peasant resistance. *Journal of Peasant Studies*. 13(2). 5–35.
Sengupta, Arjun, K.P. Kannan and G. Raveendran. (2008). India's common people: Who are they, how many are they and how do they live? *Economic & Political Weekly*. 43(11). 49–63.
Sengupta, Dipak. (2007). Walking the Buddha path. *Prabuddha Bharata (Awakened India)*. 112(11). 636–640.
Sethi, Aman Quint. (2016). *Inside Mayawatis quest to unite UPs Dalits*. Retrieved from https://www.thequint.com/quintlab/inside-mayawatis-quest-to-unite-ups-dalits/. [Accessed 22 July 2020].
Shah, Alpa, Jens Lerche, Richard Axelby, Dalel Benbabaali, Brendan Donegan, Jayaseelan Raj and Vikramaditya Thakur. (2018). *Ground down by growth: Tribe, caste, class and inequality in twenty-first century India*. New Delhi: Oxford University Press.
Shankar, Kripa. (1993). Agricultural labourers in Eastern UP. *Economic & Political Weekly*. 28(24). 1211–1241.
Shankar, Kripa. (1996). Bonded agricultural labour in India of 1996. *Economic & Political Weekly*. 31(33). 2197–2253.
Sharma, Miriam. (1985). Caste, class and gender: Production and reproduction in North India. *Journal of Peasant Studies*. 12(4). 57–88.
Sharma, Rita and Thomas T. Poleman. (1994). *The new economics of India's green revolution: Income and employment diffusion in Uttar Pradesh*. New Delhi: Vikas Publishing House.
Silver, Beverly J. and Giovanni Arrighi. (2001). Workers North and South. *Socialist Register*. 53–76.
Singh, Shrinath. (1976). *Modernisation of agriculture: A case study in eastern Uttar Pradesh*. New Delhi: Heritage Publishers.
Singh, S.S. (2013). Intervention, identity and marginality: An ethnographic account of the Musahars. *Economic & Political Weekly*. 48(20). 52–59.

Singh, Yogendra. (1970). Chanukhera: Cultural change in Eastern Uttar Pradesh. In Vandana Madan (ed.). *The village in India* (Ch. 5). New Delhi: Oxford University Press.

Sinha, Arun. (1982). Class war, not 'atrocities against Harijans'. *Journal of Peasant Studies*. 9(3). 148–152.

Srinivas, M.N. (1957). Caste in modern India. *The Journal of Asian Studies*. 16(4). 529–548.

Srinivas, M.N. (1966 [1995]). *Social change in modern India* (Revised ed.). New Delhi: Orient Blackswan.

Srinivas, M.N. (1977). The changing position of Indian women. *Man*, New Series. 12(2). 221–238.

Srinivas, M.N. (1987 [1994]). *The dominant caste and other essays* (Revised ed., Ch. 4). New Delhi: Oxford University Press.

Srinivas, M.N. (1989). *The cohesive role of sanskritization and other essays* (Ch. 4). New Delhi: Oxford University Press.

Srivastava, Piyush. (2011). UP farmers not against land acquisition but want better price. *India Today* [Online]. Retrieved from http://indiatoday.intoday.in/story/farmers-protest-demand-transparency- and-better-price-for-land/1/137628.html [Accessed 11 August 2012].

Srivastava, Ravi. (1989). Interlinked modes of exploitation in Indian agriculture: A case study. *Journal of Peasant Studies*. 16(4). 493–522.

Srivastava, Ravi. (1999). Rural labour in Uttar Pradesh: Emerging features of subsistence, contradiction and resistance. In T.J. Byres, Karin Kapadia and Jens Lerche (eds.). *Rural labour relations in India* (Ch. 8). London: Frank Cass.

Srivastava, Ravi. (2007). Economic change among social groups in Uttar Pradesh, 1983–2000. In Sudha Pai (ed.). *Political process in Uttar Pradesh: Identity, economic reforms and governance* (Ch. 14). New Delhi: Pearson.

Srivastava, Ravi and Rahul Ranjan. (2016). Deciphering growth and development: Past and present. *Economic and Political Weekly*. 51(53). 32–43.

Subas, Ram. (1984). Dynamics of agrarian relations in Sultanpur east Uttar Pradesh. *Social Scientist*. 12(7). 57–63.

Sud, Nikita. (2009). The indian state in a liberalizing landscape. *Development and Change*. 40(4). 645–665.

Swaminathan, Madhura and Arindam Das (eds.). (2017). *Socio-economic surveys of three villages in Karnataka*. New Delhi: Tulika Books.

Swaminathan, Madhura and Vikas Rawal. (2015). *Socio-economic surveys of two villages in Rajasthan*. New Delhi: Tulika Books.

Tanner, Clare L. (1995). Class, caste and gender in collective action: Agricultural labour unions in two Indian villages. *Journal of Peasant Studies*. 22(4). 672–698.

Thorat, S. and S. Madheswaran. (2018). Graded caste inequailty and poverty: Evidence on role of economic discrimination. *Journal of Social Inclusion Studies*. 4(1). 3–29.

Thorner, Alice. (1982). Semi-Feudalism or capitalism? Contemporary debate and modes of production in India. *Economic & Political Weekly*. 17(51). 2061–2066.

Tripathi, Purnima S. (2004). A surplus of problems. *Frontline*. 21(5) [Online]. Retrieved from www.frontlineonnet.com/fl2105/stories/20040312006602200.htm [Accessed 8 August 2012].

Trivedi, Prashant K., S. Goli, Fahimuddin and S. Kumar. (2016). Identity equations and electoral politics: Investigating political economy of land, employment and education. *Economic and Political Weekly*. 51(53). 117–123.

Turton, Andrew. (1986). Patrolling the middle-ground: Methodological perspectives on 'everyday peasant resistance'. *Journal of Peasant Studies*. 13(2). 36–48.

Usami, Y. and Vikas Rawal. (2018). *Changes in the structure of employment in India*. SSER Monograph 18/2. Retrieved from http://www.networkideas.org/wp-content/uploads/2018/08/Changes_Structure_Employment_ India.pdf [Accessed 25 January 2019].

Varshney, Ashutosh. (2009). *The challenge in Uttar Pradesh*. India in Transition, Centre for the Advanced Study of India, University of Pennsylvania [Online]. Retrieved from http://casi.ssc.upenn.edu/iit/varshney [Accessed 11 August 2012].

Varun, Dangli Prasad. (1976). *Deoria*. Lucknow: Department of District Gazetteers, GoUP.

Verma, A.K. (2011). Farmers' suicides and statehood demand in Bundelkhand. *Economic & Political Weekly*. 46(28). 10–11.

Verma, Smriti, A. Gulati and S. Hussain. (2017). *Doubling agricultural growth in Uttar Pradesh: Sources and drivers of agricultural growth and policy lessons*. Working Paper No. 335. New Delhi: Indian Council for Research on International Economic Relations Series.

Vij, Shivam. (27 January 2020). 'The Mayawati era is over. Bye Bye Behenji'. *The Print*. Retrieved from https://theprint.in/opinion/the-mayawati-era-is-over-bye-bye-behenji/354887/ [Accessed 22 November 2021].

Wadley, Susan S. (1994 [1996]). *Struggling with destiny in Karimpur, 1925–1984*. New Delhi: Vistaar Publications.

Walker, Kathy Le Mons. (2008). From covert to overt: Everyday peasant politics in China and the implications for transnational agrarian movements. *Journal of Agrarian Change*. 8(2–3). 462–488.

White, Christine Pelzer. (1986). Everyday resistance, socialist revolution and rural development: The Vietnamese case. *Journal of Peasant Studies*. 13(2). 49–63.

Wilson, Kalpana. (1999). Patterns of accumulation and struggles of rural labour: Some aspects of agrarian change in Central Bihar. In T.J. Karin Kapadia Byres and Jens Lerche (eds.). *Rural labour relations in India* (Ch. 8). London: Frank Cass.

Wiser, William and Charlotte Wiser. (2001 [2004]). *Behind mud walls: Seventy-five years in a North Indian village*. New Delhi: Chronicle Books.

Wolf, Eric R. (1969). *Peasant wars of the twentieth century*. London: Harper & Row.

World Bank. (2008). *Agriculture for development* [Online]. Retrieved from http://siteresources.worldbank.org/INTWDR2008/Resources/WDR_00_book.pdf [Accessed 2 March 2009].

World Bank. (2020). *Employment in agriculture (% of total employment, modeled ILO estimate)* [Online]. Retrieved from https://data.worldbank.org/indicator/SL.AGR.EMPL.ZS?locations=IN [Accessed 8 July 2020].

Index

For Product Safety Concerns and Information please contact our EU
representative GPSR@taylorandfrancis.com
Taylor & Francis Verlag GmbH, Kaufingerstraße 24, 80331 München, Germany

www.ingramcontent.com/pod-product-compliance
Ingram Content Group UK Ltd.
Pitfield, Milton Keynes, MK11 3LW, UK
UKHW020007200926
475702UK00015B/2518
9781032229065